WHAT IS A JUST PEACE?

What is a Just Peace?

Edited by
PIERRE ALLAN and ALEXIS KELLER

OXFORD
UNIVERSITY PRESS

OXFORD
UNIVERSITY PRESS

Great Clarendon Street, Oxford OX2 6DP

Oxford University Press is a department of the University of Oxford.
It furthers the University's objective of excellence in research, scholarship,
and education by publishing worldwide in

Oxford New York

Auckland Cape Town Dar es Salaam Hong Kong Karachi
Kuala Lumpur Madrid Melbourne Mexico City Nairobi
New Delhi Shanghai Taipei Toronto

With offices in

Argentina Austria Brazil Chile Czech Republic France Greece
Guatemala Hungary Italy Japan Poland Portugal Singapore
South Korea Switzerland Thailand Turkey Ukraine Vietnam

Oxford is a registered trade mark of Oxford University Press
in the UK and in certain other countries

Published in the United States
by Oxford University Press Inc., New York

British Library Cataloguing in Publication Data

Data available

Library of Congress Cataloging in Publication Data

Data available

Typeset by SPI Publisher Services, Pondicherry, India
Printed in Great Britain
on acid-free paper by
Biddles Ltd., King's Lynn, Norfolk

ISBN 978–0–19–927535–9 (Hbk.)   978–0–19–954571–1 (Pbk.)

1 3 5 7 9 10 8 6 4 2

Unjust and Just Peace: Preface for the Paperback Edition

Work on Just War is essential and continues. Work on Just Peace is no less important. We further need to study the numerous attempts to achieve peace and justice separately as well as together—with the consequence of often obtaining neither. In 2006, when the first edition of this book was published, we chose a title 'What is a Just peace?' ending with a question mark because we wished to provoke a discussion on peace and justice, two terms widely used together, but insufficiently conceptualized together. This paperback edition allows us to correct a number of small mistakes left in that first publication. Moreover, this new preface gives us the opportunity to provide readers with some elements of the concept's empirical grounding.

Just Peace describes a process whereby peace and justice are reached together by two or more parties recognizing each others' identities, each renouncing some central demands, and each accepting to abide by common rules jointly developed. The aim of our approach is to propose an accommodation process whereby negotiators seek to agree to a fair and lasting peace by crafting it in a manner deemed just by all relevant protagonists. Peace achieved in this way is just because it entails gradual recognition by the negotiating parties of a series of conventions. It is just because it is expressed in a shared language that respects the sensitivities of all parties. Indeed, the definition of justice itself will be negotiated between the parties involved, recognizing that there is some inevitable tension between the idea of justice and the idea of reconciliation. Based on our language-oriented approach (see Chapter 9), we claim that four conventions or principles are required to negotiate a peace perceived as just and legitimate, that is, a Just Peace: thin recognition, thick recognition, renouncement, and a common rule. They are adjusted to prevailing circumstances and are prerequisites for a Just Peace as well as the steps making it possible. As in Just War theory, all conditions are necessary, and if together all are satisfied, then they are sufficient for a Just Peace. However, unlike the Just War doctrine, our conventions also describe a process and not simply a set of requirements.

Our concept is a formal one. It neither specifies some general rules of justice nor the content of the peace, but focuses on some very general forms the process of a Just Peace needs to proceed through. As the world changes and history continues, a specific Just Peace formula will not necessarily be, as in a Kantian perspective, a perpetual one. Just Peace needs to be maintained, and therefore adapted to changing societal circumstances, in order to survive. Since the existence of many collective identities is a central feature of the world and cannot be ignored in exploring the demands for recognition, this human diversity implies that each peace is, in a sense, a particular one, accommodating the specific identities involved.

This perspective allows us to deepen our understanding of Just Peace along two complementary approaches: the study of what it is not—that is, the study of unjust peace; and a historical-comparative study. Analysing when and how a peace is almost or near just, or when it is more clearly unjust, allows us to better understand Just Peace by focusing on the concept's borders, when its discriminating features are at the forefront. In this respect, let us mention an important category of peace in which there are plenty of instances where justice has been absent: imposed peace. However, the imposition of peace is not necessarily foreign to a potential leading eventually to a Just Peace. The question then becomes: Why does an imposed and unjust peace acquire some legitimacy over time? In what ways can the original injustice leave way for a gradual perception of normalcy increasingly acquiring legitimacy over time?

Another kind of peace has a similar potential to evolve toward justice: 'stable peace'—whereby the mere possibility of war is absent from people's minds. Even a violent civil war can, in a matter of a few generations, lead to a collective experience whereby the current societal arrangements become perceived as just. This simply stems from the fact that the protagonists are no longer alive and the integrated society of their grand-children has other concerns. The history of many modern nation-states, originally born out of violence, provides us with numerous examples of this kind of process. With years passing by, unjust historical situations often acquire some legitimacy simply because of the passage of time.

Therefore, starting from a specific war ending or peace treatise, not only its features in terms of our four Just Peace criteria need to be examined, but the post-treatise period also needs careful analysis. Focusing on these kinds of events, empirical cases should be selected on basis of the 'possibility principle': one is not inquiring into all kinds of peace and conflict situations in order to extract the ones that satisfy the four necessary and sufficient conditions for Just Peace. Rather, this methodological rule limits the perspective to the cases that could be reasonably envisaged as having the mere possibility of satisfying these requirements—and thus considerably limits the number of irrelevant cases.

Methodologically, such concerns should be substantiated by a systematic and comparative study of historical instances of unjust and Just Peace. History does provide us with peace processes where some elements of justice were taken into account. The treaty of Augsburg (1555) reached between protestant and catholic States in the Holy Roman Empire, the Royal Proclamation of 1763 in which the British Crown set out its relations with the Amerindian nations, the treaty of San Francisco (1951) between Japan and the United States, the 'Two Plus Four Treaty' of 1990 which accepted German reunification in its present border, the constitutional negotiations in South Africa between 1990 and 1994 are all seen as examples of 'just' settlements in that they incorporate a certain sense of 'justice' in the legal and moral sense. How then should historical cases be selected? We would argue that we should not focus on recent history nor only examine the classical treaty literature between modern nation-states. Rather, we need to pay close attention to peace agreements between peoples of various cultural persuasions. It is in those circumstances that the peace made will be most diverse and—prima facie— the most difficult to reach given the different societal and ideological viewpoints involved. In that respect, an anthropological approach defining law as a process would enrich this analysis.

Indeed, more and more international lawyers and legal historians accept that the confrontation of Europe from the 1500s onwards with the world beyond Europe was of the utmost importance for the formation of modern international law. Nevertheless, like international relations theorists, they have generally paid much too little attention to what precisely a Just Peace could mean. The story they tell builds on a narrative, either expressed or implied, that the legal rules and principles adhered to were the exclusive by-products of the Western legal tradition brought to the rest of the world. In that sense, they are still marred by something that some call 'conceptual colonialism'. They offer a deep analysis of the notion of sovereign equality—indeed, one of the most pervasive images of international legal order posits a community of equals engaging in relations through juridical forms. They show how the European nations began to distinguish—by means of a standard of civilization—those countries able to enter into a full range of relations from those unable to do so. They insist on the discrepancy between formal equality and substantial political and social inequality, paving the way for the theory and practice of compensatory inequality. But they nevertheless provide for a history from the point of view of the colonizer, the colonized having to accept the colonizer's conceptual and legal idiom.

It is however essential to consider international law because it plays two key roles with respect to peace agreements. First, to the extent that peace agreements themselves form legal documents, law plays a role in their implementation. Second, international law has a relationship to peace agreement negotiation and content, in an enabling or regulatory capacity. In addition, international lawyers have also paid attention to so-called unequal treaties.

This notion has its origins in the law of contracts and is an outgrowth of the natural law concept of a fair price. Differently put: we have no hope of explaining what is—or is not—a Just Peace unless we pay more attention to the intellectual context in which international law was formed. This way of putting it will sound familiar to those aware of the debate on the linguistic turn, identified with the form of historical critique developed by the Cambridge School and its followers. It consists in the historical adaptation of Ludwig Wittgenstein's method of dissolving philosophical problems by examining the conventions that governed a language during a period of time in which both problems and solutions arose.

When discussing the law of nations, which was transformed, in the eighteenth century, into international law, modern theorists redefined the normative foundations of the society of states created by the expansion of Europe. Thus, they codified the terms for membership in this community of states. They drew the boundaries between those who belonged to the society and those who did not. Those who did belong formed a moral community bound by mutually agreed rules of conduct. And fundamental to this community was the idea that its members were not obliged to treat non-members according to the norms that applied to relations between themselves. By codifying rules that excluded many non-European entities and individuals, international law—and the law of treaties which was part of it—was consistent with (and supported) an international society that was unjust in the way it treated different peoples as unequal. If we do recognize this historical conjunction between the emergence of international society and European expansionism, then international law is faced with the problem of solving some conflicts, especially conflicts involving different cultures. If modern theories of international law played an historical role in justifying the destruction of indigenous people's cultures, how can international law achieve a peace perceived as just by culturally diverse entities? Does international law have the capacity to conceptualize such a peace, which first implies the adoption of a common language, understood and accepted by all conflicting parties?

We should therefore give a special empirical and historical place to the so-called Encounter era (seventeenth and eighteenth centuries) between European and non-European peoples in analysing Just Peace—or its absence—between them. In that period, the power relationships among potential colonizers and colonized was not yet overwhelmingly favourable to the Europeans. Thus, they could not avoid dealing with non-Europeans or confronting the conceptions of justice that indigenous peoples applied to their relations with the strange newcomers to their lands. The importance Europeans attached to their dealings with other cultures is evidenced by the large number of well-known European and Anglo-American names appearing in the history of these relations during the seventeenth- and eighteenth-century era which witnessed hundreds of treaties and agreements. We are fortunate that there exists a relatively rich archive of legal resources where opposing visions of American Indian, Asian, African, and Pacific indigenous peoples' rights have been recorded and preserved. Extraordinary documents in their own right, the records of the colonial period treaty conferences between the European powers and aboriginal societies still constitute nowadays a literary type that has been rather neglected by contemporary scholars. In countless reiterations, the Encounter era treaty literature affirms the sovereign capacity of indigenous peoples to engage in bilateral governmental relations, to exercise power and control over their lands and resources, and to maintain their internal forms of self-government free of outside interference.

By looking more deeply into this body of literature, we should be able to provide a greater appreciation of the different conceptions of peace available to both Europeans and non-European peoples. These visions converge in a distinctive language of multicultural diplomacy that indigenous peoples and Europeans used to conduct their treaty relations with each other. This indigenous diplomatic language functioned paradigmatically to prescribe what the actors within the Encounter era treaty system might say and how they might say it. The majority of the treaties analysed should primarily be ratified treatises; these are reasonably easy to define, for the process usually included parliamentary authorization and/or formally appointed and instructed commissioners negotiating for the sovereign authority. Nevertheless, although there are no set of criteria for determining what makes an 'un-ratified treaty', we should also take into consideration numerous cases in which agreements between European and non-European peoples did not get through the formal ratification process. This is of course especially crucial for the latter, for whom we will study the 'functional' equivalents of ratification.

Perhaps, one of the most important reasons for trying to develop a better understanding of the essential interplay between peace and justice is the challenge posed by multiculturalism to modern world politics. To this extent, there is much to be learned from unearthing the long-neglected history of cross-cultural confrontations, accommodations, and diplomatic negotiations between non-European peoples and colonizing Europeans found in the literature. Further work on this relatively neglected body of knowledge on peace between various cultures should help us better understand the reasons why some of the traditional peace efforts made in Europe were met with success while others were a simple parenthesis between continuing conflicting periods. In this respect, the early Encounter era reflects its singular time in legal history with respect to cultural group relations. It was a time of intense crises and confrontation. Radically different peoples were required to negotiate as rough economic, military, and political equals for survival on the land. No one group's narratives occupied a privileged or dominant position in the new type of society that was emerging on the multicultural frontiers of seventeenth- and eighteenth-century North America. Throughout the Encounter era, numerous and distinct cultural groups, indigenous and European, can be found negotiating with each other at arm's length about the competing visions of peace and justice that would govern their mutual relations. More often than our histories might suggest, these groups agreed to create multicultural alliances of law and peace. Therein lies the significance of this empirical material.

This return to history—both just and unjust—should more clearly show the implicit conflict-solving rules that exist within a liberal quasi-universalistic approach, rules that solve the problem intellectually, but not necessarily historically. It should also provide us with further arguments speaking for the Just Peace concept we propose in this book.

Geneva, February 2008

Pierre Allan and Alexis Keller

Preface for the Hardback Edition

This volume grew out of philia, out of an intellectual friendship that developed when we started teaching an advanced seminar on international relations ethics to a small and a diversified student body at the University of Geneva during the winter term of 1998–9. Teaching elements of Just War theory, we realized that no equivalent body of doctrine or conceptual thinking lay behind the often jointly used terms of justice and peace. Compared to the Just War doctrine, and conceptually, little intellectual effort has been devolved to define a Just Peace equivalent.

Therefore, in the fall of 2001, we organized a round-table meeting on the theme 'What is a Just Peace?' at the University. This academic manifestation was inscribed in a series of events commemorating the first Nobel Peace Prize given in 1901 to Henry Dunant, who founded the International Committee of the Red Cross. It is telling that Dunant, whose life was devoted to making war more just and humane, shared the prize with a pacifist, Frédéric Passy. We invited four academics and a practitioner to debate that topic two evenings in a row, on 30 and 31 October. The theme, the date, and the choice of our debaters explain the extraordinary interest that this debate aroused. More than 1,000 people intensely followed our public round-table meeting. Members of the Geneva international and diplomatic community, or students and colleagues from the University of Geneva, all sat quietly for hours following the debate, with a number of them participating at the end of each evening.

Everyone present vividly remembers the electric atmosphere of both evenings, especially the second one with the direct exchange between Edward Said and Yossi Beilin on peace between their peoples. Said passionately pleaded for justice and, ultimately, for a single state in the Middle East for Palestinians and Israelis alike. Beilin made a strong plea for a search for peace first, more importantly than the attainment of Justice. Both recognized the grave historical errors that had been made—and that were still being made—on all sides. Both had been, and were still, intimately involved in that history. The culturalist spoke of the necessity of accepting to think about two histories together, contrapuntally. The practitioner reminded the audience that whereas it may have appeared to the parties that not making peace was justified, in hindsight it had become clear that greater injustice, in fact, lay in not making peace. The Palestinian asked for the same rights and institutions of common secular citizenship with at first two equal states, and then a unitary one. The Israeli cautioned that the price paid by both sides for abstaining from making peace at junctions where such an act was possible, because it seemed unjust, was too dear.

The Professor of Comparative Literature asked for secularization, which requires demystification, courage, and above all, an irrevocably critical attitude towards self, society, and the other. At the same time, it requires keeping in mind the imperatives of justice and peace. Therefore, it also requires a narrative of emancipation and enlightenment for all, not just for one's own community. The former Minister of Justice warned of the great danger in talking about 'Just Peace' because peace can only be defined as such if it is not unjust— since there is no greater justice than peace. So, what really is a Just Peace?

The four debaters present in Geneva subsequently rewrote and extended their papers, while Stanley Hoffmann wrote a prologue for this volume. Based on these contributions, the two editors wrote their own chapters and a joint concluding chapter, which attempts to synthesize the whole volume by developing a concept of Just Peace that echoes the debates.

Nevertheless, we owe our contributors both an apology for having made them wait to see their work in print and an explanation for this delay. Having been solicited in October 2000 by the *Fondation pour Genève* to organize an academic event in relation to the commemoration of Henry Dunant, we wanted from the start to implicate not only academics but also a practitioner who could participate in a high-level debate as a politician and statesman, not as an official of his country. Yossi Beilin readily accepted our invitation in the spring of 2001. Then, in August 2001, Alexis Keller had the idea that we could offer Beilin the possibility to complete, in Switzerland, the unfinished Taba negotiations. Indeed, in January of that year, the Israeli Government and the Palestinian Authority had directly negotiated in that Egyptian resort. Their positions had come closer than ever before. Beilin had participated in these talks as a member of the Labor Government of Ehud Barak, who was driven from power when he lost against Ariel Sharon a few weeks later. In fact, we did not know that Yossi Beilin was then already discussing ways to resume negotiations with Yasser Arafat's Minister of Information, Yasser Abed Rabbo. After some exploratory discussions in Geneva to discuss the parameters of the negotiation, Beilin and Rabbo accepted our help in hosting meetings in Geneva and elsewhere in Switzerland. Several of these engagements were held in the spring of 2002. The main issues were discussed in detail by a small team that prepared the work of the two delegations.[1]

But then, difficulties stemming from the Second Intifada made further joint meetings impracticable, and Alexis Keller accepted becoming the intermediary between the two parties. In this function, he spent a considerable

---

[1] See Menachem Klein, A Possible Peace between Israel and Palestine. An Insider Account of the Geneva Initiative (New York: Columbia University Press, 2007).

amount of time from June 2002 until 1st December, the date of the public launching of the Geneva Accord by its signatories. This agreement is the first—and up to now, the only—full-fledged Israeli–Palestinian text based on a two-state solution.[2] This did not speed the preparation of the present volume, but it did give us food for thought, as we maintained our discussions on peace and justice. Additionally, we continued developing our ideas on the complex interrelationships between these two concepts, especially from the perspective of an implementation of a Just Peace.

To come back to the voices of Yossi Beilin and Edward Said—at both the scientific and political level—the latter argued for 'some basic agreement, a compact or entente whose outlines would have to include regarding the Other's history as valid but incomplete as usually presented, and second, admitting that despite the antinomy these histories can only continue to flow together, not apart, within a broader framework based on the notion of equality for all'. And we should heed the call of the former, too: 'The great danger in the term Just Peace is, naturally, legitimizing the terms Unjust Peace. It is not a big stretch from its academic use to a political one, and may justify opposition to peace by claiming that it is unjust. Since no peace treaty can address the needs of both sides in their entirety, a newly legitimized excuse may be provided for those opposing it.' The 'academic scribbler'—to use John Maynard Keynes's famous quote on the influence of economists and political philosophers on 'practical men' and 'madmen in authority'—has been warned. His duty, however, lies not only in conceptualizing Just War but also in developing its peaceful emulator.

In assembling and organizing these essays, the editors have incurred numerous debts. We are especially grateful to our contributors for being so patient through numerous delays and requests for revision. They all took up the task of seriously thinking about Just Peace beyond their own disciplinary backgrounds while listening to the voices of others. Our thanks also extend to our students and colleagues both in Europe and the United States, who are too numerous to thank individually and whose criticisms were helpful— although we did not always follow them. The contribution of three anonymous Oxford University Press reviewers also needs to be recognized whose numerous points were well received and constructive. One of them—of a liberal and legalistic bent—was quite trenchant. Although we did not follow the advice given, our text benefited from the criticisms of this referee. They made us articulate our concept of Just Peace in a clearer way with respect to a classic liberal conception based on universal principles of law and justice.

---

[2] See Alexis Keller, *L'Accord de Genève: un pari réaliste* (Paris and Geneva: Seuil and Labor et Fides, 2004).

Finally, we would like to express our deep gratitude to our two research assistants, Sylvie Guichard Friesendorf and Steven J. Barela, who provided competent and diligent help in putting all of it together. We are beholden to the *Fondation pour Genève* for its generous financial help without which this work could not have been done. And, last but not least, we are particularly obligated to our two families whose understanding and caring attitude truly 'supported' this work—in the French meanings of the term.

Geneva, April 2005

P. A. and A. K.

Contents

Contributors

Pierre Allan is Professor of Political Science at the University of Geneva.

Yossi Beilin Dr. Beilin, a member of the Knesset, held several ministerial positions in the Israeli government, including Minister of Justice, and was one of the chief negotiators for the Geneva Accord of 2003.

Stanley Hoffmann is the Buttenwieser University Professor at Harvard University.

Alexis Keller is Professor of History of Legal and Political Thought at the University of Geneva.

David Little is Professor of the Practice in Religion, Ethnicity, and International Conflict at Harvard Divinity School and Faculty Associate at the Weatherhead Center for International Affairs.

Sir Adam Roberts is Senior Research Fellow of the Centre for International Studies in Oxford University's Department of Politics and International Relations. He is also an Emeritus Fellow at Balliol College, Oxford. He was the Montague Burton Professor of International Relations at Oxford University from 1986 to the end of 2007.

The late **Edward W. Said** (1935–2003) was University Professor of English and Comparative Literature at Columbia University.

1

Introduction: Rethinking Peace and Justice Conceptually

Pierre Allan and Alexis Keller

As Just War has attracted considerable attention for centuries, the words peace and justice have been, and are still, often used together. While an old doctrine of Just War exists, surprisingly little conceptual thinking has gone into what constitutes a peace that is a just one. This book debates this *problématique* and develops the concept of a Just Peace.

The problem with the idea of a Just Peace is that striving for justice may imply a Just War, or at least 'justifiable violence', as Adam Roberts, one of the contributors to this book argues. Peace and justice do clash at times. Therefore, one often starts from a given view of what constitutes justice, but this a priori approach leads—especially when imposed from the outside—straight into discord. This book presents various—and at times conflicting—viewpoints on this question from perspectives originating in political science, history, international law, political philosophy, cultural studies, and theology in particular, as well as from a policy perspective. In that respect, it takes into account the process of the Geneva Accord—the first comprehensive Israeli–Palestinian peace plan—with which one author and the editors were closely associated.

This book presents complementary approaches to a Just Peace and the editors, building on the different contributions, propose the concept of a Just Peace as a language-oriented process. It is just, because it is based on conventions that are negotiated and accepted by the parties. Recognition, renouncement, and rule are central. In this sense, the Geneva Accord embraces some of these conventions. Thus the book ends up challenging a liberal view of peace founded on norms claiming universal scope. This liberal conception has difficulty in solving conflicts such as civil wars characterized typically by fundamental disagreements between different communities. Cultures make demands that are identity-defining, and some of these defy the 'cultural neutrality' that is one of the foundations of liberalism.

War was, and has continued to be, a problem that has plagued people's existence and begged for civility and restriction in its use. Partially because of its humanly constructed nature, and also because of great necessity—made all the more essential and urgent with the development of weapons of mass destruction—constraints to war are felt as vital by everyone, even if for some this is only lip service. It is too often overlooked that four nuclear armed countries all chose defeat rather than to deploy these highly destructive weapons.[1] This occurred when the Soviets were engaged in Afghanistan, the French in Algeria, and in separate instances when the Chinese and the Americans were waging war in Vietnam. Since their first and only use in the Second World War, states have thus far not encountered a situation in which they could justify the use of nuclear weapons to themselves, or to the rest of the world. It also raises the question of whether the logic of war, in which all available means may be applied to protect the state, has reached some kind of limit.

Most often, the idea behind going to war has been based on assuring a place for peace in the not so distant future, whether the motivation was normative as within the Just War doctrine, or more simply the hope of victory leading to the end of organized violence. As Saint Thomas Aquinas states in his *Summa Theologiae*, '[t]hose who wage war justly aim at peace'.[2] So if peace has so often been the end, one must ask the question why it has not been possible to achieve this peace through the means of war. In other words, alternative and non-violent ways to peace need to be contemplated. Although the path through justice is a demanding one, its accomplishment opens the way to a durable settlement accepted by the parties initially engaged in conflict. Clearly, the more ambitious goal of peace with justice can lead to smaller chances for success. Indeed, it may derail the whole enterprise and keep the flames of violent conflict alive through the search for 'justice'—alas it is not the same on both sides of the fence!

The point of departure in this discussion of the complex interrelationships between violent conflict, peace, and justice is *Peace and Justice: A Prologue* (Chapter 2) by Stanley Hoffman. He presents a sketch of the international arena in which a belligerent justice is seen as a last resort that can at times justify the use of violence. To describe this notion, Hoffman uses the potent representation of a justice that 'no longer resembles the traditional image of a scale, but instead the image of a fighter with his sword'. This conviction that there are moments in which all reasonable options have been exhausted, leaving only recourse to the use of force, acts as a baseline that frames

[1] Cf. Jonathan Schell, *The Unconquerable World* (New York: Metropolitan Books, 2003).
[2] Cf. http://ethics.acusd.edu/Books/Texts/aquinas/justwar.html

Hoffman's philosophy. Because there is no 'all-powerful Olympian judge' to preside over international conflicts and impose an objective justice, self-defence must remain an available remedy. Hoffman also proposes that the lack of an international judicial system means that the leaders of nations must take into consideration the perceptions of injustice that can stem from their decisions. Since it is widely recognized that any evaluation of conditions will not come from an objective authority, but rather a national one, all conclusions will be interpreted as subjective. This being the case, conflicts are bound to arise over differing interpretations. Therefore, to avoid creating large-scale resentment it is necessary to allow feelings and perceptions to be a part of political calculations. Otherwise the subjectivity of justice becomes predominant and the resolution of conflict comes down to traditional concepts of power.

This last point also relates to Hoffman's reference to Kant in which the internal transformation of states is viewed as the best antidote to war. This alteration is based on a 'transition to the rule of citizens in representative democracies'. In such a system where universal suffrage is accepted and all are regarded as valuable members of the society, each person's perspective matters. Kant proposes that in such a constitution, a 'perpetual peace' is possible because there, citizens

will have great hesitation on embarking on so dangerous an enterprise. For this would mean calling down on themselves all the miseries of war, such as doing the fighting themselves, supplying the costs of the war from their own resources, painfully making good the ensuing devastation, and, as the crowning evil, having to take upon themselves a burden of debt which will embitter peace itself and which can never be paid off on account of the constant threat of new wars.[3]

Justice, Peace and History: A Reappraisal (Chapter 3) by Alexis Keller investigates how international law and its predecessor, the law of nations, was, at crucial junctures of its history, a form of cultural imperialism. Keller claims that 'we have no hope of explaining what is—or is not—a Just Peace unless we pay more attention to the intellectual context in which international law was formed'. Indeed, in the early phases of European expansion the indigenous peoples were granted rights by modern theories of international law but these rights were gradually eroded in response to the changing demands of European settlers. Over a period of four hundred years following the conquest of Mexico, there was a progressive retreat by Europeans from conceding sovereign rights to specific non-European Peoples. During this time, Keller argues, international legal thought progressed from recognizing

---

[3] Immanuel Kant, *Political Writings*, ed. Hans Reiss (Cambridge: Cambridge University Press, 1991), 100.

sovereignty in indigenous peoples to recognizing conditional sovereignty to eventually denying it. This was especially the case with peoples labelled as 'barbarians' or 'uncivilized'. Important moments in these developments were the adoptions by natural law theorists of Locke's vision of history and Locke's labour theory of property. Also relevant was the emergence of a 'universalizing discourse about law' mainly Eurocentric, based on the equation: 'culture = nation = state'.

In his survey of modern theories of international law, Keller shows that there was nevertheless a tradition of thought that recognized and accommodated cultural diversity. Such a tradition can be found in the writings, among others, of Montesquieu, Rousseau, and US Chief Justice John Marshall. These 'dissenters' did shape the usual authoritative way of comprehending 'otherness' and offered new ideas to accommodate cultural differences. They did not presume that modern European cultures were superior and the base requirement for individual freedom. They underlined the necessity to preserve diversity inasmuch as what was applicable to relations between European states was not necessarily appropriate to relations with other civilizations.

One of Keller's principal claims in his chapter is that these writers proposed one of the cornerstones of the concept of Just Peace: *the principle of recognition*. They developed this notion from an effort to understand not only another's point of view, but also the deeper context from which another perspective arose. They rooted this principle in the conviction that the law of nations of their time was inappropriate. They pleaded for the Other to become a part of a new We, and knowing that this did not need to lead to the loss of Self.

Consequently, the tracing of this principle of recognition through the history of the law of nations gives a new perspective to the idea of justice in international society. Although many might turn to international law in the belief of an equalizing tradition, there are identifiable shortcomings to be found in its origins that cannot be overlooked, especially when dealing with intercultural conflicts. Contemporary international law can surely help redress the legacy of its hegemonic history. For instance, were it to be adopted, the Draft United Nations Declaration on the Rights of Indigenous Peoples would be an important set of norms against which to measure the moral legitimacy of individual states. But international law still needs to address the issue of whether it possesses the standards to achieve peace that is not only just, but also perceived as such.

In *Just Peace: A Cause Worth Fighting For* (Chapter 4), Sir Adam Roberts presents his thesis. The reader is offered a series of different themes exploring the avenues and pitfalls of how we might arrive at a Just Peace. Through his investigation what becomes most apparent is the difficulty of achieving this lofty goal. This is by no means to say that this author doubts the possibility of Just Peace, however it is all the more important to recognize the size and complexity of a task before undertaking it with any seriousness. Prescriptive methods simply revealing a cultural bias, a diversity of ideas concerning justice, and an inclination to impose an 'ideal' model are all dangers to be aware of in this endeavour. Additionally, conflicts between justice and peace might be more prolific than normally acknowledged and the language of justice has often been co-opted to frame arguments in international affairs that can make positions inflexible. These are all possible pitfalls, and so it is best to identify them at the outset so that we may be properly alert to their presence in our discussions.

One of the principal ideas presented in this chapter is, as seen in the Hoffman piece, that it may sometimes be necessary to fight in order to secure and construct the foundation of a Just Peace. This does not, however, mean that Roberts approaches the topic from a realist perspective in which efficacy is related to a baseline of force. Rather, his work illustrates the importance of using coercion at times to put into effect understandings of justice, without losing sight of the undermining effect this might have on legitimacy and thus peace. Although Roberts indicates a dearth in serious academic research into the popular civil resistance that has brought about peaceful political change in the nineteenth and twentieth centuries, he holds fast to his analysis that there are times when force can, in fact, be justifiable. As a scholar who has published extensively on humanitarian law, Roberts is aptly familiar with the theory of Just War, and this is why he advocates the use of a similar, yet substantially different, term: *justifiable force*. 'This would move the tradition away from appearing to approve a war as a whole, and toward recognizing something more conditional and cautious—that the threat and use of military force by a particular state or group of states may in particular circumstances be justifiable.'

One other topic that should not be overlooked is the notion of 'assisting change through the magnetic power of successful example' or 'induction' that Roberts examines through the Helsinki Process. There is much literature and speculation about the European Union and how its presence and structure will shape the future of international relations. Roberts writes about how this development has had an impact on the nations of this region and how it has already opened the concept of 'induction' through adherence to human rights law to become a part of the Union. One of the points that Roberts makes clear is that it is through processes at the regional level and not only through the United Nations, that we can find positive illustrations of how justice can be maximized without the introduction of force. This brings us back to the original notion that war that is waged justly aims at peace. And since a desire to proliferate the 'good' has been what has long shaped human relations, this examination of the Helsinki process provides an admirable example of how an internal focus on justice can create an environment that witnesses promulgation.

In *Measuring International Ethics: A Moral Scale of War, Peace, Justice, and Global Care* (Chapter 5), Pierre Allan goes beyond Just Peace in a comparative perspective, distinguishing it in particular from its closest 'moral' neighbours, a stable (but usually unjust) peace and positive peace. Allan develops an international ethical scale to evaluate different acts from a moral standpoint, with conflict as the baseline of ethical behaviour. The more extreme the discord, the worse it is considered on the scale he has created, and the more harmonious, the better.

Allan's scaling proceeds on the basis of two dimensions independent of each other—a consequentialist one and a deontological one—that are used in tandem. He argues that the end points of his moral scale—the complete eradication of humankind on one hand, and paradise on the other—actually correspond to a vanished humanity. The worst that can now be carried out by a national leadership could lead to a nuclear holocaust in which none survive. At the other end of the spectrum, a society in which only agape, love for each and all, existed, would leave no need for moral principles, and thus would no longer be human. In other words, it is only within a limited range that ethics applies.

Arguing that absolute unhappiness and absolute happiness are not of this world, Allan presents eight intermediary moral situations, all of an empirical content, each being superseded by the next one in ethical terms. The first four types correspond to various kinds of conflict: genocide, war, (Hobbesian) non-war, and Just War. His scale then proceeds to stable peace, Just Peace, positive peace (or minimizing structural violence), and 'global care'. These are the four categories that he considers of an ethical 'good' in ascending order.

Allan criticizes modern theories of justice which claim universality while addressing themselves to free and competent adults only. What place then for dependants in such schemes? Briefly analyzing some extreme cases such as Auschwitz, Himmler, and Hitler, Allan shows that humanity—in the sense of empathy and a humane attitude to close relations—is in fact never absent. This is the foundation for his ethic of 'global care'. He develops it using feminist theories of care, religious, and secular declarations on a global ethic, evolutionary theory arguments, and a critique of a liberal human rights approach. Both encompassing justice and superseding it, the concept of global care is morally superior to positive peace because caring also includes an affective and a cultural dimension. It also means consideration, sympathy, and compassion at both the individual and collective levels. Two basic responsibilities are at its core: treating others humanely—a duty beyond the liberal right to be treated equally; and, observing the Golden Rule—which implies a universality of humanity, as Allan shows. These two responsibilities are complemented by the values of non-violence, tolerance, and solidarity.

In *Just Peace: A Dangerous Objective* (Chapter 6), Yossi Beilin argues somewhat sceptically. As a practitioner—as well as political scientist—involved directly in conflict negotiations he brings a valuable contribution to this book. Beilin was a former chief negotiator for the Israeli government in the Oslo process at Camp David and Taba. After fulfilling his post as the Minister of Justice for the Israeli government, he became one of the lead Israeli representatives in the Geneva Accord negotiations. In his work here, Beilin points to the possible dangers of speaking about a combination of the concepts of justice and peace, as he believes there clearly cannot be one without the other. In addition, he shows that history is flush with examples in which political leaders have bypassed opportunities for peace because they did not deem the conditions just, and thus perpetuated conflict with untold costs.

Beilin begins by examining European history and describing the notions of peace that developed over time on this particular continent. The concept was largely absent of what would be considered justice for the peoples of each nation, and instead focused on what might suit the royalty or courts. Beilin highlights a string of peace treaties that ended conflict through some kind of a territorial partition, regardless of inhabitants' wishes. This formula seemingly created a sort of perpetual state of war in which there were always unsatisfied grievances that could be used as pretext for reinstating hostilities. It was this approach that was once again used to punish the defeated in the Versailles Peace Treaty, and that many attribute as one of the causes of the Second World War. Only after the rejection of this notion of retributive justice had been internalized by the Europeans has a more stable peace and future been able to be realized.

Beilin also explores the enduring Israeli–Palestinian conflict that has been at the centre of his life and career. He draws attention to the many moments in history in which a possibility for peace was presented to each party to a conflict, and subsequently rejected because the political leaders at the time thought that justice would not be served by accepting the terms on offer. It is this compelling point that Beilin addresses in this book. If people are overly seduced by the notion of a Just Peace, they will be blind to ending conflict when the opportunities present themselves. Beilin claims that a genuine definition of peace already, in fact, includes the notion of justice and that to perpetuate a term that might cause missed opportunities is unjust in itself.

'Since justice is always relative', the notion of qualifying peace with such a subjective term could in fact be dangerous.

In *Peace, Justice, and Religion* (Chapter 7), David Little raises many questions of international legality in addressing the finer concepts of peace enforcing, peacekeeping, peacemaking, and peace building. In discussing these four issues, the author accentuates the rule of law, democracy, and human rights as foundations for each of these stages towards peace. It is through the notions of international legality that Little attempts to bring the concept of justice to the idea of building a more stable and lasting peace. By looking towards collectively accepted international treaties for a concept of justice, Little taps into the notion of legal validity that is at least partially composed of a legitimacy that emanates from the people themselves. This is quite important because, ultimately, it is the people involved in a conflict who will determine whether a peace is just, and therefore lasting. It is the theory of *iusnaturalism* that is based on the idea that each of us has an innate understanding of basic human principles and thus serves as the logic of law to find and follow. If we accept such a view, it means that the international treaties that have been largely, if not universally, ratified by current states bring a certain authority, or legitimacy, to what one can conceive of as justice in international affairs. So by turning to legality in its global form, Little uses for the baseline of his analysis the closest that international society has thus far been able to construct in terms of a justice that we all share. Although we find valid reasoning for questioning who has been allowed to participate in this process of uncovering what might be considered natural law, protecting the human rights of all and labelling it justice does not seem to create an untenable starting point.

In one of his treatments of religious influence on Just Peace, Little discusses the unconventional thinking of peace enforcement through non-violent measures. He raises the question of whether there is any place for the use of 'legitimate' force in the field of enforcing our notions of peace. Due to the recent respectability gained through its effective implementation, it would seem that Little properly pushes the discussion of Just Peace in the direction of dealing with recalcitrant conflict by employing means that could best avoid reproach. If the instrument used is absent of violence, it is all the more difficult to criticize and claim that injustice has been perpetrated, and thus justify reprisals. However, Little also rightfully queries if these methods can truly be put into practice when violent measures are already driving a current conflict.

Little often returns to the idea that the best effort that we can make to approach a notion of justice, particularly because of its subjective nature, is through the international legal framework that has evolved over centuries and expanded almost exponentially in the previous sixty years. He believes that 'the promotion of internationally recognized human rights provides a unifying theme, and thereby serves to connect justice and peace in a particularly compelling way'.

A Method for Thinking about Just Peace (Chapter 8) by the recently deceased Edward Said presents a vivid and passionate depiction of the ongoing conflict that he has experienced first-hand as a Palestinian. Interestingly, he is of the firm belief that a type of secularization of the Israeli–Palestinian conflict is required to keep it from fomenting and intensifying further. As a culturalist, Edward Said is not in concrete disagreement with David Little's assessment of religion's restorative potential in conflict, but it is clear that personal experience has played a major role in shaping each of these intellectuals' contributive chapter.

Said usefully identifies that one common trait in conflict is that rhetoric tends to be tremendously, with his own terminology, 'contrapuntal'. This potent idea and method highlights what should be considered an important part of the nature of war: each side tends to present only binary propositions for how to view the opposition and the solutions themselves. So what ends up dominating the discourse are 'us versus them' options that attempt to remove the complexity of what is inevitably a part of each and every dispute. It is through Said's previous study of imperialism that he comes to identifying and accentuating this common feature of conflict that he believes must inevitably be addressed. It also provides him with his method:

A comparative or, better, a contrapuntal perspective is required in order to see a connection between coronation rituals in England and the Indian durbars of the late nineteenth century. That is, we must be able to think through and interpret together experiences that are discrepant, each with its particular agenda and pace of development, its own internal formations, its internal coherence and system of external relationships, all of them co-existing and interacting with others.[4]

In Said's chapter, we also find a discussion of the centuries-old battle for Northern Ireland. Here, he is able to artfully and effortlessly discuss the literary works of Lloyd George, Frank Pakenham, Maria Edgeworth, and Brian Friel. Through the use of these illustrations, Said is able to begin to bring to life the antagonisms that the common soul suffers day to day when discord between groups of peoples is aggravated. It is for this reason, among others, that for Said the idea of Just Peace is one that is 'very fluid, rather than a stable, concept'. Inevitably, the notions of peace and justice will be based on individuals, which means that there will always be an element of capriciousness that cannot be removed from the equation. This might be disconcerting

---

[4] Edward W. Said, *Culture and Imperialism* (London: Vintage, 1994), 36.

to some, but these are the only tools with which we have to work when dealing with ideas that are constructed by and carried out by humans.

In his discussion of the Israeli–Palestinian conflict, Said makes the extremely important point that 'their histories and cultures—inextricably linked for better or worse—together, contrapuntally, in symbiotic, rather than mutually exclusive term'. This acknowledgement is pivotal and can be related to the concept of 'thick recognition' put forward in the concluding chapter by Allan and Keller. When this appreciation of the situation has occurred, it no longer seems as viable to eliminate opposition, because there will always be a tomorrow in which retribution will be demanded by those who feel that an unjust peace had been forced upon family members or previous generations. This is why Said has emphasized the need to think about, and work towards resolving, two histories that have become interwoven. This is despite the fact that many have tried to define each in contradictory terms. Part of arriving at a Just Peace would entail recognizing a shared identity and common history even if this approach highlights differences. Clearly, this might be a monumental task considering the trials and tribulations that have come to pass, but for Said an 'abridged memory' is not an option that will lead to Just Peace.

In the concluding chapter, *The Concept of a Just Peace, or Achieving Peace Through Recognition, Renouncement, and Rule* (Chapter 9), Pierre Allan and Alexis Keller propose a process-based approach rather than defining justice on the basis of a pre-existing set of universal principles. Just Peace is perceived as such by parties in a peace process based on four necessary and sufficient conditions. The first is 'thin recognition' of the other as an autonomous entity, in a liberal perspective. Second, there must be 'thick recognition' whereby each party needs to understand the other's core features of its identity; this allows for an inter-subjective consensus of what each side profoundly needs to remain 'self', and thus, satisfied in this culturalist perspective. Third is *renouncement*, when some real concessions need to be made by each of the parties. The last condition is *rule* in which the inter-subjectivity of the first three conditions and the features of the just solution need to be objectified by a 'text' in the wide sense of the word, including symbolic features, and specifying the particular rules by which the parties agree to abide.

By advocating this approach based on a language-oriented process among directly concerned parties, Allan and Keller go beyond liberal and culturalist perspectives. They claim that negotiators need, throughout the process, to build a novel shared reality as well as a new common language. This allows for an enduring harmony between previously clashing peoples. It develops an inter-subjectivity for those both inside and outside of a conflict by increasing the likelihood of observation through a shared understanding. This point leads into one of the liberal objections that has been raised to the approaches generally put forth in this book. The concern is that the idea of Just Peace might reflect a manner in which the resolution to hostility has been treated previously. Allan and Keller point out that what has largely been advocated formally has looked to ideas of justice through adherence to already drafted and ratified international legal norms. As discussed in this book, there are weaknesses in this idea because of the culturally biased form in which the law of nations emerged. So there would be an inherent inadequacy in advocating observance of regulations that chronically marginalized the influence and existence of different societies. Although there is a respect here for working arrangements and agreements, there is also an explicit recognition that inclusion into the decision-making process helps create the feeling of personal investment into the final negotiated product.

So finally, what is a Just Peace? The reader will certainly not agree with all she or he will find in the coming chapters. All contributors however hope that this book will help each one in rethinking peace and justice conceptually.

2

Peace and Justice: A Prologue

Stanley Hoffmann

1. A WORLD UNJUST AND BELLIGERENT

Peace can be defined in two ways. The broad definition belongs to Giraudoux who describes it as 'the intervals between wars' (which he considers, as did Raymond Aron, to be the essence of international relations). A narrowly construed definition sees peace as referring specifically to peace treaties and their consequences for the former warring parties and the international realm. This is the definition that I will be using here, modified slightly to take into account those cases when, such as in 1945, the final ratification of treaties was prevented by the breaking up of the alliance which defeated Germany. These treaties were replaced with agreements that were both temporary and limited. But as some have said, there is nothing more permanent than that which is temporary.

Georges Bidault once said that a good diplomatic agreement was one with which all parties were equally dissatisfied. This is an elegant way to acknowledge that the purpose of peace treaties was more to balance out injustice than to have justice prevail. (We can look here to the case of Poland, which lost its eastern border but was 'compensated' with parts of Prussia and Germany's Silesia region.) In fact, many peace treaties that were imposed by the victors were seen as unfair (not only by the vanquished, but also by some of the victors themselves such as in the case of Italy after 1918). The Versailles Peace Treaty is a classical example. The accords of Yalta and Potsdam, which allowed Russia to impose its dominion over Eastern and Central Europe (I will not enter here into the debate over the margin of choices available to its allies), were seen as profoundly unfair by those behind what became the Iron Curtain. The peace treaty signed by Egypt and Israel in 1979 was seen as unfair not only by the Palestinians, who were left out, but also by a sizeable portion of the Arab world. The status given to Austria, once it was finally determined in 1955, was unjust not because it was too harsh, but because it cast in the role of victim a nation that had for the most part fully embraced Hitler.

Conversely, justice is often belligerent when it no longer resembles the traditional image of a scale, but instead the image of a fighter with his sword. I am reminded here of wars, or guerrilla wars, against the oppression and the domination of the colonizers. Similarly there have been those interventions in cases of human rights violations which are often more effective in establishing or reestablishing justice, as was the case with the wars stemming from the dissolution of Yugoslavia, than is the stubborn adhesion to the principle of non-intervention, as was the case with Rwanda. In addition, there are antiterrorist operations, the purpose of which is to bring aid to the victims of terror, insecurity and fear. The expulsion of al-Qaeda and the Taliban from Afghanistan is a good example of belligerent justice.

Violence, therefore, is something just, or justifiable, when there is an emergency and when all other avenues have been exhausted. Armed interventions in ethnic conflicts, aimed at ending massive human rights violations (as was the case in Yugoslavia) fall into this category. (In contrast, in the case of Rwanda, it was the lack of intervention/non-intervention that proved unjust.) The decision by Great Britain and France to go to war after the inglorious injustices of the 'appeasement' might have also fallen into this category, had the all-out war against Fascism and Nazism not taken aim at so many civilians and thus violated the long-standing principle of the Just War doctrine: the protection of non-combatants. As for peace, it has at times existed—I am thinking here of the fate of West Germany and Japan after the Second World War. This time there was no manifestation of the retaliatory violence which drove Hitler before and after his rise to power, and which was similarly apparent in the *Organisation de l'Armée Secrète*, at the time of the Evian Accords in 1962. This was not due only, or even primarily, to the military presence of the Western victors or the new threat posed by the USSR.

Why then has peace been so often unjust and why has justice been more often belligerent than peaceful? There are many reasons for this. First, there are many different types of peace. Peace was often imposed by the victor on either the vanquished or the unfortunate 'little' countries trapped between the Great Powers. This was the case in Europe after Yalta, when one side was occupied by the Soviets and the other found itself under the imperfect influence of the Americans and the British. Thankfully, there has also been peace which stems from a compromise and creates little, or less, resentment. There is also grandiose peace that reshuffles the world order, such as the Westphalia Treaty or the peace following the Napoleonic wars or First World War. Here, the adoption of new principles and the bartering over territory led to a patchwork of decisions, which governments or people considered unjust, and of attempts to repair past injustices, which are often inextricable. The former are usually perceived as unpalatable and the latter are less celebrated than we could imagine. Finally, there are peace or armistices which serve only to put a temporary end to violence and leave all sides, or at least some of them, feeling dissatisfied (as is the case with the Israeli–Arab conflicts or the war over Kashmir).

Second, there is a wide array of definitions of justice. The preliminary question is: justice for whom? For the States involved in a conflict? For the individuals who are often victims of the compromises constructed by the States? Let us consider the Accord of Evian in 1962. Both Algeria, which had obtained its independence, and France, which had freed itself from the Algerian quagmire, had good reasons to find these agreements acceptable. Could the same be said, though, of the *harkis* or of the members of the *Organisation de l'Armée Secrète*? Peace achieved through compromise has often entailed large transfers of populations and thus individuals have suffered the consequences of the actions taken by States.

Moreover, there are different types of justice. Criminal justice, which deals with perpetrators of war crimes or crimes against humanity (even if they happen to be statesmen) is perceived as just by the victims (e.g. the victims of Milosevic), but is seen as partial and vindictive by those who had supported and even inspired those same criminals. The current ambivalence of the USA with regard to international criminal justice is quite typical: the Americans supported the creation of tribunals in the cases of Yugoslavia as well as Rwanda, where they had not wanted to intervene, but they have renounced the International Criminal Court because it could—theoretically—incriminate American nationals.

Distributive justice is the subject of even more fierce controversy because it can be viewed in many ways: equal opportunity, fairness (as defined by Rawls), equality of results. In all these aspects, the opposition between States and individuals can at times be dramatically felt. In other words, this is the area where it might be most difficult to achieve an agreement between adversaries or rivals.

Although procedural justice is perceived as less contentious, it can nonetheless be very hard to achieve, particularly when the very type of procedure selected (recall the arguments over the shape of the table) can determine the outcome of a conflict.

The nature of international relations is another obstacle to the ideal of Just Peace. The universe in which these relations occur is by definition ruled by partiality. This is true in two ways: each actor tends to see things only from its own point of view (think back to de Gaulle with respect to Israel during the Six Day War), and there is no impartial judge empowered to decide what is just and impose its decisions on the parties. In the Hobbesian universe, the Leviathan alone defines what is just and it is therefore an arbitrary decision. No such global Leviathan exists today. Therefore, in a world where state and non-state actors abound (from Doctors Without Borders to unscrupulous terrorists), each side tends to have its own idea of justice (which fuels wars if said actors are armed), and, of course, its own interests.

Finally, the traditional shortcomings of the 'anarchical society', so well analysed by Hedley Bull, are accentuated by contemporary international relations. Preoccupations with justice have intensified as the public, which plays a role in foreign policy, has gotten more and more democratized. This general public acts less like an inert object in the hands of diplomats or military professionals and more as a large group of concerned actors wanting to have their say. Between the end of the Napoleonic wars and the end of the French–Prussian war, the habit of treating entire populations like cattle lost its legitimacy. Consequently, the negotiation of peace accords went from attempting to strike a balance between competing interests to attempting to achieve a weakening or a quieting of passions, which is much more difficult. Demands for self-determination have greatly sparked the political tinderboxes and have added fuel to the fires of wars, as was the case with internal demands and revolutions to obtain democracy.

As contemporary international relations have intensified, they have also worsened. This is due to the nature of modern warfare. With the increased sophistication of weapons, able to strike harder and farther, with armies becoming more and more civilian (as opposed to professional armies), wars which were once fairly limited, now expose to view the most inflamed passions such as patriotic or chauvinistic fervour, terror, and brainwashing, to name a few. Injustice has multiplied in a way commensurate with modern warfare. (On 11 September 2001, why were victims targeted in New York, but not in Chicago or San Francisco?)

2. WHAT CAN BE DONE?

Political philosophy, which has always been more interested in the *polis*, or State, rather than the relations between the units, has focused its attention on the opposition between order and justice. In order to maintain the established order, grave injustices are often condoned, the resolution of which initially carries the risk of engendering disorder, if not civil war. It bears remembering here the saying attributed to Goethe: better injustice than disorder. This is the near universal mantra shared by almost all right-leaning people such as Kissinger. In the realm of international relations, there is, however, a third participant: peace (or war, as the case may be). It is rare for regional or world order to be established without both injustice *and* violence. I am reminded here of the order imposed by the colonial empires. Although decolonization brought back a certain brand of justice, this was often achieved by the use of force (by the 'decolonizers') and resulted in a perilous state of disorder. Many authors have viewed, or continue to view, empires (ancient or modern) as a form of government that puts justice below order and peace. But in reality, such peace is usually a 'peace of cemeteries', where maintaining order is a constant preoccupation and in the end, there is neither stable order, nor assured peace or justice.

What can be done then if one wishes (not as a naïve idealist but as a realist, horrified by constant oppression, the human and material cost of modern warfare and by the surge in passions stoked by injustice) to get closer to a form of order that is both more just and more peaceful? The reader is well aware that such a vast subject cannot be addressed in just a few paragraphs. I will, therefore, limit myself to a few comments that are more consistent than might at first appear.

1. If it is at all possible to choose, it is almost always preferable to try to achieve justice through peace rather than war. Justice, like democracy, can rarely be established with foreign gun power. It was much better that apartheid was abolished by an agreement between Blacks and Whites rather by way of a war between enemy races, which would have created a profound sense of injustice for the losing side.

2. Precisely because there is no all-powerful Olympian judge able to define 'objectively' what constitutes justice, it behoves the leaders of nations to concern themselves with the feelings of injustice created by their decisions, rather than focusing solely on objective justice. Objectively, the ragged edges of the Versailles Treaty were not scandalously unjust. But whereas a century ago the victors had refrained from humiliating the French, this time around the vindictiveness of the victors and the clause on the German responsibility left a sizeable portion of the Germans feeling humiliated. Peace which feeds resentment is a bad peace. (However, peace which does not seek to bring to justice the perpetrators of horrific acts from the victors' own camp, is neither wise nor just.)

3. States engaged in armed conflict often choose to bid farewell to arms (at least temporarily), rather than to continue their exhausting fighting. More often that not, outside mediators also tend to focus on achieving a ceasefire above all else. However, if the victory over violence is not followed by an effort to resolve the root causes of the conflicts and to reach an agreement which is acceptable (if not wholly satisfactory) to the warring factions, then peace will remain fragile enough, and the feelings of injustice strong enough, for violence to start anew. For proof of this, we can look to the

Middle East from 1947 to present or Kashmir. One should not mistake the temporary and deceptive order created by military reprieves for an order that is both peaceful and just, which should remain the primary objective.

4. In today's world establishing or re-establishing justice (or eliminating injustice) often requires the use of force. Therefore, in order to legitimize this recourse, it is necessary to endow the United Nations with its own armed forces that would be able to act quickly upon orders from the Security Council. This would be beneficial on two accounts. First, it would be more efficient, and serve more as a deterrent, than improvising a collective action in times of crisis. Second, it would prevent some actors, who might be guided solely by their own self-interest, from acting unilaterally.

5. From a Hobbesian perspective, if the international system becomes as dangerous for the survival of the habitants of Earth as civil wars, it is therefore necessary that States abandon their state of nature. Hobbes considered the state of nature to be less harmful for the states than the one individuals experienced before understanding the necessity to transfer their powers to a State able to protect them against the war of all against all, and to ensure them with a modicum of justice. The logic of the Leviathan calls then for the creation of a world State, as was understood by Morgenthau during the advent of the nuclear age. This remains true, in my opinion, in the age of transnational terrorism. For various reasons (well understood by Kant) the world is not ready for this leap. This does not preclude us, however, from taking steps towards this goal, by strengthening the power and legitimacy of international and supranational organizations. By the same token, it is of paramount importance to reduce the injustices caused by the global economy, by making certain that the market is not ruled by the law of the jungle in areas ranging from trade, to foreign investment and the environment. Here too, a just order will only be achieved if the cooperation between States and private actors leads to common rules and regulations.

6. Kant corrects Hobbes in so far as he is less concerned about the survival of individuals than about their sense of civic duty. For Kant, what constitutes the best antidote to war (whether civil war or war against outside forces) is not the transfer of the use of force to the State, or a confederation of States, but the internal transformation of the States: the transition to the rule of citizens in representative democracies, which would prevent arbitrary rule and put a damper on the warring tendencies of the Leviathans both at home and abroad. This is why the slow process towards justice and peace must include free speech and the respect for human rights.

7. This brings us back to the true foundation of international relations: not States or transnational groups but individuals. Although democracy is

often promoted as a guarantee for peace (with respect to relations between democracies), it can nonetheless be a cause of injustice and violence, unless individuals endeavour to establish three conditions. The first has to do with viewing individuals in a manner that is closer to Kantian liberalism than to the oft-weakened liberalism of the previous century. This latter liberalism tends to be concerned mainly with the rights of individuals: the primacy of individual rights over the common good, the primacy of freedom through independence over freedom through participation. Kant insists on the duties, the categorical imperatives present in the consciousness of the people, more than on freedoms. Second, despite an electoral process where the short term tends to prevail, it behoves the individuals who make up the democracy to find the necessary resources to put long-term interests ahead of short-term preoccupations. (This is possible only if there already exists a modicum of order, peace, and justice.) There are several forces that can enable, or at least help, citizens to rise above this tendency. Inside the States, a style of education is needed which is antiracist, antinationalist, and universalist (not, however, antipatriotic). Outside, international institutions need to focus on the common interest rather than the specific interest of groups or nations and need to favour the long-term view over the short-term view. Third, in the mind of citizens, reason and humanism must win over, not only the secular religion of totalitarianism and the dark passions it ignites, but also the religious fanaticism which calls stridently for the death of those who are ungodly, infidels, or 'different'. A tall order indeed. . . .

In order to achieve justice and peace despite human nature, the nature of nations and the nature of international relations, it is necessary to affect both institutions and values. As far as the latter are concerned, imagination, which allows one to understand the points of view and grievances of the Other, and its sister, compassion, are especially important. (I do not speak here of tolerance as there are all manner of injustices and violence which are intolerable.) As for institutions, it is necessary gradually to circumvent and subvert the Westphalian order and the vast area of international law that stems from it. We need to both chisel away at sovereignty and create a series of obstacles to extreme sovereignty, which is one of the worst contributors to violence and injustice.

I recently had the opportunity and the sombre pleasure of rereading *The Pest* by Camus. This, in my opinion, is not only the most beautiful novel of the twentieth century, but it is also the most convincing guide for the twenty-first century. It does not promise that rats will disappear once and for all, but it does demonstrate to us why and how we must fight against them.

3

Justice, Peace, and History: A Reappraisal

Alexis Keller

1. INTRODUCTION

Political and moral philosophy have primarily focused on the idea of a Just War. Countless books have examined the relationship between war and justice from a legal, political, or moral perspective,[1] while many studies on peace refer to 'negative peace', 'positive peace', 'armed peace', 'perpetual peace', and 'universal peace'.[2] There has, however, been little research on the concept of Just Peace and its history. Also, paradoxically, although it is now quite common to talk about Just Peace, the term is by no means easy to define. Yet recent history provides us with examples of peace processes where some elements of justice were taken into account. The post-Second World War settlement reached between France and Germany, the constitutional negotiations in South Africa between 1990 and 1994, the Dayton agreements on Yugoslavia providing for the creation of an international war crimes tribunal are all seen as examples of 'just' settlements in that they incorporate a certain sense of justice.[3]

There are several ways of examining the link between peace and justice. One is to apply methods of research on conflict resolution, which focus on the negotiating process and the way in which it is affected by the 'call for justice'.[4]

---

[1] See Michael Walzer, *Just and Unjust Wars* (New York: Basic Books, 1977).

[2] See David Barash, *Approaches to Peace* (Oxford: Oxford University Press, 2000); Joseph J. Fahey and Richard Armstrong (eds.), *A Peace Reader: Essential Readings on War, Justice, Non-violence and World Order* (New York: Paulis Press, 1992).

[3] Here, the term justice can be defined narrowly referring to its *legal* dimension. This includes condemnation of people accountable for a conflict and compensation for the wrongs suffered by the victims.

[4] Many works have been published on this subject. See, among others, Barbara Walter, *Committing to Peace* (Princeton, NJ: Princeton University Press, 2002); Paul Stern and Daniel Druckman (eds.), *International Conflict Resolution after the Cold War* (Washington, DC: National Academy Press, 2000); William Zartman, Daniel Druckman, Lloyd Jensen, Dean G. Pruitt, and H. Peyton Young, 'Negotiation as a Search for Justice', *International Negotiation*, 1/1 (1996), 79–98.

Theorists and practitioners in this field look at the extent to which such calls influence the outcome of talks. They compare case studies to extrapolate the conditions required for a Just Peace. And they insist on the importance of cultural differences, emphasizing how the individual or collective attitudes of conflicting parties and psychological factors can shape relations between negotiators.[5] Basically, for them, a 'culturalist' approach is inevitable since any process of communication is profoundly affected by differing cultural conventions, norms, meanings, assumptions, ideals, and perceptions.[6]

Another way of approaching the concept of Just Peace is to base the discussion on research into political psychology and international relations. Here, the emphasis is on the role of 'perception' and 'motivation' in decision-making process and conflict management.[7] An expanding body of literature has emerged in this field, focusing very much on the vision that individuals (be they decision-makers or not) have of the world in general and/or of a specific political situation. For example, in his book *Justice and the Genesis of War*, David Welch analyses the role of injustice in shaping decisions in international relations.[8] He shows that 'while national leaders are keenly aware of their own concern for justice, they are often insensitive to the role of the justice motive in the behaviour of others, with the result that they seriously misjudge their protagonists' interests, objectives, and resolve'.[9] Welch maintains that we can get around the inherent problem of cultural diversity (different perceptions of justice) by adopting a common conception of international justice, adding in chapter 7 that such a conception 'can only mean what *states* agree that it means; . . . in the absence of such an agreement, he explains, there is no such thing as international justice or injustice'.[10] Welch's argument is thus rooted within the liberal conception of international law based on a society of states. In such a perspective, a Just Peace is reached

[5] See Roger Fisher, *Getting Together: Building a Relationship that gets to YES* (Boston, MA: Houghton Mifflin, 1988); William B. Gudykunst and Stella Ting-Toomey, *Culture and Interpersonal Communication* (Newbury Park: Sage, 1988); William B. Gudykunst and Stella Ting-Toomey, 'Culture and Affective Communication', *American Behavioral Scientist*, 31/3 (1988), 384–400.

[6] See Raymond Cohen, *Negotiating Across Cultures: Communication Obstacles in International Diplomacy* (Washington, DC: United States Institute of Peace Press, 1991).

[7] See Robert Jervis, *Perception and Misperception in International Politics* (Princeton, NJ: Princeton University Press, 1976); and David O. Sears, *Oxford Handbook of Political Psychology* (Oxford: Oxford University Press, 2003).

[8] David Welch, *Justice and the Genesis of War* (Cambridge: Cambridge University Press, 1993).

[9] Ibid., Introduction, 2.

[10] Ibid., 200.

between what John Rawls describes as 'well-ordered peoples', which presupposes the existence of 'reasonable pluralism'.[11]

My approach in this chapter is rather different, more *historical*. I shall try to show that we have no hope of explaining what is—or is not—a Just Peace unless we pay more attention to the intellectual context in which international law was formed. Throughout the seventeenth and eighteenth centuries, attempts were made to structure a system of international relations, which reflected the new balance of power between states. Political and legal theorists were called upon to remove war and peace from their traditional theological context and redefine them on the basis of a descriptive and prescriptive understanding of nature. Various plans also emerged during this period to tackle a wide range of goals and concerns. Some initiatives aimed at bringing peace to Europe through a political solution, like Sully's 'grand design' for Henry IV in 1638, or Leibniz's plans for Europeanism. Other thinkers, such as Emeric Crucé and William Penn, clearly saw peace as the product of new relations between European states.[12] If it is true that Penn and, more specifically, his fellow Quaker, John Bellers, believed that these relations were coloured by ethical concerns, all agreed to say that peace was essentially a matter of *law* created and protected by *institutions*.[13]

The flaw in all these peace plans is that they were tailored for Europe and its monarchs. No account was taken of regions outside Europe. Tzvetan Todorov's *The Conquest of America*, Anthony Pagden's *Lords of all the World*, Richard Tuck's *The Rights of War and Peace*, and James Tully's *Stange Multiplicity* each, in their own distinctive way, have provided useful insights into the dynamics of European encounters with non-Europeans. They convincingly argue that discovery and colonization of America offered a new way of resolving the whole issue of individuals' and states' natural rights.[14] When discussing the law of nations, which was transformed, in the eighteenth

---

[11] John Rawls, *The Law of Peoples: with 'The Idea of Public Reason Revisited'* (Cambridge, MA: Harvard University Press, 1999), 4–5.

[12] Emeric Crucé, *Le Nouveau Cynée ou Discours des occasions et moyens d'établir une paix générale et la liberté de commerce par tout le monde* (Paris, 1623); Maximilien de Béthune de Sully, *Mémoires des sages et royales Oeconomies d'Estat, domestiques, politiques et militaires de Henri le Grand* (Amstelredam: 1638); William Penn, *Essay towards the present and future Peace of Europe* (London, 1693); John Bellers, *Some Reasons for a European State* (London, 1710).

[13] See Olivier Christin, *La paix de religion* (Paris: Seuil, 1997), 34–8.

[14] Tzvetan Todorov, *The Conquest of America: The Question of Other* (New York: Harper Torch, 1992); Anthony Padgen, *Lords of All the World: Ideologies of Empire in Spain, Britain and France, 1500–1800* (New Haven, CT: Yale University Press, 1995); Richard Tuck, *The Rights of War and Peace: Political Thought and the International Order from Grotius to Kant* (Oxford: Oxford University Press, 1999); James Tully, *Strange Multiplicity: Constitutionalism in an Age of Diversity* (Cambridge: Cambridge University Press, 1995). I should add that I have been greatly influenced by Tully's work.

century, into international law, early-modern theorists redefined the normative foundations of the society of states created by the expansion of Europe.
Thus, they codified the terms for membership in this community of states.
They drew the boundaries between those who belonged to the society and
those who did not. Those who did formed a moral community bound by
mutually agreed rules of conduct. And fundamental to this community was
the idea that its members were not obliged to treat non-members according to
the norms that applied to relations between themselves.

The story of the expansion of international society to one that embraced
the world as a whole has too often been written as one of *states* and the rivalry
between them. But it is also the story of the subjugation and domination of
others that are frequently overlooked by the emphasis on *interstate* conflicts.
Therefore, the history of the formative period of international law is important in that it outlines the gradual emergence in the seventeenth and eighteenth centuries of a *universalizing discourse* about law based on the equation:
culture = nation = state.[15] Other attitudes towards diversity and customs
were discarded in favour of one centralized legal conception, eloquently
exposed by Immanuel Kant and the natural law tradition. In the search for
'universal peace'—which is very different from a Just Peace—no effort was
made to integrate non-European *peoples* and non-European visions of
history. Debate was restricted to peace as expressed in normative, European,
and legal terms, based on a *homogenous* view of cultures.[16]

By codifying rules that excluded many non-European entities and individuals, international law was consistent with—and supported—an international
society that was unjust in the way it treated different peoples as unequal. As
Tuck put it: 'It cannot be a coincidence, seen from this perspective, that the
modern idea of natural rights arose in the period in which the European
nations were engaged in their dramatic competition for the domination of

---

[15] In his brilliant and inspiring study, Paul Keal defines a 'universalizing discourse' as 'one
that either has pretensions to, or is regarded as having, universal application. It is one that seeks
increasingly to include more people, societies, organizations or states into terms of reference as,
for instance, does the discourse of human rights. A universalizing discourse is accordingly one
that either expands, or has the potential to expand, the boundaries of the community to which it
refers.' See Paul Keal, *European Conquest and the Rights of Indigenous Peoples* (Cambridge:
Cambridge University Press, 2003), 85–6.

[16] It does not mean that classic international law was either a *universalizing discourse* or a
form of *cultural imperialism*. 'Parts of it', says Paul Keal, 'applied only to particular non-
European entities and did not involve the imposition of European cultural values. International
law regulated, for instance, relations between the Ottoman Empire and Europe, but was not
used to justify European domination and to deprive the peoples of the Ottoman Empire of their
rights. The development of international society brought with it different kinds of international
law depending on the nature of the relationship it was meant to regulate.' Keal, *European
Conquest and the Rights of Indigenous Peoples*, 85.

the world, and in which there were urgent questions about how both states and individuals adrift in a stateless world behave to one another and to newly encountered peoples.'[17] If we do recognize this historical conjunction between the emergence of an international society and European expansionism—and I think we should—then international law is faced with the problem of solving some conflicts, especially conflicts involving different cultures.[18] If classic theories of international law played a historical role in justifying the destruction of indigenous people's cultures, how can international law achieve a peace perceived as *just* by culturally diverse entities? Does international law have the capacity to conceptualize such a peace, which first implies the adoption of a common language, understood and accepted by *all* conflicting parties?[19]

I shall accordingly divide my chapter into three parts. The first focuses on some arguments about 'barbarians' elaborated by theorists of the natural rights tradition in the seventeenth and eighteenth centuries. The second concerns the American and French debates on the definition of the terms 'constitution' and 'nation' at the end of the eighteenth century. I shall use these examples to illustrate the rise of a uniform way of apprehending otherness and law. The third turns to another body of thought, which approached non-Europeans and native peoples completely differently. I shall try to show that some thinkers accepted—to a certain extent—the idea of cultural diversity and introduced the principle of *recognition*. They challenged the exclusionary view of the law of nations of their time. They put into question the moral legitimacy of the international society in which they lived. Finally, in the conclusion, I shall venture to offer some suggestions for a possible way of building the concept of Just Peace. Those who are only interested in the story may disregard the theory; those who are only interested in the theory may disregard the story. My aim is to suggest a theory rooted in history.

---

[17] Tuck, *The Rights of War and Peace*, 14–15.

[18] We adopt Stella Ting-Toomey's definition of intercultural conflict as 'the perceived or actual incompatibility of values, norms, processes, or goals between a minimum of two cultural parties over content, identity, relational, and procedural issues. While everyday intercultural conflicts are often based on cultural ignorance or misunderstanding, it is obvious that not all intercultural conflicts are based on miscommunication or lack of understanding. Some intercultural conflicts are based on deep-seated hatred, and centuries-old antagonism often arising from long-standing historical grievances.' See Stella Ting-Toomey, *Communicating Across Cultures* (New York: The Guilford Press, 1999), 194.

[19] That does not mean that international law nowadays cannot play a crucial role in reclaiming and entrenching the rights of indigenous people. See James Anaya, *Indigenous Peoples in International Law* (Oxford: Oxford University Press, 1986) and Keal, *European Conquest and the Rights of Indigenous Peoples*, especially ch. 4.

2. THE LAW OF NATIONS AND THE RIGHTS
OF NON-EUROPEAN PEOPLES

After the European discovery of the 'New World', two questions became increasingly important to the reflections on war and peace. These were whether Europeans had the right to occupy the land inhabited by non-Europeans and whether the use of force against them was justifiable. As explained by Tuck, the principal thinkers engaged in this task were grounded in one of the two traditions of thinking about war and peace current at the beginning of the seventeenth century.

One, the more familiar to modern historians, was the scholastic tradition, represented principally by the Dominicans and Jesuits of Spain and Portugal, which persisted in judging warfare by the Thomist criteria, and which was therefore inevitably critical of much actual modern military activity (and in particular the conquest of Central America). The other was... the humanist tradition, which applauded warfare in the interests of one's *respublica*, and saw a dramatic moral difference between Christian, European civilization and barbarism.[20]

Hugo Grotius played a primary role in inventing a new way of talking about international order. He was recognized even by his contemporaries as a key figure in the history of the law of nations.[21] In both *De Jure Praedae Commentarius*, which Grotius himself called *De Indis*, and his later *De Jure Belli ac Pacis*, he addressed questions related to legal position of non-European peoples. He based his arguments on two significant claims. First, that there is no significant moral difference between individuals and states and that both may use violence in the same way and for the same ends. Second, that natural man was sociable—in an Epicurean sense—and that this *thin* notion of sociability was resting on a general view of the role of self-interest in the natural world.[22]

Like his Spanish predecessors—Las Casas, Sepulveda, and Vitoria—Grotius worked from the precepts of natural law, but by the time he wrote, states had begun to loom larger and with them the need for a new law of nations. According to him, such law of nations was clearly differing from natural law. Humans had to shape it through consensus, without reverting to natural

[20] Tuck, op. cit., 78.

[21] Prior to the seventeenth century the term 'law of nations' was a literal translation of the Roman *jus gentium*, which was Roman law concerned with relationships among individuals and was law the Romans applied to themselves and to foreigners. For chronological purposes, I will assume that *jus gentium* is operating from the sixteenth to the beginning of the seventeenth century, whereas the law of nations prevails since then to the end of the eighteenth century, leading up to the inception of international law as a purported branch of public law and an embryonic scientific discipline.

[22] Tuck, op. cit., 78–108.

law.[23] Hence, he argued that knowledge of the law of nations was not inherent, but derived from jurisprudence, which explains the number of historical and biblical examples used to back up his principles. Drawing comparisons with the individual, Grotius defined *states* as the sole agents capable of promulgating the law of nations. Unlike the laws of each state that were to do with the interests of that state, the law of nations represented certain laws that originated between all states. It was the expression of a common consent.

Grotius believed in the possibility of a law common to all peoples. He insisted on legitimizing treaties with non-Christians and condemned attempts to convert the latter through religious wars (notably in his 1604 work, *De Indis*).[24] Nevertheless, his understanding of the law of nations remained deeply *Eurocentric*.[25] It was very much about conquering the world and justifying Dutch commercial expansion. For example, endorsing the humanist argument over the right to inflict violence on barbaric peoples, Grotius supported an international 'right to punish', which was relevant for the law of nations. In 1625, he wrote:

It is proper also to observe that kings and those who are invested with a Power equal to that of Kings, have a Right to exact Punishments, not only for Injuries committed against themselves, or their Subjects, but likewise, for those which do not peculiarly concern them, but which are, in any Persons whatsoever, grievous Violations of the Law of Nature or Nations. For the Liberty of consulting the Benefit of Human Society, by Punishments, which at first, as we have seen, was in every particular Person, does now, since Civil Societies, and Court of Justice, have been instituted, reside in those who are possessed of the supreme power.... War may be justly undertaken against those who are inhuman to theirs Parents... [against those who kill Strangers that come to dwell amongst them] [*a sentence found only in the 1625 edition*]; against those who eat human Flesh...; and against those who practice Piracy... War is lawful against those who offend against Nature.[26]

While Grotius tempers his judgement somewhat a few paragraphs further on, he is clearly espousing a position legitimizing European action against indigenous or colonized peoples. In doing so, he retraces some of the arguments used by the Spanish to justify their conquest of the New World.

[23] For a general account of Grotius' views about natural law, see Alfred Dufour, 'Grotius et le droit naturel du dix-septième siècle', in *The World of Hugo Grotius: 1583–1645* (Amsterdam; Maarssen: APA-Holland University Press, 1984), 15–41.

[24] These arguments have led numerous scholars to praise Grotius's enlightened attitude towards non-European peoples. An excellent example of such view is to be found in Charles Alexandrowicz, *An Introduction to the History of the Law of Nations in the East Indies* (Oxford: Oxford University Press, 1967).

[25] See Joan-Pau Rubiés, 'Hugo Grotius's Dissertation on the Origin of the American Peoples and the Use of Comparative Methods', *Journal of the History of Ideas*, 52 (1991), 221–44.

[26] Grotius, *De Jure Belli ac Pacis*, book II, ch. 20, 40, trans. by Tuck, *The Rights of War and Peace*, 102–3.

Another example concerns Grotius' position on the right of property, as set out in book II, chapters 2, 3, and 4 of *De Jure Belli ac Pacis*. Two arguments are used here. The first highlights the link between property and uncultivated land, later expanded on by John Locke.[27] Grotius claims that barren and waste land in a territory must be given to foreigners who request it, and may even be occupied by foreigners, since there can be no ownership of uncultivated land. A nation or indeed a group of individuals with an institutional identity can therefore appropriate land that is not being processed in any way and is thus losing its potential for cultivation. Grotius' second argument draws on the law of the Sea and distinguishes between *property* and *jurisdiction*:

> As to what belongs to no Body, there are two Things which one may take Possession of, Jurisdiction, and the Right of Property, as it stands distinguished from Jurisdiction... Jurisdiction is commonly exercised on two Subjects, the one primary, *viz.* Persons, and that alone is sometimes sufficient, as in an Army of Men, Women, and Children, that are going in quest of some new Plantations; the other secondary, *viz.* The Place, which is called Territory...[28]

On the one hand, in its 'primary' sense, sovereignty is jurisdiction over persons; in its other, secondary, sense, it relates to the possession of territory. Practically, foreigners could acquire ownership rights to territory in another state, without interfering with the sovereign jurisdiction that a ruler has over his or her subjects.[29]

Both examples demonstrate the extent to which Grotius' law of nations was tailored to Europe and its expansionism. The underlying premise appears to be that state-building is inevitable and indigenous populations non-existent. Civil and religious peace were undeniably central concerns in Grotian ideology, but they were wedded to a Eurocentric vision of the law of nations, feeding arguments to those seeking to justify nascent European expansion.[30] As Tuck explains, 'far from being an heir to the tradition of Vitoria and Suarez, as was assumed by writers at the beginning of the century [the twentieth], he [Grotius] was in fact an heir to the tradition Vitoria most mistrusted, that of humanist

---

[27] Several scholars have noticed the affinities between Grotius's thinking here and the subsequent arguments of Locke and other liberal political theorists, noting especially Grotius's use of the American Indians to illustrate a contemporary people that still lived in the simplistic, natural manner of communal property and therefore where the natural right of *occupatio* might still be exercised by colonial settlers in his own time. See Barbara Arneil, *John Locke and America: The Defence of English Colonialism* (Oxford: Clarendon Press, 1996), 46–54.

[28] Grotius, *De Jure Belli ac Pacis*, book II, chs. 3–4, translated by Tuck, *The Rights of War and Peace*, 106–7.

[29] Ibid., book II, ch. 12.

[30] On Grotius' irenicist thought, see Peter Haggenmacher, 'La paix dans la pensée de Grotius', in Lucien Bely (ed.), *L'Europe des traités de Westphalie* (Paris: Presses Universitaires de France, 2000), 55–79.

jurisprudence ... Grotius endorsed for a state the most far-reaching set of rights to make war which were available to the contemporary repertoire. In particular he accepted a strong version of an international right to punish, and appropriate territory which was not being used properly by indigenous peoples.'[31]

Hobbes clearly resurrected Grotian 'humanist' reasoning on war and peace, although his theoretical assumptions on the 'state of nature' were radically different. The analogy between the state of nature and the international order, and the idea that indigenous peoples were merely *users* of the land they inhabited were central to Hobbes's thought.[32] Tuck shows how Pufendorf strongly disagreed with Grotius on the right to settle land that was of no use or at least not properly used by its alleged owners. He did not accept Grotius' theory that the possession of the material world, which is useful for our personal consumption, was a fundamental right. Pufendorf fine-tuned the idea of man's inherent sociability, thus paving the way for a less aggressive interventionist concept of the law of nations, which deemed colonization to be incompatible with the ethics of a modern trading nation. Kant was to share that view. But it was Locke, in his response to Hobbes and Pufendorf, who drew on Grotian arguments on the nature and goal of the law of nations and provided arguments to secure the expansion of European 'nations'.

Like his contemporaries, Locke was also called upon to justify land appropriation by the British Empire. He had to apply Grotius' theory to a world in which there was no 'explicit agreement between all co-owners'.[33] Locke built his position around two theories which came to have a major bearing on modern political philosophy and are particularly significant for this chapter: (1) an evolutionist theory of history and (2) a theory of property.

(1) Discarding both Hobbes and Pufendorf, Locke defined the state of nature as one characterized by equality and freedom. Seen in this way, the state of nature is not entirely irreconcilable with the civil state since it already constitutes a social state of sorts. The law of nature stipulating self-preservation and preservation of the human species is an integral part of civil society. However, war can erupt at any point in the state of nature, since there is no common judge to punish violence. Locke saw the state of nature as a delicate balance between war and peace, a balance that may be tipped at any point since we all act as our own judges. Civil society is formed when humans

---

[31] Tuck, op. cit., 108.

[32] From this perspective, Hobbes represents the culmination of the humanist tradition concerning the thinking about war and peace. See Tuck, *The Rights of War and Peace*, 138.

[33] On Locke and natives peoples, see James Tully, *An Approach to Political Philosophy: Locke in Contexts* (Cambridge: Cambridge University Press, 1993), especially the chapter 'Rediscovering America: The Two Treatises and Aboriginal Rights', 137–78; see also, from the same author, 'Placing the Two Treatises', in Nicolas Phillipson and Quentin Skinner (eds.), *Political Discourse in Early Modern Britain* (Cambridge: Cambridge University Press, 1993), 253–82.

renounce their right to exercise executive authority and adopt a constitution based on a declaration of their natural rights. Society's sole task is to safeguard those rights. Locke links the duty of self-preservation with the moral imperative of protecting the common good. Individual sovereignty is reined in by the public good. The state of nature, however, exists *between nations* since there is no higher power to which civil societies can yield their executive authority. The solution is to build a law of nations binding *nations* in the same way that the declaration of natural rights binds civil society, in other words, create a legal bond to maintain peace.

This vision of the state of nature was the basis for Locke's evolutionist theory of history. It enabled him to deny indigenous peoples the right to call themselves 'nations'. He saw them as the oldest and most primitive members of the human species. In his *Second Treatise of Government* (§ 49, 108) Locke explained that 'in the beginning, all the World was *America*, and more than that is now', and added a few chapters further on that '*America . . .* is still a Pattern of the first Ages in *Asia* and *Europe*.'[34] European societies were at the forefront of evolution and civilization, whereas America had remained in the state of nature. It had neither people's sovereignty nor genuine territorial authority. It was a continent of hunters and gatherers, which put it at the first stage of economic civilization and prevented it from being considered a 'nation'. As such, America could not be subject to the same criteria as European nations.

(2) It is no secret that Locke did not share Hobbes's belief in a war of all against all. He agreed with Hobbes that natural law was rooted in the individual's survival instinct, but had a very different perception of that instinct as a result of his theory of property. That theory also helped him to deny colonized peoples any property rights.

Locke proposed a new definition of property as the *product of labour*, thus making it an extension of the individual. Property can exist in the state of nature, since labour does. Hence, 'Man (by being Master of himself, and *Proprietor of his own Person*, and the Actions or *Labour* of it) had still in himself *the great Foundation of Property*.'[35] In a new departure from traditional thinking, Locke defines property as autonomous, private, and personal. He makes no distinction between self-preservation and the protection of property. Society's purpose is to maintain civil peace *and* protect property. The concept of property sums up and expands the concept of the individual. It covers life, liberty, and wealth. According to Locke (*Second Treatise*, § 123),

---

[34] John Locke, *Two Treatises of Government*, ed. Peter Laslett (Cambridge: Cambridge University Press, 1988), 301 and 339.

[35] Ibid., 298.

'tis [it is] not without reason, that he [man] seeks out, and is willing to joyn in Society with others who are already united, or have a mind to unite for the mutual *Preservation* of their Lives, Liberties and Estates, which I call by the general Name—*Property*.'[36]

Locke's definition of property is relevant to our discussions here. Since 'Indians' were still in a state of nature, their property rights were limited to the product of their labour. They 'owned' the fruit and nuts they gathered, the wild grain they harvested, and the meat they hunted, but *not* the land they inhabited.[37] Representatives of civilized societies, on the other hand, had *governments* and *laws* defining land ownership rules. They cultivated the land and were entitled to impose harsh peace terms on them for any damage sustained. Remaining in the state of nature, Indians could be punished or destroyed 'as a *Lyon* or a *Tyger*, one of those wild Savage Beasts, with whom Men can have no Society nor Security'.[38] According to Locke, peace existed between 'nations', whose very existence meant they were no longer in a state of nature. Locke accepted that some indigenous peoples were organized in nations and subject to a type of government, but did not equate their customs with 'constitutional' laws. In other words, he remained trapped in a view in which 'sovereignty', 'law', and 'constitution' were defined according to European legal criteria. In fact, as Tully explains, Locke's purpose, at least in part, was 'to legitimate and to celebrate the superiority of English colonial market agriculture over Amerindian hunting, gathering, and replacement agriculture that it forcefully displaced'.[39] Throughout the eighteenth century the arguments underpinning Locke's first and second theories were widely applied to describe dealings between 'peoples'. They shaped debate on the law of nations, both by those in favour of it, like Vattel, or those who critized it, like Rousseau.

It is true that opposition to the European expansion intensified as of 1730, fuelled by the naturalists and anthropologists of the Enlightenment. For example, in his *Considérations sur les causes de la grandeur des Romains et de leur décadence* [*Considerations on the Causes of the Greatness of the Romans and their Decline*], Montesquieu fleshed out the argument that Roman conquerors lost their civic virtues as they built their Empire. He reviled conquest for turning armies into a Praetorian Guard. Occupying forces could be more usefully employed in defending their own territory.[40] The eighteenth century

---

[36] Ibid., 350.
[37] Ibid., on this point, see especially §. 28, 30, 34, 41–3, 48–9.
[38] Ibid., 274.
[39] Tully, *An Approach to Political Philosophy*, 162.
[40] Montesquieu, 'Considérations sur les causes de la grandeur des Romains et de leur décadence', *Œuvres complètes*, 2 vols. (Paris: Gallimard, 1949), 69–209; see especially chapters 9 and 10.

saw an entire intellectual movement violently attack expansionist ambitions and deconstruct the myth of empires. At its helm were figures such as Hume, Diderot, Condorcet, and Abbé Raynal. As Hume explained in his essay, *Of the Balance of Power,*

enormous monarchies are, probably, destructive to human nature, in their progress, in their continuance, and even in their downfall, which never can be very distant from their establishment. The military genius, which aggrandized the monarchy, soon leaves the court, the capital, and the centre of such a government, while the wars are carried on at a great distance, and interest so small a part of the state.... This is the necessary progress of human affairs; thus human nature checks itself in its airy elevation; thus ambition blindly labours for the destruction of the conqueror, of his family, and of everything near and dear to him.[41]

Nonetheless, it was broadly accepted that there could be no return to 'the old order of things'. It was not possible to send settlers back home, drive them out of the towns they had built and away from land that they had cultivated for years. No one was suggesting withdrawal in the modern sense of the term. Criticism of empires, or what Hume termed 'enormous monarchies', was aimed at bringing about economic rationalization, ushering in a new era in which social ties were based primarily on trade.[42] We should therefore not be fooled by the seemingly radical nature of criticism levelled against wars fuelled by kings. The law of war might have been questioned because of its underlying immoral view of human relations, but it was by no means discarded. War and peace were still described in terms of 'laws' and 'nations'. While colonial expansion had fallen out of favour, relations between Europeans and non-Europeans were still governed by Locke's arguments.

That same view was held by Emmer de Vattel, who in 1758 published *The Law of Nations, or Principles of the Law of Nature*, one of the texts most widely quoted by members of America's constituent assembly. Underpinning Vattel's philosophy is the idea that mankind is split into nations. He saw Europe as a balance of powers, prompting him to reject the notion of *civitas maxima* developed by his mentor, Christian Wolff.

A nation or a state is, as has been said at the beginning of this work, a body politic, or a society of men united together for the purpose of promoting their mutual safety and advantage by their combined strength. From the very design that induces a number of men to form a society which has its common interests, and which is to act in concert, it is necessary that there should be established a Public Authority, to order and direct

---

[41] David Hume, *Theory of Politics*, ed. Frederick Watkins (Austin, TX: University of Texas Press, 1953), 192.

[42] On this point, see Anthony Pagden, *Lords of all the World: Ideologies of Empire in Spain, Britain and France, 1500–1800* (New Haven, CT; London: Yale University Press, 1995), 156–77.

what is to be done by each in relation to the end [objective] of the association. This political authority is the Sovereignty; and he or they who are invested with it are the Sovereign.[43]

Vattel believed that humanity was destined to form nations. As such, he echoes Grotius, despite protesting otherwise. Society's objectives are pursued through the mediation of states, rather than in a universal context. Politics is a feature of a society of states bound by common interests and recognized rules and institutions. Nations sign treaties for the exact same reason humans leave behind the state of nature. Treaties give tangible shape to the 'social contract' between nations.

Vattel's system of international order was one in which individual human beings were excluded as direct subjects of international law. Peoples could only assert rights against the state and were therefore cut off from appeal to international society. And there were implications to equating the idea of nation with that of a state or sovereign people. It automatically excluded from international order any population not organized into a 'nation', such as native peoples. It also implied a territorial perception of the state, with all its limits and needs. Vattel conceded that, 'no nation can lawfully appropriate to herself a too disproportionate extent of country, and reduce other nations to want subsistence, and a place of abode',[44] but, like Locke, believed that

the cultivation of the soil deserves the attention of the government, not only on account of the invaluable advantages that flow from it, but from its being an obligation imposed by nature on mankind. The whole earth is destined to feed its inhabitants; but it would be incapable of doing this if it were uncultivated. *Every nation is then obliged by the law of nature to cultivate the land that has fallen to its share*; and it has no right to enlarge its boundaries, or have recourse to the assistance of other nations, but in proportion as the land in its possession is incapable of furnishing it with necessaries. Those nations (such as the ancient Germans, and some modern Tartars) who inhabit fertile countries, but disdain to cultivate their lands and choose rather to live by plunder, are wanting to [failing] themselves, are injurious to all their neighbours, and *deserve to be extirpated as savage and pernicious beasts*. There are others, who, to avoid labour, choose to live only by hunting, and their flocks. This might, doubtless, be allowed in the first ages of the world, when the earth, without cultivation, produced more than was sufficient to feed its small number of inhabitants. But at present, when the human race is so greatly multiplied, it could not subsist if all nations were disposed to live in that manner.... Thus, though the conquest of the civilized empires of Peru and Mexico was a notorious

[43] Emmer de Vattel, *Le droit des gens ou principes de la loi naturelle* (London, 1758), book I, ch. 1, § 1–2. (my translation from the 1916 Washington edition).

[44] Ibid., book II, ch. 7, § 86 (my translation).

usurpation, the establishment of...colonies on the continent of North America *might, on their confining themselves within just bounds, be extremely lawful. The people of those extensive tracts rather ranged through than inhabited them.*[45]

Through Vattel's work, colonization gained legitimacy, and weaker states or 'nations' were urged to join leagues forming blocs of equal strength. And so, while acknowledging the need of moral conscience in the law of nations, Vattel ultimately concluded that to secure legal status, international law would have to be and remain morally flawed. In his own words:

The effect of the whole is, to produce, at least externally and in the eyes of mankind, a perfect equality of rights between nations..., *without regard to the intrinsic justice of their conduct*, of which others have no right to form a definitive judgment....It is therefore necessary, on many occasions, that nations should suffer certain things to be done, though in their own nature unjust and condemnable, because they cannot oppose them by open force, without violating the liberty of some particular state, and destroying the foundations of their natural society.[46]

Kant, who is often viewed as the founding father of liberal political thinking, dissociated himself from Grotius, Pufendorf, and Vattel, calling them the 'sorry comforters' in his essay on perpetual peace.[47] Looking at the various texts in which Kant discussed peace and world order, it is clear that humanity can achieve freedom and moral progress if it fulfils certain conditions, broadly set out in his perpetual peace project. His three definitive articles correspond to the three legal categories required for perpetual peace, that is, civil law, international law, and cosmopolitan law. They are: (*a*) 'The Civil Constitution of every State shall be Republican'; (*b*) 'The Right of Nations shall be based on a Federation of Free States'; and (*c*) 'Cosmopolitan Right shall be limited to Conditions of Universal Hospitality'. Perpetual peace has to be born of a federation of republican states. Kant saw no use for a law of nations to be based on a law of war. Seen in this light, the latter is not a law but rather a set of maxims.[48] Kant's analysis is underpinned by a powerful notion: that the prerequisites for a republican order in a state are not only the regulations of the international system, but also a cosmopolitan legal framework which will unite all peoples and individuals as world citizens, thus eliminating war.

---

[45] Emmer de Vattel, *Le droit des gens ou principes de la loi naturelle* (London, 1758), book I, ch. 7, § 81 (my translation and my italics).

[46] Ibid., Prolegomena, § 21 (my translation).

[47] Immanuel Kant, *Political Writings*, ed. Hans Reiss (Cambridge: Cambridge University Press, 1991), 103.

[48] On this point, his views differ significantly from those of Grotius, Pufendorf, and Vattel.

Although Kant firmly eschewed the 'sorry comforters', his vision of peace, like that of his predecessors, was still rooted in a legal tradition based on a European vision of law and on the idea of representative government.[49] In his own words, 'to accord with the concept of right, it [the government] must be based on the representative system. This system alone makes possible a republican state, and without it, despotism and violence will result, no matter what kind of constitution is in force.'[50] This imperative emerges clearly in his discussion on the foundations of cosmopolitan law. Kant argues that a lasting alliance between peoples must be backed by a constitution, which requires a certain moral disposition on the part of its signatories. That moral disposition is neither instinctive nor easily attained, creating a tension. For want of the requisite moral predisposition, a cosmopolitan law is unrealistic, yet the sovereignty of states cannot be sacrificed for a global state. Kant's answer is to develop a philosophy, which restores the evolutionist vision of history, a type of socialization of mankind. He describes human as the only living being who must 'produce everything out of himself. Everything had to be entirely of his own making—the discovery of a suitable diet, of clothing, of external security and defence..., as well as all the pleasures that can make life agreeable.'[51] Their self-education conflicts with the emergence of social groupings. The first source of conflict lies in 'mankind's unsociable sociability', in the 'tendency to come together in society, coupled, however, with a continual resistance which constantly threatens to break this society up'.[52] Freedom in society paves the way for wide scale conflict, which in turn shapes freedom itself by spawning common laws within a nation and then between all states, to protect individual rights. The ultimate goal in Kantian thinking is clearly the creation of republican institutions, in which mankind continues to progress towards moral freedom through its 'unsocial sociability'. Kant could therefore conclude that native peoples—hunters and gatherers—had not fully evolved since they had no constitution or government. They had yet to farm the land. Increased trade would initiate these backward peoples in the advantages of farming and, to a certain extent, republican constitutions. 'In this way,' Kant concluded, 'continents distant from each other can enter into peaceful mutual relations which may eventually be regulated by public laws, thus bringing the human race nearer and nearer to a cosmopolitan constitution.'[53]

---

[49] On this point, see Jerome B. Schneewind, *The Invention of Autonomy: A History of Modern Moral Philosophy* (Cambridge: Cambridge University Press, 1998), especially the final chapter.

[50] Kant, 'Perpetual Peace: a Philosophical Sketch', *Political Writings*, 102.

[51] Kant, 'Idea for a Universal History with a Cosmopolitan Purpose', *Political Writings*, 43.

[52] Ibid., 44.

[53] Kant, 'Perpetual Peace', *Political Writings*, 106.

Notwithstanding his vision of history, Kant categorically condemned the excesses of colonial wars, which he deemed unjust and horrendous. In doing so, he rejected Locke's views on the 'right of acquisition'. In a famous passage from his *Metaphysics of Morals* (chapter II), Kant argued that

the question arises how far does authorization to take possession of a piece of land extend? As far as the capacity for controlling it extends, that is, as far as whoever wants to appropriate it can defend it—as if the land were to say, if you cannot protect me you cannot command me. This is how the dispute over whether the sea is *free* or *closed* also has to be decided; for example, as far as cannon shot can reach no one may fish, haul up amber from the ocean floor, and so forth, along the coast of a territory that already belongs to a certain state. Moreover, in order to acquire land is it necessary to develop it (build on it, cultivate it, drain it, and so on) ? No.... When first acquisition is in question, developing land is nothing more than an external sign of taking possession, for which many other signs that costs less effort can be substituted.

Commenting on the right to colonize uninhabited regions or those inhabited by 'American Indians' or 'Hottentots', Kant concluded that, 'such way of acquiring land is therefore to be repudiated'.[54]

Despite some gaping differences in opinion, all the natural law theorists we have seen perceived relations with indigenous peoples through a 'standard' prism of law, which required integration, if necessary by force. Natives were not seen as a fully-fledged 'people', 'nation', or 'state' and therefore had no place in the legal system developed by those building the law of nations. *The peace offered to indigenous peoples was on European terms, forcing them to choose between exclusion and assimilation.*[55] Both Locke and Kant admittedly put forward arguments to support the constitutional recognition of colonized peoples, but their theories on the original contract (the mythical 'state of nature'), their analysis of private property and their definition of the modern state presented a world view in which indigenous peoples were very much marginalized. The law of nations was built on a rather monolithic understanding of culture, leading to inequality in international order. At the end of the eighteenth century, the 'empire of uniformity', using Tully's words, had choked off political and legal pluralism, preventing genuine recognition of cultural diversity across the world.

[54] Kant, 'Doctrine of Right', *The Metaphysics of Morals*, ed. and intro. Mary J. Gregor and Allen Wood (Cambridge: Cambridge University Press, 1996), 416–18. It must be said that Kant's position on the right of acquisition is sometime ambiguous, as the end of paragraph 15 shows. He thus concludes that 'this problem (of the sole, original external acquisition) [is] the hardest of all to solve'.

[55] See Pablo Gutierrez Vega, 'The Municipalization of the Legal Status of the Indigenous Nations by Modern (European) International Law', in René Kuppe, Richard Potz (eds.), *Law and Anthropology. International Yearbook for Legal Anthropology* (Leiden : Martin Nijhoff Publishers, 2005) vol. 12, 17–54.

3. ASSIMILATING NON-EUROPEANS: THE AMERICAN AND THE FRENCH REVOLUTIONS

The American and French revolutions merely exacerbated the trend I have described. America in 1787 bore no resemblance to France in 1789, but both were convinced of the need for a representative system, in one case to create the modern republic, in the other to replace an absolutist regime by creating a new political order. To this end, they crafted a system, which enshrined the principles of individual autonomy and collective authority. They devised a new 'common' language for modern politics based on a new perception of what a constitution should be and how a nation should be defined.

In a major study, Gerald Stourzh demonstrated that the US founding fathers had no uniform understanding of the concept of constitution in the late eighteenth century.[56] In a nutshell, they could adopt two meanings. First, the term had conventionally an institutional dimension, whereby a constitution structures political and legal authority. It described the arrangement of elements in a political body. A constitution sets out the organization and operation of public authorities and authorizes various political entities to carry out specific tasks. Seen in this light, the Philadelphia Convention draft was indeed a constitution. The second meaning of the term constitution was that of a prescriptive text enshrining constitutional law as supreme. In that perspective, the constitution was the highest norm in a hierarchy of legal standards. It was supreme because it originated in the constitutive power of the people, who held ultimate sway in the political and legal order. According to Stourzh, '[T]he rise of the constitution as the *paramount law*, reigning supreme and therefore invalidating, if procedurally possible, any law of a lower level in the hierarchy of legal norms, including "ordinary" legislator-made law, is *the* great innovation and achievement of American eighteenth-century constitutionalism.'[57] In other words, 1787 saw the US founding fathers adopting the idea of a constitution as a means of structuring authority, with one major change: for the first time ever, they defined constitution as a supreme law.[58] In doing so, they echoed the views of Pufendorf and Vattel, who, in 1758, described a constitution as, 'the fundamental regulation that

---

[56] Gerald Stourzh, 'Constitution: Changing Meanings of the Term from the Early Seventeenth to the Late Eighteenth Century', in Terence Ball and J. G. A. Pocock (eds.), *Conceptual Change and the Constitution* (Lawrence, KS: University Press of Kansas, 1988), 35–54.

[57] Ibid., 47.

[58] See Judith N. Shklar, 'A New Constitution for a New Nation', in A. E. Dick Howard (ed.), *The United States Constitution: Roots, Rights and Responsabilities* (Washington, DC: Smithsonian Institution Press, 1992), 136.

determines the manner in which the public authority is to be executed'.[59] Like Thomas Paine, they expounded a modern theory of constitutionalism, based on rational and, above all, *uniform* principles.

This is also reflected in the *Federalist Papers'* interpretation of what constitutes the 'people'. Admittedly the definition was somewhat ambivalent in those turbulent months of 1787 and 1788, as exemplified by Madison. He saw 'people' as a dynamic concept, and emphasized the plurality of an America made up of different states. He also stressed the unity of the American people, identifying them as a distinct entity, ranked higher than federal or state governments.[60] But it is worth noting that he remained firmly wedded to a vision of the 'American people' that excluded the indigenous peoples, described in the *US Declaration of Independence*, in 1776, as, '*merciless Indian Savages whose known rule of warfare, is an undistinguished destruction of all ages, sexes and conditions*'.[61] Although the *Federalists* subscribed to the pluralist school of thought, allowing for various factions as an expression of freedom, Madison in particular still clung to an exclusive, narrow-minded understanding of the 'American people'. As Gordon Wood put it, 'Americans had begun the Revolution assuming that the people were a homogenous entity in society set against the rulers. Such an assumption belied American experience, and it took only a few years of independence to convince the best American minds that distinctions in the society were various and unavoidable, so much so that they could not be embodied in the government.'[62]

A similar kind of debate marked discussions on the definition of the 'French nation' in 1789.[63] The French revolution had identified the nation as the sovereign entity, but had yet to give shape to this notion, which could no longer be defined by using Old Regime terminology. In post-revolutionary France, nation-building was closely linked to the fight against diversity, ultimately equated with privilege. The year 1790 saw efforts get under way to standardize language and root out dialects. In his *Rapport sur la nécessité et les moyens d'anéantir les patois et d'universaliser l'usage de la langue française* [*Report on the Need and Means for Wiping Out Dialects and Enforcing Use of*

---

[59] Emer de Vattel, *Le droit des gens ou principes de la loi naturelle*, book I, ch. 3, § 27 (my translation).

[60] Alexander Hamilton, James Madison, and John Jay, *The Federalists Papers with Letters of 'Brutus'*, ed. Terence Ball (Cambridge: Cambridge University Press, 2003), especially no. 39 and no. 46.

[61] The US Constitution Online, *The Declaration of Independence*, http://www.usconstitution.net/declar.html (my italics).

[62] Gordon Wood, *The Creation of the American Republic, 1776–1787* (Chapel Hill, NC: University of North Carolina Press, 1969), 606.

[63] Among the vast literature on this topic, see Marcel Gauchet, *La révolution des droits de l'homme* (Paris: Gallimard, 1989) and Claude Nicolet, *Histoire, Nation, République* (Paris: Odile Jacob, 2000).

the French Language] presented to the Convention in 1794, Abbé Grégoire argued that a common language was the cornerstone of a single indivisible republic.[64] It was necessary for the state to work towards the same goal of unity. As of 1792, French government sought to introduce the tools and techniques needed to structure society. The decision was taken to standardize weights and measures. A law passed on 7 April 1795 enshrined the decimal metric system. In its first article, it urged citizens to, 'prove their commitment to a united indivisible republic by using the new measures in their calculations and business transactions'.[65]

This call for unity cut across all the French revolutionary discourse. In 1789, the 'nation' was perceived as a homogenous entity opposed to the Old Regime's *société des corps* [society of bodies] and described by Sieyès as 'the great body of citizens'. Camille Desmoulins most eloquently expressed public sentiment on this point, asking:

Is there now any distinction between provinces? Do you wish to separate us, break us up apart? Are we not one big family, one large body? Are there divisions in the founding assembly? Do we not all share one and the same home? ... In one of his fits of eloquence, Saint Paul wrote 'you have all been born again in baptism. You are no longer Jews, Samaritans, Romans or Greeks; you are all Christians.' In the same way, we have been born again in the National Assembly. We no longer hail from Chartres or Montlhéry, Picardy or Brittany, Aix or Arras; *we are all French, all brothers.*[66]

The goal was patently to streamline and assimilate all in sight, to create a sense of national identity. In the words of Sieyès, 'assimilation was the first prerequisite for *a true nation, a single united people.*'[67]

No one more than Condorcet understood the Revolution's ambiguous philosophy on dealings with other cultures. In his *Esquisse d'un tableau historique des progrès de l'esprit humain* [*Historical Overview of Advances in Human Thinking*] (1794), he attacked colonialism, reserving particular bile for Christian overseas missionaries. He applied the adjectives conventionally used to describe 'barbarians' (bloodthirsty, tyrannical, and ignorant) to colonizers, missionaries and those on the old continent who clung to ancient 'superstitions'. The new task at hand, however, was to educate, emancipate, and civilize. The sanctity of religion gave way to the sanctity of civilization.

---

[64] See Michel de Certeau, Dominique Julia, and Jacques Revel, *Une politique de la langue: la Révolution française et les patois* (Paris: Gallimard, 1975).

[65] Quoted in Pierre Rosanvallon, *L'Etat en France de 1789 à nos jours* (Paris: Seuil, 1990), 103 (my translation).

[66] Camille Desmoulins, *Oeuvres de Camille Desmoulins* (Paris, 1874), vol. I, 218–19 (my translation).

[67] Sieyès, 'Sur le projet de décret pour l'établissement de l'instruction nationale', *Journal d'instruction sociale*, no. 5, 6 July 1793, 146 (my translation).

Condorcet's text clearly points to the same ultimate goal. Enlightenments must civilize other cultures just as missionaries had sought to convert all of humanity to Christianity. In a well-known passage, he urges readers to

examine the history of our endeavours and settlements in Africa or Asia. There you will see trade monopolies, betrayal, violent contempt for those of a different colour or faith, outrageous land-grabbing, overzealous proselytising and plotting on the part of our priests. These actions destroyed the respect and kindness initially secured through our more enlightened philosophy and ability to trade. However, the time is coming when we will offer them more than corrupt tyrants, becoming instead useful catalysts, benevolent liberators. Europeans will then confine themselves to free trade and value their own rights too much to flout those of other peoples. They will finally honour the independence they have hitherto so brazenly violated.... When that day comes, men will spread the word to all nations of the truths that will make them joyful and enlighten them as to their interests and rights. The pursuit of truth is a passion that should be shared with distant lands, once it has rid our shores of gross prejudice and grievous misconceptions. These vast lands are home to countless peoples crying out for *civilisation*, waiting for us to lead them there. They see *Europeans as their brothers and yearn to befriend them, to become their disciples....* Nations under the tyrant's yoke...; virtually wild populations...; or conquering hordes.... The latter two categories will be slowest to move forward, and their path will be stormy. They may even shrink in the face of civilized nations to the point of *disappearing altogether or being absorbed.*[68]

Condorcet had no doubts predicting that civilization would wear down savage nomads until they were literally or culturally wiped out. Spreading the message of 'civilized' expansion was still the dynamic way forward in his eyes, even after his rejection of territorial conquests.

There is no need to spell out the instant impact this philosophy had on the law of nations. Secure in the belief that they had the unique model for nationhood and were at the forefront of civilization, French revolutionaries saw no reason to doubt their hierarchical vision of the peoples. Emancipation was open to all peoples, but not all could achieve it in the immediate future. Between 1789 and 1791, revolutionaries made the case for a very similar hierarchy of peoples. The uppermost level contained the French, Swiss, English, and Americans, who all had constitutional governments and, one way or another, acknowledged the European notion of human rights. At the very bottom, we found the Spanish, Russians, and Austrians, with their dictatorial governments. Inhabitants of the colonies were not even mentioned. In 1791, the outbreak of war in Europe transformed the revolutionaries' attitude towards the civil society of nations. The law of nations was

---

[68] Condorcet, *Esquisse d'un tableau historique des progrès de l'esprit humain* (Paris: 1794), 334–38 (my translation).

staring down the barrel of a gun. The universal defence of human rights changed from a long-term goal to an urgent task. A new approach to the law of nations emerged, with the thirst for conquest back at the fore. The French nation was no longer based on universal brotherhood and mutual respect for natural law. Instead it preached a new right of conquest inspired by the revolution and a renewed focus on national interests. The law of nations was once again used to justify territorial expansion, and the republic was on course to become another empire.

In *Reason and Rhetoric in the Philosophy of Hobbes*, Quentin Skinner unequivocally demonstrates how Hobbes pitched his political and legal theory to undermine the humanist culture of the Renaissance, as exemplified by common-law tradition. He rejected the notion of dialogue inherent in humanists' moral philosophy (*audi alteram partem*), which held that criteria for such a dialogue were applied on a circumstantial or contextual basis, rather than being essential or universal. Hobbes sought to overcome the 'uncertainty' propagated through humanist philosophy, opting for a scientific and monological footing by setting a hypothetic-deductive method. In Skinner's words, Hobbes first initiated 'the shift from a dialogical to a monological style of moral and political reasoning'.[69] In their work on the law of nations, the philosophers I have looked at so far followed closely in Hobbes's footsteps. They may have differed considerably on occasion, but they all forged their systems of international order on a uniform vision of law, which ruled out any dialogue with non-European cultures. Notwithstanding efforts on the part of Pufendorf and Kant, not one of them defined peace in terms of *recognition* or *fairness*. They defined peace in *legal* terms, using a language that completely ignored the structure and 'political' systems characteristic of colonized peoples. They came up with a 'liberal' theory of natural law that could justify territorial expansion.

4. THE PRINCIPLE OF RECOGNITION: MONTESQUIEU, ROUSSEAU, AND JOHN MARSHALL

A closer look at the tradition I have described reveals that some writers did not perceive the law of nations from quite the same perspective. While they borrowed some of their contemporaries' arguments and, as such, belong to the natural law tradition, they differed in their take on relations between

---

[69] Quentin Skinner, *Reason and Rhetoric in the Philosophy of Hobbes* (Cambridge: Cambridge University Press, 1996), 16.

peoples. They turned away from the homogenous view of culture that under-pinned the legal and political tenets of their day. Instead, they acknowledged the importance of cultural diversity in crafting the law of nations and sought to defend what I shall call, using Tully's terminology, the *principle of recognition.*

Montesquieu's role here was crucial. He himself admitted that his reading of the law of nations was a conventional one, drawing on natural law tradition for his arguments.[70] States were like men, in that one was entitled to kill in self-defence, the other to wage war if its existence was under threat. *Commerce* was, however, an alternative way of preserving peace between states. Lasting peace could be achieved if nations relied on each other to satisfy mutual needs. Trading partners think twice before going to war. Trade was the proof, hallmark, and guarantee of peace, its cause and consequence.

In fact, a truly pluralist vision of modern society lies behind his vision of the law of nations. Montesquieu was fascinated by the diversity of laws and ethics across the nations, intrigued by the wealth of beliefs and customs throughout time and space.[71] In *The Spirit of Laws* (1748), he explains that, he 'began by examining men, and [he] believed that, amidst the infinite diversity of laws and mores, they were not led by their fancies alone'.[72] In the second part of his *Defence of the Spirit of Laws*, Montesquieu adds that, 'those with sense will see at first glance that this work addresses the laws, customs, and practices of all peoples on this earth'.[73] He makes a compelling case for legal pluralism and, to a certain extent, for legitimizing other religious, moral, and political values, while refuting sceptical tenets.

In the seventeenth century, one of the major challenges facing natural law tradition was to counter the arguments of the sceptics, who drew their views on the writings of Carneade and Sextus Empiricus and were also reflected in the works of Montaigne, Charron, and Pascal.[74] Grotius, Hobbes, Pufendorf, and other rationalists argued that man, being endowed with reason, could deduce what was compatible or incompatible with the law of nature, thus forming even a *thin* basis for universal ethics. In other words, there were moral principles as irrefutable as mathematical facts. Nonetheless, they could

---

[70] See Montesquieu, *Pensées* n° 1863, ed. Louis Desgraves (Paris: Robert Laffont, 1991).

[71] On this point, see the illuminating article of Cecil P. Courtney, 'Montesquieu and the problem of *la diversité*', in Giles Barber and Cecil P. Courtney (eds.), *Enlightenment Studies in Memory of Robert Shackleton* (Oxford: The Voltaire Foundation, 1988), 61–81.

[72] Montesquieu, *The Spirit of Laws*, ed. Anne M. Cohler, Basia C. Miller, and Harold S. Stone (Cambridge: Cambridge University Press, 1989).

[73] Montesquieu, *Défense de l'esprit de lois*, ed. Robert Derathé (Paris: Garnier, 1990), II. 429 (my translation).

[74] See Richard Tuck, *Philosophy and Government 1572–1651* (Cambridge: Cambridge University Press, 1993).

not deny the existence of absurd laws and customs. In response to the sceptics' arguments, they insisted that the focus should be firmly placed on civilized countries, to identify their wise laws which, more importantly, were very much in line with the law of nature. The fact that not all men could perceive rational truths no more invalidated ethical truths than mathematical rules controverted mathematical truths.

At the beginning of the eighteenth century, Montesquieu was highly influential in this debate. In *The Spirit of Laws* he leaves little room for doubt as to his general opposition to scepticism, but he is much more ambiguous in his earlier writings. As shown by Ronald Grimsley, the *Persian Letters* are extremely subjective and sceptical on the issue of reason, indicating that the young Montesquieu was following in libertine footsteps.[75] Similarly, in his *Discours sur Cicéron* [*Speech on Cicero*] Montesquieu not only shows strong admiration for Stoic philosophy but praise, above all, for the way in which Cicero destroys the notions of 'prejudice' and 'error'. Montesquieu enthusiastically talks about

the joy in seeing him [Cicero] in *On the Nature of the Gods* examining all sects, astounding all philosophers and crushing each prejudice! He fights these monsters; he scoffs at philosophy. The champions he creates wipe each other out. One is bested by another, who in turn is defeated. All systems crumble one after the other until all that remains in the reader's mind is scorn for philosophers and admiration for critics. What utter satisfaction to read his book *On Divination* and witness him free the Romans of the ridiculous yoke of haruspices [aruspices] and their attendant rules. They had disgraced pagan theology since their appointment by magistrates in the beginning. They were a mark of uneducated peoples and were undermined once these peoples became more enlightened.[76]

We should not, however, get carried away by the sceptical tone of Montesquieu's early writings. He does not recognize the importance of diversity through the eyes of a sceptic or relativist. He does not merely defend each person's right to be judged according to his own laws. The blanket rejection of despotism that pervades *The Spirit of Laws* could not have been built out of relativism. His work is in fact a fundamental attempt to articulate universalism and relativism rather than a decision to adopt one or the other. On the one hand, we have natural law and associated forms of government; on the other, the general spirit of each nation, which stems from a blend of geographical conditions, economic and cultural structures, and history. Each

---

[75] Ronald Grimsley, 'The Idea of Nature in the *Lettres persanes*', *French Studies*, 5 (1951), 293–306.
[76] Montesquieu, 'Discours sur Cicéron', *Œuvres complètes* (Paris: Gallimard, 1949), I. 94 (my translation).

decision involves an assessment of all factors, to determine what is universal and what is not. Extreme relativism is a mere illusion, but it is impossible to go back to a universal philosophy that ignores cultural plurality and the individual's quest for equality. Montesquieu's 'epistemological globalism' enables him to understand other cultures: comparing a feature of their civilization with one of ours makes little sense, but much can be gained from examining it in context, together with other traits from the same culture. This, in a nutshell, is the basis of the *principle of recognition*.

Montesquieu's views on religious tolerance illustrate his position nicely. He believes that the law should protect religious diversity in a nation, thus regulating pluralism and inducing harmony. But he also says, in Book 25, Chapter 9 of *The Spirit of Laws*, that laws should ensure that religions do not undermine the state or do not disturb each other.[77] In other words, Montesquieu goes beyond both tolerance and the idea of a state religion. Clearly, the ultimate evil is despotism, characterized by the uniformity it requires. By rejecting complexity in society and power, despotism cannot allow any human ability. It shows 'no tempering, modification, accommodation, terms, alternatives, negotiations, remonstrances, nothing as good or better can be proposed. Man is a creature that obeys a creature that wants.'[78] The despot, in his love of simplicity, obliterates the dialectic dimension of consent, obedience, the universal, and the specific. *The Spirit of Laws* provides us with a powerful comparison, likening the despot to one who would chop down a tree to pluck its fruit.

Further proof of Montesquieu's belief in the principle of recognition may be found in his analysis of the sources of law. Lawmakers should respect the plural nature of states and, as such, are not the sole sources of law. They should also take into account the different types of law. Civil law is not to be dealt with in the same way as political law; family law should not be confused with criminal law, and so on. Montesquieu shows us a pluralist vision of law. Law is enriched through reform that comes without upheaval, eschewing violent contradiction of a people's beliefs. Therefore, we should 'reform by laws what is established by laws and change by manners what is established by manners, and it is a very bad policy to change by laws what should be changed by manners'.[79]

His position on customs is also telling. In eighteenth-century France, customs were generally viewed as synonymous with rigid tradition. Critics railed against the status of long-standing habit and denounced the arbitrary whims, self-interest, ignorance, and superstition shown by self-styled legislators and interpreting judges. All backed Voltaire in decrying the 'confused

---

[77] Montesquieu, *The Spirit of Laws*, 488.   [78] Ibid., 29.   [79] Ibid., 315.

jumble of our many different customs',[80] as a result of which, 'in a single European province, between the Alps and the Pyrenees, over forty peoples... call themselves compatriots... despite being as unlike each other as Tonkin and Cochin China'.[81] Montesquieu had a very different take on this. Recognizing that people were very attached to their customs, he saw them, in Book 28 of *The Spirit of Laws*, as important, 'new regulations', 'remedies pointing to a present ill', a 'continuous accidental situations' that introduced 'new usages'.[82] They are part of historical continuity, he explained, a vital expression of social diversity. Unlike his predecessors, Montesquieu rejected the theory whereby societies develop in stages and, by extension, the idea that customs are a mere phase in the evolution towards modern societies. Hence, Montesquieu is claimed to be one of the founding fathers of anthropology, having linked legal differences to the multiple, social, and economic conditions prevailing in a given society.[83]

As a defender of equality, Rousseau also stamped his mark on the eighteenth century's conception of the law of nations. Spurred on by Abbé de Saint-Pierre's *Project for Perpetual Peace*, Rousseau outlined his thoughts on peace, which were based on a radically different vision of the state of nature. In the Hobbesian state of war or unstable sociability defined by Pufendorf and Locke, the state of nature had always been considered a state in which human interaction was governed by natural law. Rousseau, however, saw it first and foremost as a state of solitude, autonomy, and freedom. As such, without too much overemphasizing the gulf between him and his predecessors, he waved aside both Hobbes and Pufendorf, with two major consequences.

First, Rousseau believed that the natural man was driven by moderate feelings, designed to meet limited needs. He did not accept the idea that the natural man instinctively wished to destroy fellow humans. Conflict might pitch him against his neighbour, with both vying for the same object. One of them might even die, but then the conflict would have run its course. War does not exist between men, only between states.[84] Second, Rousseau

---

[80] Voltaire, 'Lettre à Etienne de Beaumont (7 juin 1771)', *Œuvres* (Paris, 1820), 36. 332 (my translation).

[81] Voltaire, *Dictionnaire philosophique*, article 'Lois', *Œuvres* (Paris, 1818), 19. 366 ss. (my translation).

[82] Montesquieu, op. cit., 547 and 600.

[83] Peter Stein, *Legal Evolution: The Story of an Idea* (Cambridge: Cambridge University Press, 1980), 18.

[84] On this topic, see especially his 'Discourse on the Origin and Foundations of Inequality Among Men', ed. Victor Gourevitch, *The Discourses and other early Political Writings* (Cambridge: Cambridge University Press, 1997) and 'The State of War', ed. Victor Gourevitch, *The Social Contract and other later Political Writings* (Cambridge: Cambridge University Press, 1997).

transposed to civil society the natural law theories that Hobbes and Pufendorf had devised for the state of nature. He conceded that the state of war existed, but saw it as a feature of civil society. In his own words, 'Hobbes's error [was] therefore not to have established the state of war among men who are independent and have become sociable but to have assumed this state to be natural to the species, and to have given it as the cause of the vices of which it is the effect.'[85]

As such, the role of politics in institutionalizing social cohesion takes on fresh significance in Rousseau's writings. He does not see the social contract as the keystone of civil society, describing it instead as a means of enabling humans to safeguard their freedom, which is under threat in the state of nature. Following this mode of reasoning, the law of nations can only be forged through *agreements* signed between nations. It is not common to all peoples, unlike natural law. Rousseau clearly makes his point in a 1760 letter to Malesherbes: 'Natural law applies to all men, to whom nature has given a common yardstick and set limits not to be crossed. The law of nations, on the other hand, is rooted in human institutions. It is not absolute; it varies and indeed should vary from one nation to another.'[86]

This view of international order does not necessarily imply unconditional respect for otherness, but it does firmly place Rousseau among the advocates of 'the principle of recognition'. His entire work is a forceful plea for equality and fairness. Unlike contemporary philosophers, he did not just call for equality between men (implying compassion towards indigenous peoples) but also between peoples. This belief led him to condemn all wars of conquest and any attempt to govern through force. He returned to the theme time and again, especially in his reply to Mr Bordes on the *Discourse on the Sciences and the Arts*:

Let us look at the immense continent of Africa, [to the interior of which] no mortal is bold enough to penetrate, or lucky enough to have remained unscathed in the attempt. Thus on the grounds that we have been unable to penetrate [to the interior of] the continent of Africa, that we are ignorant of what goes on there, we are made to conclude that its peoples are laden with vices; that would indeed have been the conclusion to draw if we had found a way of introducing our vices there.... America offers us spectacles that are no less shameful for mankind. Especially since the Europeans are there.[87]

---

[85] Rousseau, 'Geneva Manuscript', ed. Victor Gourevitch, *The Social Contract*, 159.

[86] Letter of 5 November 1760 to Malesherbes, quoted by Robert Derathé, *Rousseau et la science politique de son temps* (Paris: Vrin, 1988), 396 (my translation).

[87] Rousseau, 'Last Reply', ed. Victor Gourevitch, *The Discourses*, 80.

This tirade against colonization should be examined in conjunction with Rousseau's criticism of modern civilization. He argued that increased commerce would only offer an illusion of peace, concealing the true war of all against all. 'Modern' man was largely driven by competition, jealousy, thirst for glory and power, greed for riches, suspicion of one's neighbour, widespread defiance, ever-present fear and fierce hatred made more potent by the fact that it had to be kept secret. On this subject, Rousseau foresaw, 'a massacre, ten thousand men with their throats slit; mounds of corpses, the dying trampled underfoot horses, death and pain wherever you look. That is the outcome of pacific institutions!'[88]

Rousseau understood very early the importance of the 'principle of recognition' for his social theory. He pointed out that you have to know someone before you can recognize him. In his own words,

although the inhabitants of Europe have for the past three or four hundred years overrun the other parts of the world and are constantly publishing new collections of travels and reports, I am convinced that the only men we know are the Europeans.... One cannot open a travel book without coming upon descriptions of characters and morals; yet one is utterly astounded to find that these people who have described so many things have said only what everybody already knew.... Hence that fine adage of ethics so much harped on by the ruck of Philosophasters, that men are everywhere the same, that, since they everywhere have the same passions and the same vices, it is quite useless to seek to characterize different Peoples; which is about as well argued as it would be to say that it is impossible to distinguish between Peter and James because both have a nose, a mouth, and eyes.[89]

Rousseau offers an alternative to this biased, unsound knowledge. Following the path of the ancient philosophers, mankind has to, 'shake the yoke of the National prejudices, to get to know men by their conformities and their differences, and to acquire that universal knowledge that is not exclusively of one century one country but of all times and all places, and thus is, so to speak, the common science of the wise.'[90]

Throughout his writings, Rousseau underlines two ways of 'knowing' other cultures. The first step is to pinpoint what is specific about each people and, by extension, the ways in which they might differ from us. It calls for an informed attitude, with no ulterior motives, since Rousseau does not tolerate missionary zeal. It also requires jingoistic prejudice and ethnocentric preconceptions to be cast aside, but even then the job is only half done. Once differences have been identified, the next step is to resurrect a universal

---

[88] Rousseau, 'Ecrits sur l'abbé de Saint-Pierre', *Œuvres complètes* (Paris: Gallimard, 1964), III. 609 (my translation).

[89] Rousseau, 'Second Discourse', ed. Victor Gourevitch, *The Discourses*, 209–10.

[90] Ibid., 210.

perception of humanity, assimilating all empirical knowledge acquired. Rousseau makes this clear in chapter 8 of his *Essay on the Origin of Languages*: 'When one proposes to study men one has to look close by; but in order to study man one has to learn to cast one's glance afar; one has to begin by observing the differences in order to discover the properties.'[91] By observing relations with other peoples, Rousseau strives to combine *interest* and *objectivity*. In other words, his intent is to seek out the truth. Anything else is tantamount to reiterating what is already known. It means, 'seeing what one believes, rather than what is there. Everything can be explained in the light of our preconceptions, and we only accept a perceived error by convincing ourselves that we committed it through a lack of attention rather than insight.'[92] Therefore, Rousseau urges us to avoid thinking like missionaries or merchants, who only seek confirmation of their own thoughts and beliefs from other peoples. As he put it in 'Emile', the traveller only sees what he desires to see; if it is self-interest, it engrosses the whole attention of those concerned.[93]

According to Sankar Muthu, the arguments used by Montesquieu and Rousseau to support the 'principle of recognition' were also used by some eighteenth-century anti-imperialist authors such as Diderot and Herder.[94] Indeed, Herder was the main source of inspiration for the emergence of cultural nationalism among the oppressed populations of the Austro-Hungarian, Ottoman, and Russian empires. The same ideas were also revisited later on in a famous decision handed down in 1832 by US Supreme Court Chief Justice John Marshall. His judgment has particular bearing on our topic since he voiced the *principle of recognition* of indigenous peoples in the language of rights.[95]

From the outset, policy on native Indians in the United States was a mixture of freedom and violence, free trade, and state intervention. The government constantly sent out mixed signals to Indians, violently suppressing them one day and paternally guiding them the next. Its Janus face could be seen in the actual appropriation of land and in the way the settlers legitimized their actions, by citing treaties, the rights of farmers or even demands for a Just War. Land shortage spawned a whole series of wars in the late eighteenth century, when American expansion across to the Pacific coast became the

---

[91] Rousseau, 'Essay on the Origin of Languages', ed. Victor Gourevitch, *The Discourses*, 266.

[92] Rousseau, 'Rousseau, juge de Jean-Jacques', *Œuvres complètes* (Paris: Gallimard, 1959), I. 742 (my translation).

[93] Rousseau, 'Emile', *Œuvres complètes* (Paris: Gallimard, 1969), IV. 831 ss.

[94] Sankar Muthu, *Enlightenment against Empire* (Princeton, NJ: Princeton University Press, 2003).

[95] On this point, see James Tully, 'Aboriginal Property and Western Theory: Recovering a Middle Ground', *Social Philosophy and Policy*, 11 (1994), 153–80.

cornerstone of US policy. *Indian Removal* was a policy devised by Jefferson and continued by his successors before being formally imposed on southern Indians by Andrew Jackson as of 1820. It offered Indians the opportunity of moving out from the West, provided they gave up their ancestral lands. Although Indians effectively had no choice, the *Indian Removal* policy meant that they could be expropriated with a semblance of respect for the law. In fact, they were forced to accept their own subjugation.[96]

By the early nineteenth century, the Indians had been displaced through treaties or defeated in battle and were left in the government's 'care'. The tribes were deemed 'wards' by the Supreme Court in its decision on the *Cherokee Nation v. State of Georgia* (1831). Their relationship with the US government was likened to that of a child to its guardian. Under no circumstances could they claim the title of fully-fledged 'nation'. Careful scrutiny of the 1831 decision reveals that it was not passed unanimously. Moreover, it was over-turned by a second Supreme Court decision handed down a year later, which completely redefined relations between the US government and the Amerindian nations. In *Worcester v. State of Georgia* (1832), Samuel Worcester led a team presenting the case for Cherokee sovereignty, and Supreme Court Chief Justice John Marshall awarded Indians the status of 'nations', a ruling with significant legal implications.

America, separated from Europe by a wide ocean, was inhabited by a distinct people, divided into *separate nations*, independent of each other and of the rest of the world, having institutions of their own, and governing themselves by their own laws. It is difficult to comprehend the proposition, that the inhabitants of either quarter of the globe could have rightful original claims of dominion over the inhabitants of the other, or over the lands they occupied; or that the discovery of either by the other should give the discoverer rights in the country discovered, which annulled the pre-existing rights of its ancient possessors.[97]

In the text of his ruling, Marshall reviews the various treaties signed and draws on this extensive summary to justify his decision. He refers to the Royal Proclamation issued on 7 October 1763 in which the British Crown set out its

---

[96] On the American Indian question, see, in particular, Michael Paul Rogin, *Fathers and Children: Andrew Jackson and the Subjugation of the American Indian* (New York: Knopf, 1975) and, from the same author, *Ronald Reagan, the Movie and other Episodes in Political Demonology* (Berkeley, CA: University of California Press, 1987), especially ch. 4 ; see also Robert M. Utley, *The Indian Frontier, 1846–1890* (New Mexico: University of New Mexico Press, 1984); Vine Deloria and Clifford M. Lytle, *American Indians, American Justice* (Austin, TX: University of Texas Press, 1983); see also the old but classical book of Helen Hunt Jackson, *A Century of Dishonor* ([1881] New York: Dover Publications, 2003).

[97] *Worcester vs. the State of Georgia*, 6 Peter 515 (U.S.S.C. 1832), p. 542, reprinted in John Marshall, *The Writings of John Marshall, Late Chief Justice of the United States, upon the Federal Constitution* (Littleton, CO: FB Rothman Press, 1987), 426–7 (my italics).

perception of its relations with the Amerindian nations. The Proclamation itself was based on treaties signed since 1664, various royal commissions on Indian affairs since 1665, royal instructions to colonial administrators since 1670, the Board of Trade's 1696 recognition of Indian sovereignty (Locke was a Board member at the time) and advice from Sir William Johnson, Superintendent of Indian Affairs in North America.

Marshall clearly states that the Crown negotiators in 1763 did not subject indigenous populations to criteria that only fitted European nations and had not concluded that they were 'savages' in a state of nature. The negotiators had even identified similarities between European and Indian cultures and political structures. They had recognized the sovereignty of indigenous nations and applied to them the same legal provisions to which other European nations were subject. Following the British Crown's position, Marshall reaffirms that the term *nation*—meaning a 'distinct people'—should be applied to Indians and the US constitution should acknowledge that they have the authority to enter into treaties. Even if 'the words "treaty" and "nation" are words of our own language, selected in our diplomatic and legislative proceedings by ourselves,' says Marshall, '. . . We have applied them to Indians, as we have applied them to other nations of the earth. They are applied to all in the same sense.' The USA should stand to the Aboriginal nations just as it does to 'the crowned heads of Europe'.[98]

Marshall's position is basically a reflection of what Tully named the 'convention of continuity'. Irrespective of the number of treaties signed between the Indian nations and the US government, both parties retained their sovereign identity, just as they would have done under an international treaty. They did not lose their culture, social structure, or existing constitution. 'The settled doctrine of the law of nations is, that the weaker power does not surrender its independence, its right to self government, by associating with a stronger, and taking its protection. A weak state, in order to provide for its safety, may place itself under the protection of one more powerful, without stripping itself of the right of government, and ceasing to be a state. . . .'[99] Chief Justice Marshall's 1832 decision enshrined the *principle of recognition* in the American law tradition. He distanced himself from the Eurocentric view of international law with its uniform understanding of law. In doing so, he paved the way for peace through respect for cultural diversity and recognition of legal pluralism.

---

[98] John Marshall, *Writings of John Marshall*, 445.   [99] Ibid., 446.

5. CONCLUSION: SOME ELEMENTS TO
ACHIEVE A JUST PEACE

Stories often have morals. They may suggest what we are and what we could be. When they do, they help us not only to understand our past but also to build our future; understanding that the past is the first step towards understanding ourselves. Moreover, a sound grasp of past beliefs enables us to alter current thinking, thus shaping future action. Historians' account of the past becomes actions in the present. New perspective enables us to change our behaviour and beliefs. Where does that leave us on peace and justice? What does the study of the formative period of international law tell us about the capacity of such a law to play a role in building a Just Peace?

In this chapter, I have sought to outline how the classic tradition of international law is based on a vision of law and justice that allowed little room for the *principle of recognition*. In its formative period, it denied indigenous peoples the status of independent 'nation' and flowed from a uniform perception of culture, which took no account of diversity or idiosyncrasies. European theorists progressively conceptualized native peoples in ways that dehumanized them and represented their cultures or civilization as inferior. The belief in their own superiority allowed Europeans to ignore the problem of mutual understanding between themselves and those who were 'different' or perceived as 'uncivilized'. By using concepts such as 'nation', 'constitution', 'people', 'civilization' that were essentially European, and placing them above other conceptions of government and culture, Western theories of the law of nations not only denied cultural pluralism as a problem, it also imposed European values as universal standards.

I have also suggested that there were some theorists inside this dominant tradition who draw our attention to the *principle of recognition* within international order. Although a minority, they did value difference, not only for its own sake but also because to do otherwise would be to privilege only *one* understanding of what it is to be human over others. In Rousseau's terms, they did reject assimilation unless it was the free choice of the individual or people being assimilated. If they were perfectly aware that the dominant settlers' societies were not going to go away, they pleaded for a mutual agreement about the conditions for sharing space and land. It was clear for them that a lasting peace and a just reconciliation between indigenous people and settlers required recognition, mutual consent, and negotiations in a respectful manner on a nation-to-nation basis. Unfortunately, those few who supported cultural diversity and were willing to recognize the others they encountered, were not always taken seriously by their opponents, as shown by the fate of Chief Justice Marshall's decision.

After leading ruthless wars of slaughter against the Greek and Seminole, General Andrew Jackson, 'Sharp knife', was elected president in 1829. On hearing of Marshall's judgment in defence of the Cherokee nation, ..., he flatly responded, 'John Marshall made his decision, let him enforce it'. President Jackson then ordered the forced removal of the five 'civilised' tribes (Cherokee, Choctaw, Chicksaw, Creek and Seminole) from their ancestral lands and their relocation hundreds of miles westward. ... Their lands were stolen, possessions plundered and schools converted to taverns for the incoming settlers. The atrocities were so abhorrent that an enquiry was set up in 1841. ... The government did not release the report.[100]

In Chapter 13 of *Leviathan*, Hobbes dwells on the significance of political conflict, adding that one of the key triggers is, '...a word, a smile, a different opinion, and any other sign of undervalue, either direct in their Persons or by reflection in their Kindred, their Friends, their Nation, their Profession, or their Name'.[101] Unfortunately, international law is still partially rooted in the solutions proposed by Hobbes and the writers of the dominant tradition of the law of nations. It is therefore unlikely to suffice alone in resolving intercultural conflicts, which pitch radically different codes, rites, terms, and beliefs against each other. It is true that international law has recently played a major role in reclaiming the rights of, in particular, native peoples. International lawyers appear, in this case, to be actively revising an understanding derived from their predecessors and to be doing so ahead of state leaders. Nevertheless, there are still thorny issues to be resolved. For example, indigenous peoples' claims on self-determination are resisted, in part, because of the way self-determination has been understood as an attribute of statehood. Native peoples also reject Europeans notions of sovereignty in which the state exercises authority over civil society. In New Zealand, debate about sovereignty has thus centred on the difference between how Maori and Pakeha (the dominant white society) understand the meaning of the term in the 1840 Treaty of Waitangi.

This suggests that a *just* settlement, or one perceived as such, should be achieved through mediation, which implies the necessity to adopt the *principle of recognition*, as 'dissent' thinkers like Montesquieu, Rousseau, and Chief Justice Marshall have indicated. Some have argued that the concept of 'international society' can help redress the legacy of its historic expansion by acting as a standard bearer. I welcome this idea and hope that it may become an acceptable vehicle to accommodate indigenous peoples and consider the

---

[100] Tully, *Strange Multiplicity*, 210.
[101] Hobbes, *Leviathan*, ed. Richard Tuck (Cambridge: Cambridge University Press, 1996), 88.

political arrangements needed for states to satisfy indigenous claims. But the *principle of recognition* and its successor, the *principle of reconciliation*, should be key elements in this process.

Nowadays, there is general consensus on the pressing need to find a way of ending intercultural conflict. Racial, national, ethnic, religious, and linguistic animosities have become a key feature of international relations. All evidence suggests that large-scale disruption, increased mobility and greater inter-action between peoples as a result of globalization will exacerbate cultural antagonisms. Throughout the world the 250 million Aboriginals or native peoples are still waiting for the recognition and accommodation of their 12,000 diverse cultures, governments, and environmental practices. They are still fighting to be recognized as first nations in international law which has been imposed over them during the last 500 years of European expansion. There is thus a need to find a new *language* to address these issues. The question of our time is not whether one or another claim can be recognized. Rather, the question is whether a settlement—or a peace—can give recognition to the legitimate demands of members of *diverse cultures* in a manner that renders everyone their due, so that all would freely consent to this form of *Just Peace*.

4

Just Peace: A Cause Worth Fighting For[1]

Sir Adam Roberts

1. INTRODUCTION

How is peace within and between states best attained? The central argument of this chapter is that issues relating to justice must be taken into account in any serious discussion of international peace. Preventing future war is not simply a matter of establishing a system of order in which uses of force are effectively restricted: any system of order needs also to incorporate a strong element of justice. This means justice for states, groups, and individuals. The concept of justice needs to encompass, not just specific human rights and humanitarian norms, but also general ideas of legitimacy and fairness; and it needs to focus on the processes, procedures, and means of struggle through which justice can be achieved. The paradox in the title is intentional: it may sometimes be necessary to fight in order to secure the basis of a Just Peace.[2]

In most cultures and civilizations the principles of justice and peace have been seen as linked. Peace—and the role of both justice and power in it—is a subject which has preoccupied practitioners and writers for centuries, and has been the subject of a distinguished and rigorous body of scholarly analysis.[3] No general scheme for international peace has neglected issues of justice entirely. The unavoidable incorporation of such issues helps to explain the

---

[1] This chapter is a revised and expanded version of remarks made at the Round Table on 'What is a Just Peace?', Geneva, 29–30 October 2001, and takes into account comments of participants. In addition, I am grateful to Dr Mary-Jane Fox for her responses to draft versions. Part 4 of the present chapter draws on material in Adam Roberts, 'Order/Justice Issues at the United Nations', in Rosemary Foot, John Gaddis, and Andrew Hurrell (eds.), *Order and Justice in International Relations* (Oxford: Oxford University Press, 2003).

[2] Just Peace is rendered with capital initials throughout this chapter. This is to indicate that it refers to a body of ideas and practice potentially comparable with Just War, and to avoid possible confusion with 'just' in the sense of 'no more than'.

[3] See F. H. Hinsley's masterly survey, *Power and the Pursuit of Peace: Theory and Practice in the History of Relations Between States* (Cambridge: Cambridge University Press, 1963).

perception of those who have thought about it that 'peace is certainly a far more complex affair than war'.[4]

In the post-1945 era, on which this survey mainly concentrates, there has been explicit acceptance, especially in the framework of the United Nations (UN), that justice is a necessary foundation for peace. Yet the notion of Just Peace remains hugely problematical, and is much harder to summarize in a few simple propositions than is its close relative, the notion of Just War. This is largely because the Just Peace, assuming it means that justice is a necessary foundation for peace, embodies two built-in and unavoidable problems. (*a*) Is the denial of one or another principle of justice a legitimate basis for resorting to war or other acts of violence? (*b*) Must a state, in seeking to preserve its security or indeed international security generally, restrict its relations with unjust regimes? These two questions point to the risk that the Just Peace, if pursued logically and zealously, could easily end up digging its own grave. How can justice be seen as a foundation for peace without undermining the very building it is supposed to support?

When faced with a subject that involves logically insoluble problems such as those outlined, it is useful to focus on practice as much as on theory. Only practice—in other words history—can show how such problems can be addressed effectively even if not solved finally. This chapter attempts, no doubt awkwardly, to straddle the twin currents of theory and practice.

Part 2 of this survey examines some hazards in the pursuit of the concept of Just Peace. Part 3 considers how the idea of Just Peace does or does not relate to the Just War tradition of thought, and suggests some possible directions for it, and a possible new label, 'justifiable force'. Part 4 looks at the ongoing and remarkably rich interactions of the principles of order and justice in the United Nations. Part 5 focuses particularly on action on a regional scale; and puts forward the idea of change brought about by 'induction', as practised in Europe over the past three decades. Finally, Part 6 suggests that the state has a place in any notion of Just Peace; and, while accepting that there is also a role for the use of force, indicates concern over the tendency to use an enticing vision of peace as a justification for waging war.

Before embarking on the journey thus outlined, it may be useful to illustrate briefly how long-standing is the relation between order and justice by glancing at how these issues have arisen over the past few centuries in one modest-sized European city—Geneva.

---

[4] Michael Howard, *The Invention of Peace: Reflections on War and International Order* (London: Profile Books, 2000), 1–2.

Geneva is an appropriate city in which to address the relation between justice and peace. The link was clearly seen long before international organization in its modern form emerged and changed the skyline and image of the city. As many observers noted, the links between justice and peace were particularly important in the city's social and political system. Here is how, over 240 years ago, an enthusiastic English visitor to Geneva, George Keate, saw the idea and reality of what we now call Just Peace. In the Introduction to his book, *A Short Account of Geneva*, published in 1761, he observed that in this city the Reader:

will not here meet Legions of armed Men rushing abroad into the World, and with the Thunders of War, disturbing the Peace of Mankind; but, on the contrary, he will be conveyed to the gentler Scenes of Academic Silence, where Philosophy is more studied than the Sword. He will see a People happy and free, yet who have defended themselves with Bravery on every Occasion, against the various Encroachments of Tyranny and Oppression;...and in fine, by what Regulations...five-and-twenty thousand People preserve the utmost Harmony within their Walls, and live together like one great Family.[5]

The history of Geneva yields a further and more precise indication that a general sense of the justice of an international arrangement itself contributes powerfully to peace. In 1815, at the time of the Congress of Vienna, the representative of both Switzerland and Geneva, Charles Pictet de Rochemont, urged every possible strategic and political reason why the *Pays de Gex* should be ceded by France to Geneva.[6] The British Secretary of State for Foreign Affairs, Viscount Castlereagh, opposed this: 'These arguments about natural defences and strategic boundaries are pushed too far. Real defence and security comes from the guarantee which is given by the fact that they cannot touch you without declaring war on all those interested in maintaining things as they are.'[7] The *Pays de Gex* was not ceded, and Geneva's subsequent security has indeed largely depended on the kind of 'guarantee' described by Castlereagh: a mixture of international respect for the legitimacy and security of existing arrangements, and preparedness to use force in their defence. Both through its membership of the Swiss Confederation, and through its numer-

---

[5] George Keate, *A Short Account of the Ancient History, Present Government, and Laws of the Republic of Geneva* (London: R. and J. Dodsley, 1761), 4–7. He elaborates further on the Academy's role on pp. 124–38.

[6] The strong claims advanced by Pictet de Rochemont in the 1815 negotiations may be found in *Rochemont, Pictet de, Genève et les traités de 1815: Correspondance diplomatique de Pictet de Rochemont et de François d'Ivernois, Paris, Vienne, Turin, 1814–1816*, 2 vols. (Geneva: Kündig; Paris: H. Champion, 1914).

[7] Sir Charles K. Webster, *The Foreign Policy of Castlereagh, 1812–1815: Britain and the Reconstruction of Europe* (London: Bell, 1950), 268. See also the account of Swiss questions on pp. 393–6.

ous international roles, Geneva has been part of a larger system of security based on an interest in 'maintaining things as they are'—which in turn requires a sense that the existing order is tolerably just.

Subsequently Geneva made a major contribution to international order through the humanitarian activities and bodies which developed there. Already in the eighteenth century humanitarian work had an important part in Geneva's system of social harmony. In the chapter on hospitals in the book quoted above, George Keate had written: 'There is certainly no Place, which has been more eminent for its Humanity than Geneva'.[8] He would not have been surprised when, over a century later, it was a group of men in this city, 'the Geneva Committee', that convened the 1863 Geneva International Conference on the treatment of the wounded in war. This development, in which Henry Dunant played such a key part, led in 1864 to the first Geneva Convention, and also to the creation of the International Committee of the Red Cross (ICRC). The importance of that humanitarian work, and its connection with the larger cause of international peace, was recognized in 1901 by the award of the first Nobel Prize to Henry Dunant.

When the Red Cross movement was founded in Geneva in 1863, there was no elaborate exposition of the relation of Red Cross work to international justice, or to that elusive concept and important reality, peace. Yet the spirit of shared humanity in the face of extreme adversity, which infused the initiative, was to be one enduring contribution of the Red Cross movement, and this city. The Red Cross movement, and the body of international law that it has helped to develop, has contributed importantly to our thinking about justice and peace. It does so in ways more various and complex than Dunant and his colleagues could possibly have dreamed in 1863.

Today, humanitarian and human rights norms are global issues and are the everyday subject matter of many different UN bodies, including the Security Council and the General Assembly. Both of these sets of norms have retained their strong associations with Geneva. Proof enough is the presence in Geneva of the headquarters not only of the Red Cross movement, but also of the UN Human Rights Commission. Many other international bodies and non-governmental organizations in Geneva reflect the demand for justice in several different spheres: political, legal, and economic. The fact that some of these bodies also attract huge controversy—the World Trade Organization is the most obvious example—illustrates how tangled the connections between internationalism and peace have become, even in Geneva.

[8] Keate, op. cit., 152.

2. FIVE HAZARDS IN THINKING ABOUT JUST PEACE

Recognizing that there is a strong link between justice and peace, as the history and current role of Geneva does in so many ways, is not the end of a journey but the beginning. This journey, in which thinkers about international relations have been continuously taking part over the centuries, encounters five hazards which must be noted at the outset.

The first hazard is of seeing a Just Peace in largely prescriptive terms, based round a few appealing propositions. Such an approach can be very attractive: witness the perennial interest in writings of prescriptive thinkers on the conditions of international peace. Jean-Jacques Rousseau, perhaps Geneva's most famous citizen, had excellent reason to know the hazards of being excessively prescriptive. He was incorrectly typecast as an advocate of international organization because in 1756 he was unwise enough to write a popularized version of a plan for perpetual peace written by his friend the Abbé de Saint-Pierre.[9] Rousseau never lived down the reputation thus gained, even though he was in fact deeply sceptical about the plan—and even more so about its chances of being brought to fruition. In our own time John Rawls at Harvard has also attracted interest with his challenging exploration of international issues, *The Law of Peoples*, which he describes as 'a work that focuses strictly on certain questions connected with whether a realistic utopia is possible, and the conditions under which it might obtain'.[10] Although I like the idea of 'realistic utopia', and agree with much of Rawls' analysis, I have some residual scepticism about his methodology, especially the ratio of generalization and prescription on the one hand, as compared to description on the other. The underlying hazard of prescriptive approaches is that they may tell one more about the mind and national background of the proposer than they do about the state of the world or the real possibilities of change. Perhaps a more prosaic methodology—based more on examining actual structures, treaties, proposals and events, in all their baffling variety—is more appropriate to the subject at hand.

The second and closely related hazard is of failing to recognize just how multifarious conceptions of a Just Peace are, how they differ as between regions and cultures, and how they change over time almost as much as Paris fashions. There never has been, and is not now, a single and agreed concept of what constitutes international justice, nor of how particular

---

[9] This was published five years later as Jean-Jacques Rousseau, *Extrait du Projet de Paix Perpétuelle de Monsieur l'Abbé de Saint-Pierre* (Amsterdam: Marc Michel Rey, 1761).

[10] John Rawls, *The Law of Peoples: With 'The Idea of Public Reason Revisited'* (Cambridge, MA: Harvard University Press, 1999), 5–6.

justice-related goals might be achieved. Any vision of Just Peace requires more than the mere extension onto a global canvas of George Keate's enticing portrayal of the citizens of Geneva over two centuries ago as 'a People happy and free, yet who have defended themselves with Bravery on every Occasion, against the various Encroachments of Tyranny and Oppression'. That form of internationalism based on an unspoken assumption that the rest of the world should be more like one's own society was a curse of the twentieth century that should not be inflicted on the twenty-first. The extreme case was the vision of communism as a system of justice that was supposed to prevail worldwide, conspicuously failed to do so, and in its period of existence as a messianic creed often proved an obstacle to international security and social progress. For all the fashionable talk of globalization, this remains a world in which there are fundamentally different perceptions of the past, present and future, and of how human society should be organized. Similarly, there are many narrow, distorted and conflicting visions of justice itself. Some see justice primarily in economic terms, others in terms of political reform and good governance. Some demand the righting of ancient grievances, others start from acceptance of the status quo. Some see justice primarily as a matter of the internal order of a state, others as a structural issue that must be tackled at the international level. Some see justice in relatively conventional terms, others in the light of new concerns about protection of resources and of the environment. In short, invoking justice in international debates is no simple matter.[11]

The third hazard follows from the first two: the worst possible way to approach the whole subject of Just Peace would be to develop an 'ideal type' of such a peace, and then seek to impose it. Since there is not now, and is not going to be, one single and agreed concept of Just Peace, the attempt to impose one is likely itself to become a source of conflict. Moreover, there is bound to be widespread hostility to the methods employed to impose a system on a society, and no less widespread suspicion of the motives of states and individuals involved in such acts of imposition. Nor is imposition by world government likely to be a productive approach. One of the many reasons why schemes for world government (which is one variant of the idea of Just Peace) have not been successful is that they involve subordination of all states and their peoples to a superior authority, when in reality many societies, especially those with recent memories of colonialism, are not going to subordinate themselves so completely to an outside body.

---

[11] Illustrations of many of these hazards can be found in E. H. Carr, *Conditions of Peace* (London: Macmillan, 1942), especially in the introduction.

The fourth hazard is that claims of justice often conflict with claims of peace. In the case of clashes, the claims of peace frequently have priority. During the Cold War, Western states had to make numerous compromises with injustice in order to maintain at least a semblance of détente with the Soviet Union. They did not, for example, respond with force to the Soviet-led invasion of Czechoslovakia. The end of the Cold War, although it resulted in part from a skilful pursuit by the West of *both* peace *and* justice, left us with continuing dilemmas about the relation between them. If justice is understood, for example, to require exactly the same access to military power—even to nuclear weapons—for all states, it will be widely viewed as conflicting with peace. Likewise, if justice is seen to require that all refugees should have an unconditional right to return to their place of birth, it may frustrate the achievement of some peace agreements, including on the Arab–Israel issue. The strong international rule that it is impermissible to change the frontiers of states except by mutual consent reflects the priority given to peace and stability over justice. Even in cases where frontier changes might have been desired by the majority in a particular region or state (such as in the Serb-inhabited areas of Croatia and Bosnia in 1991–5) the international community was opposed to such changes if they could not be achieved by consent. There are good reasons for this conservatism of states on the matter of unilateral changes of frontiers. In general, any notion of Just Peace that fails to understand the centrality of security concerns will be likely to derail.

The fifth and last hazard is that using the language of justice can sometimes make the conduct of international relations more difficult. Historically, states have often defended their decisions to use force by using the language of justice.[12] This tradition continues today. In the period since 1990 ideas about justice have often been a basis for using force: military action has been taken by Western powers not just to repel aggression, but also to assist terrorized populations, and to reverse the results of military coups. Equally, many rebel movements, even terrorists, have used the language of justice.[13] Such claims may be persuasive, especially in cases where fighting in support of a principle of justice can reasonably be viewed as providing a basis for a future peace. However, in many instances the appeal to principles of justice can be a serious obstacle to efforts to maintain peace or to obtain a peace agreement.

---

[12] See David A. Welch, *Justice and the Genesis of War* (Cambridge: Cambridge University Press, 1993).

[13] For example, Osama bin Laden said in May 1997 that 'jihadis' (i.e. those willing to engage in holy war) 'spread in every place in which non-believers' injustice is perpetuated against Muslims'. Steven Simon and Daniel Benjamin, 'The Terror', *Survival*, 43/4 (2001), 9. To say that terrorists use the language of justice does not imply that injustice is the root cause of terrorist campaigns, still less that terrorism is a cure for injustice. See Walter Laqueur's trenchant comments on these issues in his *The Age of Terrorism* (London: Weidenfeld & Nicolson, 1987), 299–304.

One reason why in certain past episodes the United Nations has not been a successful interlocutor between Israel and its Arab neighbours may be that the UN's commitment to well-defined principles, including participation of all the parties in an overall settlement, reduced its flexibility for working out the kinds of deals that might be necessary for a settlement. A more rooted objection to certain uses of the language of justice is that they may involve elements of deception or hypocrisy, even merging into Orwellian propaganda: if so, it could delegitimize the very international order that it was supposed to support. Sometimes, indeed, it can be healthier if states defend their positions in the language of interest rather than that of justice. To clothe statements of interest in the garments of justice is often to make them non-negotiable.

All five hazards outlined above relate in one way or another to a core problem of international relations: the human tendency to create simplified images of other societies and cultures, even to denigrate them. Many scholars and writers, including Edward Said, have usefully reminded us that the construction of distorted and simplified visions of other societies was a perennial theme in the history of European colonialism.[14] Unfortunately, such flawed visions of other societies have often in the past infected and damaged proposals for international justice; and they remain a threat to the effective formulation and implementation of ideas about Just Peace.

The Palestine–Israel problem, explored at length elsewhere in this collection, illustrates the hazards of addressing international issues in terms of justice—especially when the two sides' ideas of justice are in conflict. When the language of justice is used to support the claims of one side and to attack the other, then it risks being a cause of war. Yet in the Middle East, as elsewhere, some concept of justice—encompassing respect for the culture, concerns, interests, and honour of the adversary as well as for international standards—is and will remain an essential precondition of any lasting peace.

Although the hazards of using the language of justice are evident, any idea that peace can be discussed usefully without reference to justice must simply be dismissed. In the past decade we have had reminders of the dangers of pursing peace without taking justice issues fully into account. For example, a peace deal on Sierra Leone concluded with UN encouragement in July 1999 offered immunity to forces which had systematically raped and mutilated thousands of fellow citizens.[15] It is now seen as a model of how *not* to address negotiations to end civil wars.

[14] Edward W. Said, *Orientalism* (London: Routledge & Kegan Paul, 1978). See also the reprinted edition, containing a new preface by the author, published by Penguin Books, 2003.

[15] Peace Agreement between the Government of Sierra Leone and the Revolutionary United Front concluded at Lomé on 7 July 1999, Article IX, provided for 'absolute and free pardon and reprieve to all combatants and collaborators in respect of anything done by them in pursuit of their objectives, up to the signing of the present Agreement'. Text in UN doc. S/1999/777 of 12 July 1999.

The spirit that informs this survey is a refusal to accept that order and justice are necessarily in conflict with each other. Without any doubt, there are issues and occasions on which they point in different directions, or one principle of justice clashes with another. Unfortunately, all good things do not go together, and tragic choices sometimes have to be made. However there is real strength in the liberal position as expressed by Hedley Bull, that 'order in international relations is best preserved by meeting the demands for justice, and that justice is best realized in a context of order'.[16]

Because the relation between order and justice is always subtle and complex, there is reason to doubt the practical utility of the conceptually clear distinction between 'positive peace' and 'negative peace' that has been drawn in much peace research writing. 'Positive peace' is viewed (favourably) as 'the creation of systems where violence is unlikely to arise', whereas 'negative peace' is viewed (less favourably) as 'the prevention of violence'—for example through arms control, crisis manipulation, and deterrence.[17] While a real distinction undoubtedly exists between peace based on consent and peace based on fear, there is a risk that too much can be made of the distinction between 'positive' and 'negative' peace. They are not always identifiable categories, nor are they clear policy choices. No imaginable system of positive peace could be so obviously just, and be seen as such by all concerned, that violence is unlikely to arise even in the absence of some of the repressive mechanisms (police, armed forces) associated with negative peace.

Although in what follows I attempt to identify certain specific components that can be encompassed in the concept of a Just Peace, they are no substitute for the looser concept of 'legitimacy'. In particular episodes the idea of what is just or unjust may depend, not on any formal agreement on the elements of justice, but rather on perceptions of legitimacy. Legitimacy in international relations encompasses, not just elements of 'black-letter' international law, but also custom; natural law; ethics; notions of fairness; and interpretations of history. Legitimacy is as difficult to define as it is important to discuss.

The undoubted hazards of applying ideas of justice in the field of international relations should not discourage those who search for a Just Peace, whether globally or locally, but should rather encourage any such search to be disciplined and cautious. Since the insufficiently-formed idea of Just Peace will not go away, we had better take it seriously. This short survey looks in

---

[16] From the first of Hedley Bull's Hagey Lectures given at the University of Waterloo, Ontario in 1983, and reprinted in Kai Alderson and Andrew Hurrell (eds.), *Hedley Bull on International Society* (Basingstoke: Macmillan, 2000), 227.

[17] For early expositions of the distinction between positive and negative peace, see Johan Galtung, 'Violence, Peace and Peace Research', *Journal of Peace Research*, 6/3 (1969), 167–91; and Robin Jenkins, 'Peace Research: A Perspective', *Political Studies*, 17 (1969), 353.

turn at the following three issues: the Just War tradition as a starting point for Just Peace; evolution of ideas of Just Peace in the UN era; the search for a Just Peace today.

3. JUST PEACE, JUST WAR, AND JUSTIFIABLE FORCE

The mere mention of Just Peace echoes the familiar term Just War. The key issue here is how the concepts of Just Peace and Just War relate to each other. To some, Just Peace may sound like a replacement for Just War, but to view it thus would be misleading. To others, it may sound like a mere complement to Just War, but that too would be misleading. The ideas of the Just War tradition are far from dead, but they are having to adapt to new conditions; and in any case they need a much less misleading label than Just War. What they are really about is justifiable threats and uses of military force.

The centuries-old Just War tradition of thought about the use of force, which remains influential, is not out of date even in the twenty-first century. Its core idea, that the use of force is sometimes justified and may be necessary for the preservation of peace, is still valid. It has transcended its Catholic origins and is part of a universal discourse about war and peace. It provides a language for understanding that force can be permissible in certain circumstances, and for debating whether it is so in a particular case. Being embodied as much in the writings of specialists as in black-letter international law, it has retained considerable flexibility, and is adaptable to new conditions.

As expounded by Saint Augustine (354–430), Just War theory was based on the proposition that war was not necessarily sinful for Christians if three conditions were met. It had to be waged: (*a*) for a 'just cause', such as avenging an injury suffered, acting against a nation that fails to punish a bad act, or fighting to return that which has been unjustly taken; (*b*) with a 'right intention'; and (*c*) on the authority of a prince.

In this early version there was very little hint of any idea of a Just Peace. As Gerald Draper wrote in a survey of the evolution of legal ideas about war: 'To St Augustine, the *outcome* of the war is not the determinant of its "justness" or otherwise. That is a matter for God and the Day of Judgement.'[18] In a more secular age we are less willing to leave so basic a matter in the hands of God. Although the outcome of a war is always hard to know at the outset, the basic

---

[18] G. I. A. D. Draper, 'Grotius' Place in the Development of Legal Ideas about War', in Hedley Bull, Benedict Kingsbury, and Adam Roberts (eds.), *Hugo Grotius and International Relations* (Oxford: Clarendon Press, 1990), 180–1.

idea that a war is only worth fighting if there is at least a prospect of a better peace thereafter has gradually become embedded in traditions of thought about war. In other words, the concept of Just War has increasingly come to be seen as requiring a concept of Just Peace.[19]

As the Just War tradition evolved, it addressed certain weaknesses. (*a*) The idea that *both sides* in a war might honestly believe that they were fighting in a just cause emerged only gradually, coming to be accepted belatedly in the works of Alberico Gentili and Hugo Grotius. (*b*) The idea that a body of law limiting the *conduct* of armed conflict had to apply equally to belligerents, irrespective of the justice of their causes, only emerged slowly, and again consolidated in the seventeenth century. (*c*) The idea that *self-defence* was the principal justification for resort to force only really crystallized in the first half of the twentieth century, but it is by no means free of problems in an age in which there are pressures to use force in a wider range of circumstances. (*d*) The idea that war is so serious and fateful a business that its initiation might require a higher *authority* than a single government also evolved very slowly, and is still only half-accepted.

There can be no claim that the Just War tradition has evolved to a point of perfection. It is a language in which there are many different dialects, and in which there can also be strong disagreements. It is only when one compares it to the imprecision of thinking about a Just Peace that its seductively simple lists of criteria, still based on those of Saint Augustine outlined earlier, seem so enviable.

3.1. Limits of Pacifism

How do notions of Just War and Just Peace relate to pacifism, in the sense of a principled refusal to take part in all acts of violence? The Just War school of thought has traditionally been important as an intellectually coherent alternative to the pacifist tradition, which has existed for centuries in various religious and secular forms. When in 1901 the Norwegian Nobel Committee awarded the first Peace Prize, it was given not only to Henry Dunant, who was not a pacifist, but also to Frédéric Passy, the Founder and President of the first French peace society, who was a pacifist.[20] Yet pacifism has always suffered

---

[19] John Rawls, in setting forth six principles of traditional Just War doctrine, puts heavy emphasis on the idea of a Just Peace, especially in the first and shortest principle: 'The aim of a just war waged by a just well-ordered people is a just and lasting peace among peoples, and especially with the people's present enemy.' Rawls, *The Law of Peoples*, 94. See also the emphasis on 'a just peace' on p. 98.

[20] Frédéric Passy (1822–1912) had founded in 1867 the Ligue Internationale et Permanente de la Paix, which in a later incarnation became the *Société Française pour l'Arbitrage entre*

from certain limitations, which explain why in most countries at most times it has remained a minority position. The most common objections to pacifism still have application in the twenty-first century: (*a*) Its practice would risk leaving a community or a state vulnerable to both internal and external forces that lack the pacifists' commitment to abstain from violence. (*b*) The vulnerability of small and weakly defended territories to attack and foreign occupation can actually increase the likelihood of major powers going to war with each other—as is evidenced by the role of Belgium and Czechoslovakia in the events leading to the outbreak of the two world wars. (*c*) Further, pacifist thought has little to say regarding three key issues of particular relevance to our times: how certain uses of force can be deterred, how force can be applied in international peacekeeping operations, and how 'strategic coercion' and actual use of force can assist in ensuring observance of a wide range of international norms.

Because of these problems, the pursuit of pacifist policies by a state, however well motivated, could actually make the problems of international relations worse, by helping to create conditions for instability and intervention. In short, for a robust notion of Just Peace to develop, there is a need to move beyond the pacifist tradition as we have inherited it.

To say that the pacifist position has weaknesses is not to say that, in consequence, it should be rejected completely, or that the Just War tradition should be uncritically accepted as the obvious viable alternative. There is at least one issue on which the Just War is weak and on which the pacifist tradition may be somewhat less vulnerable to criticism. The Just War tradition has not contributed much on the subject of peaceful change. It has, for example, taken little account of the use of non-violent forms of struggle and pressure in international relations. The use of such methods is not always, indeed not generally, associated with pacifism, but some pacifists have taken part in it or seized on its potential as a possible means of overcoming the traditional limitations of the pacifist position. The experience of non-violent struggle in the nineteenth and twentieth centuries, including in anticolonial movements and struggles against dictatorial rule, may not suggest that it is a complete substitute for violence, but it does indicate some possibilities of meeting the requirements of justice without undermining peace.[21]

Nations. He was also co-founder, in 1889, of the Inter-Parliamentary Union for Arbitration and Peace. His strong belief in international arbitration—not a major focus of attention today— serves as a reminder of how ideas about key elements of Just Peace change greatly from one generation to the next.

[21] A useful introduction to the field of non-violent action is Roger S. Powers and William B. Vogele (eds.), *Protest, Power, and Change: An Encyclopaedia of Nonviolent Action from ACT-UP to Women's Suffrage* (New York: Garland, 1997).

3.2. 'Justifiable Force'

Some elements of the Just War tradition need to be incorporated in thinking about Just Peace. However, if the tradition is to maintain its relevance it may need to adapt its title and its content, and there needs to be more clarity about how it relates to Just Peace.

The term Just War is a misnomer for several reasons. It can seem to imply, absurdly, that a whole war with all its belligerent parties and aspects can be viewed as just; or that one side in a war can be completely just in its cause and its actions. A term more faithful to the real meaning of the tradition, and to its contemporary applications, would be 'justifiable force': this would move the tradition away from appearing to approve a war as a whole, and towards recognizing something more conditional and cautious—that the threat and use of military force by a particular state or group of states may in particular circumstances be justifiable.

The tradition's content also needs to adapt. The key issue is often the legitimacy of force rather than open war. This is an age in which strategic coercion and deterrence are as important as war, in which interventions in pursuit of the agreed purposes of states may assume such forms as humanitarian intervention, peaceful intervention by consent, and international peacekeeping. Not all of these are exactly 'war' as it has been commonly conceived. Moreover, the concepts of 'Justifiable Force' and Just Peace need to be developed in harness, for only if there is a coherent vision of a state of peace can any concept of justifiable force be rescued from the accusation that it may be as much part of the problem as of the solution. I return to this issue in the final part of this chapter.

4. EVOLUTION OF IDEAS OF JUST PEACE IN THE UN ERA

In the post-1945 era the UN has by no means had a monopoly on the centuries-old and still living debate about the foundations of peace. However, to obtain a picture of the place of justice-related issues in today's world, the UN is one place to start. Since its foundation in 1945, the United Nations has recognized that peace is a matter not only of order but of justice. Already enshrined in the Charter, this recognition has been reflected in numerous declarations and activities of UN organs and agencies.

Within UN bodies, debates on order/justice issues have had several unsatisfactory aspects. They have often been heated, divisive, and marked by a disturbingly high ratio of rhetoric to substantive content. Throughout the history of the UN era, states and UN bodies have been accused of inconsistency, hypocrisy, double standards, and turning blind eyes to injustice and atrocity. They have often been guilty of these charges. There even have been doubts, not always publicly articulated, about whether the UN should be preoccupied with a wide range of justice-related issues.

However, the formal commitment of the UN and its members to justice as well as order has had positive consequences, and has been a key element in the UN's survival over more than half a century. The organization's concern, not only with the maintenance of order between existing states but with a wide range of justice-related issues, helps to explain its modest but nonetheless unprecedented degree of success. It contributed to the process of decolonization; has helped to secure the interest of peoples and governments in the organization; and has resulted in some remarkable developments in the rhetoric, practices, and decisions of UN bodies.

4.1. The United Nations Charter

The UN Charter, signed on 26 June 1945, contains principles and rules that are strongly in favour of order, especially as regards non-use of force by states. However, those principles and rules also put emphasis on justice. This dualism in the Charter between order and justice has contributed to the complexity of debates on the tangled question of whether there is a right of intervention within states when they fail one or another test of justice.

The Preamble to the Charter puts heavy emphasis on justice when it declares a joint determination:

... to reaffirm faith in fundamental human rights, in the dignity and worth of the human person, in the equal rights of men and women and of nations large and small, and to establish conditions under which justice and respect for the obligations arising from treaties and other sources of international law can be maintained, and to promote social progress and better standards of life in larger freedom, AND FOR THESE ENDS ... to employ international machinery for the promotion of the economic and social advancement of all peoples, ... [22]

Likewise, the Charter's Chapter I, on the UN's purposes, contains strong commitments to justice in each of its three substantive paragraphs:

---

[22] Capitalization in the original.

1. To maintain international peace and security, and to that end: to take effective collective measures for the prevention and removal of threats to the peace, and for the suppression of acts of aggression or other breaches of the peace, and to bring about by peaceful means, and in conformity with the principles of justice and international law, adjustment or settlement of international disputes or situations which might lead to a breach of the peace;

2. To develop friendly relations among nations based on respect for the principle of equal rights and self-determination of peoples, and to take other appropriate measures to strengthen universal peace;

3. To achieve international co-operation in solving international problems of an economic, social, cultural or humanitarian character, and in promoting and encouraging respect for human rights and for fundamental freedoms for all without distinction as to race, sex, language, or religion; . . . [23]

The Charter's emphasis on such issues was not confined to the Preamble and Chapter I. Throughout the Charter there were specific commitments to take action on human rights.[24] All this did much to establish that the UN was no mere trade union of states, as the League had often seemed to be. In addition, care was taken by the UN's founders to ensure that the dreadful mistake of the League's creation was not repeated. The Covenant of the League of Nations had originated as an integral part of the peace treaties concluded at the end of the First World War—treaties that soon came to be seen as unjust. The UN Charter was a freestanding agreement, not so tainted by association with injustice.

A striking feature of the international debate leading up to the Charter was the emphasis on social and economic as well as political rights. This had its background in the New Deal and in the growing strength of welfarism and the left in many countries. The inclusion of the language of human rights and justice in the UN Charter, sometimes thought to have been a largely American achievement, was in fact the result of pressure from many states, including the Soviet Union, which had its own vision, or at least rhetoric, of a system of global justice beyond the confines of existing sovereign states.[25] The British, in numerous wartime documents about international organization from the Declaration by United Nations of 1 January 1942 to the British drafts of the UN Charter preamble in 1945, consistently favoured the commitment to

---

[23] UN Charter, Article 1.

[24] UN Charter, Articles 13, 55, 56, 62, 68, and 76.

[25] See Ruth B. Russell, *A History of the United Nations Charter: The Role of the United States 1940–1945* (Washington, DC: Brookings Institution, 1958), 777–9.

social matters and human rights.[26] One reason why the British supported the inclusion of the statement of purposes and principles in the Charter preamble was that they wanted a strong Security Council, free to act in a variety of situations.

4.2. International Court of Justice

The very mention of Just Peace immediately raises the issue of international mechanisms for settling disputes. The International Court of Justice (ICJ) illustrates the strengths and weaknesses of the contribution to Just Peace that can be made by formal judicial mechanisms. One of the six principal organs of the UN, its business-like Statute, which was adopted in 1945 at the same time as the UN Charter, wisely makes no claims at all about the relation between justice and peace. All UN member states are parties.[27] The successor to the Permanent Court of International Justice, established at The Hague in 1922, the ICJ is empowered to issue binding decisions in cases between states which have consented to its jurisdiction. It also provides advisory opinions when requested to do so by competent international organizations. In the period from its foundation in 1946 to December 2003, the ICJ delivered 78 judgments in contentious cases and also 24 advisory opinions. Its judgments have addressed such matters as land frontiers and maritime boundaries, non-use of force, non-interference in the internal affairs of states, diplomatic relations and immunities, the right of asylum, rights of passage, and economic rights. It has played a key role in certain interstate disputes; and a notable feature, especially since the early 1970s, has been the willingness of post-colonial states to take disputes to the ICJ.[28]

However, the ICJ's overall contribution to international justice has been, and necessarily remains, limited. Its work is basically restricted to those disputes which contending states agree are of a kind which can usefully be resolved in a court. Almost all the cases that actually end up being addressed in the ICJ are those in which the state that loses may be expected to give in

---

[26] See Llewellyn Woodward, *British Foreign Policy in the Second World War* (London: HMSO, 1971) II. 212, 217; Philip A. Reynolds and E. J. Hughes, *The Historian as Diplomat: Charles Kingsley Webster and the United Nations 1939–1946* (London: Martin Robertson, 1976), 166–7; and *Foreign Relations of the United States, 1942* (Washington, DC: Government Printing Office, 1960), I. 21, 23.

[27] Switzerland, although it did not join the UN until 2002, had already been a party to the ICJ Statute from 1948 onwards.

[28] Useful surveys of the ICJ and its work include Arthur Eyffinger, *The International Court of Justice 1946–1996* (The Hague: Kluwer Law International, 1996); and Shabtai Rosenne, *The World Court: What it is and How it Works*, 5th edn. (Dordrecht, The Netherlands: Martinus Nijhoff, 1995).

gracefully. A worrying indication of states' nervousness about international adjudication is that, of the 191 states that are parties to the ICJ Statute, fewer than one third have made a declaration that they accept the compulsory jurisdiction of the ICJ in all legal disputes concerning them, and even some of these states have indicated limits regarding their consent to such jurisdiction.[29] In general, because states have been reluctant to submit certain types of case to it, the ICJ has had a distinctly limited role in respect of many international issues: major territorial disputes, the legitimacy or alleged criminality of certain regimes, terrorist campaigns, and arms build-ups. Although the ICJ and other judicial bodies have an important place in any concept of Just Peace, it is illusory to view international adjudication as the sole foundation on which the idea of Just Peace stands or falls.

4.3. UN Practice: Decolonization

In UN practice, perhaps the most important justice-related principle has been decolonization. From the start, the Charter's emphasis on the sovereign equality of states and its provisions regarding non-self-governing territories (Chapter XI) and international trusteeship (Chapter XII) contained an implicit assumption that the days of European colonialism were numbered. Similarly, the proclamation in Article 1 of 'equal rights and self-determination of peoples' came to be seen as legitimation of the principle of decolonization. Through these Charter provisions, and also through its subsequent actions, the UN came to be associated with the most important single process in international relations since the Second World War: the fission of empires into states. Largely because of this fission, the UN's membership almost quadrupled, from 51 original members in 1945 to 191 at the beginning of 2005.

This association of the UN with decolonization illustrates how tangled the pursuit of international justice can be. An important constraint was the reluctance of all concerned to break up existing administrative units within empires, however arbitrary or even oppressive the frequently artificial boundaries of colonies might be. In 1960, as the process of decolonization was gathering pace, the General Assembly passed the 'Declaration on the Granting of Independence to Colonial Countries and Peoples'. This was the first of a series of declarations interpreting the Charter provisions on the relationship between order and justice. Its strong plea for decolonization was not based on

---

[29] As at 22 March 2004 sixty-two states were listed on the UN website as bound by declarations of compulsory jurisdiction made under Article 36(2) of the ICJ Statute. http://untreaty.un.org/English/access.asp

the proposition that specific ethnic groups should form states but rather on the proposition that existing political and territorial units within empires should acquire self-government. It expressed this in remarkably dogmatic terms: 'Any attempt aimed at the partial or total disruption of the national unity and the territorial integrity of a country is incompatible with the purposes and principles of the Charter of the United Nations.'[30] For all its limitations, this approach was probably a better basis for decolonization than would have been a principle that permitted wholesale redrawing of boundaries.

The UN's anticolonial stance was by no means free of excesses. The British in particular criticized the way in which, in the General Assembly and its committees, all problems in colonies were blamed on the colonial rulers; and British representatives repeatedly attacked the double standard by which overseas rule was condemned but dictatorial rule within post-colonial states was ignored.[31] This foreshadowed later concerns that the post-colonial revolution ended up by turning its initial logic on its head. What began as a movement based on justice for peoples against existing states or empires, ended up prioritizing immunity for sovereign states and their governments—never mind what injustices their people might be suffering.

4.4. General Assembly Declarations on Principles of International Order

During the period from 1965 to 1981 the UN General Assembly considered and approved certain declarations of a general character which, among other things, interpreted those provisions of the Charter that have a bearing on the relationship between order and justice. In those years, a strong coalition of post-colonial states, often assisted by the Soviet bloc, emphasized predominantly statist and non-interventionist ideas and values.

A typical example was the 1961 'Friendly Relations' Declaration.[32] The most comprehensive of the elaborations of the Charter provisions relating to peace and security, this document strengthened earlier formulations of a

---

[30] 'Declaration on the Granting of Independence to Colonial Countries and Peoples', GA Res. 1514 (XV) of 14 December 1960, Article 6.

[31] For a British insider's considered perspective on anticolonial issues at the UN, see John Sankey, 'Decolonisation: Cooperation and Confrontation at the United Nations', in Erik Jensen and Thomas Fisher (eds.), *The United Kingdom—The United Nations* (Basingstoke: Macmillan, 1990), 90–119.

[32] 'Declaration on Principles of International Law concerning Friendly Relations and Co-operation among States in accordance with the Charter of the United Nations', GA Res. 2625 (XXV) of 24 October 1970.

non-interventionist character by specifying that 'No State or group of States has the right to intervene . . .'. However, it went on to address the right of self-determination in such terms as to suggest a right to assist at least some peoples seeking self-determination. This document's belligerent implications were limited: it appeared to confine its concern to self-determination struggles in colonial territories, which meant in practice southern Africa and the Israeli-occupied territories. For the most part, like the 1960 Declaration on Colonialism and other similar documents, it contained a strong reaffirmation of the territorial integrity of sovereign and independent states. However, its references to self-determination struggles serve as a reminder that in cases where justice is denied, demands for military intervention can easily gain support. These references, which sound more like a variant of Just War than a road map for Just Peace, confirm that working out principles of international order is unavoidably rich in ambiguity and paradox.

4.5. International Economic Justice

Justice in relation to international development, trade, and finance is a vital and troublesome part of any concept of Just Peace. There has been no serious dissent about the importance of economic justice since at least the mid-twentieth century, and the matter has been addressed extensively by states, including in numerous international bodies. While the major demands for a new structure of international economic justice have mainly come from relatively less developed states, the rhetoric of justice has also been taken up by the wealthy and powerful. However, justice in this area has proved elusive, its content is the subject of disagreement, and the route by which it might be achieved remains contested.

In this matter different UN bodies have adopted different approaches, which have also changed significantly over time; and there has been a particularly striking disjunction between UN rhetoric and aspiration on the one hand and what actually happens on the other. A visit to the headquarters in Geneva of the UN Conference on Trade and Development (UNCTAD) is reminiscent of a visit to a temple of a failed faith. Whatever its achievements, which include substantial work in information and research, UNCTAD has not delivered on the hopes for a restructuring of the international economic system that were invested in it in 1964.[33] Likewise, not too many hopes are now invested, if they ever were, in the grand abstraction of the New Inter-

---

[33] These hopes were reflected in the resolution establishing UNCTAD, GA Res. 1995 (XIX) of 30 December 1964, adopted without a vote.

national Economic Order, proclaimed by the UN General Assembly in 1974.[34] The UN system in all its many aspects has remained involved in addressing global economic inequality, producing for example the essentially bland 'Agenda for Development' in 1997.[35] Widespread scepticism remains about the capacity of the UN to introduce a general transformation of what are perceived as the dominant structures of economic power.

Sharp disagreements remain, both within the UN system and more generally, about what actually assists the development process: aid or trade; protection or exposure to free markets; debt relief or firm target-related management; planning or laissez-faire. Following the collapse of the communist model of development the debates have changed, but they have by no means ended—and they are not likely to do so soon, as in many cases they reflect different interests and national experiences. A particularly corrosive element in debates about economic justice is their tendency to lead to accusations of hypocrisy. Constructive debate is difficult when Western governments preach the virtues of free trade and open markets, but then violate these principles to protect some of their industries, and when the rulers of developing states call for aid or debt relief and then stash money away in foreign banks. While the concept of a Just Peace has to have economic content that is more than mere platitudes, achieving substantive consensus on it is a slow process.

4.6. Human Rights

Perhaps the most significant contribution to the idea of Just Peace in the UN era has been in the area of human rights. The political principles, laws, and institutions relating to human rights are all seen as having a major contribution to make not just to human welfare but also to international peace and security. The fundamental logic of the focus on human rights is sound: states that mistreat their own citizens are also frequently states that invade their neighbours; and even if they do not, they may threaten international stability by causing huge refugee flows and provoking civil wars which only too easily become internationalized.

On the basis of the Charter references to human rights, successive treaties negotiated in a UN framework have established an impressive array of obligations. The main landmarks are the 1948 Genocide Convention, the 1951

---

[34] 'Declaration on the Establishment of the New International Economic Order', GA Res. 3201 (S-VI) of 1 May 1974; the accompanying Programme of Action, GA Res. 3202 (S-VI) of same date. Both were adopted without a vote.

[35] 'Agenda for Development', GA Res. 51/240 of 20 June 1997, adopted without a vote by a special meeting of the UN General Assembly.

Refugee Convention, the two 1966 International Covenants on Human Rights, and the 1984 Torture Convention. Many agreements in this field provide mechanisms whereby a range of human rights issues can be pursued. For example, the Torture Convention incorporates provision for what is commonly, if loosely, called 'universal jurisdiction': if an offender turns up in a state party to the convention, it may either prosecute or extradite him. However, the most important achievement of the body of law may be its effect on international public discourse: for example, racial and gender discrimination are now widely proclaimed to be unacceptable. This does not mean that they have in practice been abolished, but it does make it easier to challenge them.

While the development of human rights law and policy in the UN has been impressive, it has also been flawed, in ways that illustrate how easily the subject matter of a Just Peace can become the focus of international polemics. Debates about human rights have sometimes been framed in divisive and even misleading ways. In many 1960s discussions it was supposed that there was a dichotomy between economic and social rights (championed by the Soviet Union and many non-aligned states) and civil and political rights (championed particularly by Western states). It gradually came to be recognized by most states that both types of rights are not merely valuable but inherently compatible. As Amartya Sen and others have pointed out, political freedoms and independent media can assist in the satisfaction of the most basic economic rights and can help to instigate action against the devastating consequences of droughts and other disasters.[36]

UN human rights conferences and committees have often failed to address such issues, and some of them offer little or no real intellectual exchange.[37] In the 1970s and 1980s there were many UN conferences which attached the language of rights to matters which were not best addressed in that manner. The so-called 'right to disarmament' was a case in point: UNESCO's conferences on it did not advance the cause of disarmament, nor the understanding of it. Further confirmation that human rights can become a weapon of political warfare was provided at the 2001 UN Conference on Racism, held at Durban.[38] Rhetoric on such matters offers excellent opportunities for the

---

[36] See for example the detailed studies pointing to this conclusion in Jean Drèze and Amartya Sen (eds.), *The Political Economy of Hunger* (Oxford: Clarendon Press, 1990), vol. I, *Entitlement and Well-Being*, 6–7, 23–4, 146–89; and vol. II, *Famine Prevention*, 145, 153, 159–60, 190–1.

[37] On 10 April 2002, at a session of the UN Commission on Human Rights that I attended, not one speech that I heard responded to any point made in any preceding speech. Some speeches contained questionable 'facts' and preposterous arguments.

[38] World Conference against Racism, Racial Discrimination, Xenophobia and Related Intolerance, Durban, 31 August–7 September 2001. Declaration adopted 8 September 2001 following numerous disagreements.

expression of self-righteousness, the attribution of blame, and the conduct of political warfare generally. Sadly, it contributes little to the idea or reality of a Just Peace.

The consensus on human rights has obvious limits. In many parts of the world it has not transformed deep-rooted cultural practices such as the oppression of women; and many states are at best selective about how they apply human rights principles both domestically and internationally. A notable weakness of the UN approach is that states have been consistently reluctant to create strong UN-based machinery for monitoring of human rights or to fund the various bodies that have been created. Many governments, especially dictatorships of various kinds, have no wish to be challenged; and the General Assembly has been parsimonious about funding the activities of the numerous human rights bodies it has established—including the Office of the UN High Commissioner for Human Rights in Geneva.[39] In the wake of terrorist incidents of past decades there are new challenges to the primacy of human rights. While the contempt in which terrorists hold the value of life needs no elaboration, antiterrorist struggles too can pose threats to human rights. In particular, in the 'war on terrorism' the USA has perhaps unavoidably been working closely with certain regimes that show little respect for human rights, and has itself indicated that the struggle against international terrorism may have to have priority over individual human rights, especially in the case of detainees suspected of terrorist offences.

Because of the lack of a universal international consensus on how human rights norms should be implemented, some of the more effective international human rights regimes are regional, not global. The system based on the 1950 European Convention on Human Rights functions effectively because of three factors: the states concerned have similar outlooks on key issues; the Convention's provisions have become part of the domestic law of these states; and individual redress can be sought in the European Court of Human Rights, established in 1959. Perhaps the nearest equivalent in another continent is the Inter-American Court of Human Rights, established in 1978. The UN has a long way to go to achieve anything remotely comparable. This suggests that it may be possible to build a Just Peace on a regional basis, but much more difficult to do so at the global level.

The critical question for the whole concept of Just Peace is simple. Has all the UN-based lawmaking and institution-building in the human rights field created a genuine global consensus on the subject? Despite the many

---

[39] Useful critical surveys of the functioning of the existing human rights regime are Philip Alston and James Crawford (eds.), *The Future of UN Human Rights Treaty Monitoring* (Cambridge: Cambridge University Press, 2000); and Anne F. Bayefsky (ed.), *The UN Human Rights Treaty System in the Twenty-first Century* (The Hague: Kluwer Law International, 2000).

weaknesses of the UN involvement in human rights, there is consensus of a kind. The modern law in this field, as expressed in the two 1966 covenants and other documents, is no mere Western creation but the product of hard negotiations involving Western, Communist, and post-colonial states. The 1993 Vienna Conference on Human Rights proclaimed boldly that 'the universal nature of these rights and freedoms is beyond question'.[40] Human rights have become an important part of the dialogue between states: even China, a powerful one-party state with ample reasons to be cautious about the matter, has taken some hesitant steps towards accepting that dialogue on its human rights performance is legitimate.[41] In short, there has been significant movement towards a world in which slavish acceptance of the absolute sovereignty of states regardless of how they treat their citizens is replaced by some shared understandings about the respect that the state owes to the individual. This suggests a move from a minimal peace to at least recognizing the possibility of a Just Peace.

4.7. The Laws of War

In the UN era, the laws of war—often now called International Humanitarian Law—have developed in such a way as to have a significant impact on international thought and practice, even on our ideas about peace. This body of law encompasses the four 1949 Geneva Conventions, the two 1977 Additional Protocols thereto, the 1998 Rome Statute of the International Criminal Court, and numerous other agreements. Particularly in the post-Cold War period, it has had an important bearing on the concept of Just Peace in two main ways:

First, this body of law, or at least some significant parts of it, is increasingly seen as a standard by which the international community can judge conduct in wars, including civil wars. As such, it provides one basis for criticism of repressive governments in such wars, and also for demands for intervention to stop violations and even to replace repressive regimes.

Second, after a society has experienced hideous atrocities, one way in which it can get back to some kind of normality is if those who perpetrated such acts

---

[40] From the first paragraph of Article 1 of the Vienna Declaration and Programme of Action, adopted by consensus on 25 June 1993 at the World Conference on Human Rights, Vienna.

[41] China signed the 1966 UN Covenant on Economic, Social and Cultural Rights in October 1997 and ratified it in March 2001; it signed the Covenant on Civil and Political Rights in October 1998 but had not ratified it by March 2004. On the background, see Ann Kent, *China, the United Nations, and Human Rights: The Limits of Compliance* (Philadelphia, PA: University of Pennsylvania Press, 1999); and Rosemary Foot, *Rights beyond Borders: The Global Community and the Struggle over Human Rights in China* (Oxford: Oxford University Press, 2000).

are held responsible for them and punished. Otherwise there will be a tendency to put blame on all members of an adversary group, thus perpetuating the hatred that leads to new conflict.

Because of such considerations, the laws of war can be seen as part of a larger process whereby states are seen, not as having total sovereign rights to act as they please within their borders, but as having to observe certain international standards. The establishment of the three international criminal tribunals (for former Yugoslavia, Rwanda and the International Criminal Court) in the period 1993–2002 reflected this view. This process highlighted the difference between an older notion of the 'peace of states' and the developing (but by no means novel) idea of Just Peace.

With the application of the laws of war, as with other aspects of the application of justice in international relations, there can be no easy assumption that all good causes are compatible. Sometimes they are not. Although the ICRC in Geneva views international criminal tribunals as a valuable means of showing that the world is serious about the law, for its own staff to give evidence to such tribunals would risk undermining the reputation for impartiality, neutrality and confidentiality which is so important to the ICRC's work. This was painfully evident in 1999–2000 when the question arose as to whether the ICRC should produce information in connection with a trial before the Yugoslavia Tribunal. It was decided that it should not.[42]

It would be easy to criticize the increased emphasis placed on international humanitarian law, as also on human rights law. These bodies of law are not always taken seriously by states.[43] Even when they are taken seriously, both bodies of law can add new points of friction in international diplomacy, can complicate the operation of alliances, and can even on occasion contribute to decisions to use armed force. Both could thus be seen as subversive of the stability of the international order of sovereign states. Yet both of these bodies of law can have a positive practical role in the conduct of national and international politics. Both of them are compatible with the existence of strong sovereign states, which alone can implement their provisions effectively. The emphasis in both these bodies of law on respect for the individual, and their message that all states are subject to some fundamental international norms, provides a politically appealing and functionally significant grounding for Just Peace, which might otherwise seem hopelessly abstract.

---

[42] International Criminal Tribunal for the Former Yugoslavia, decision of 28 February 2000. See also separate opinion of Judge David Hunt. ICTY, *Judicial Supplement*, no. 16 (7 July 2000), 2–3.
[43] This sober conclusion is reached by Geoffrey Best in the epilogue to his *War and Law Since 1945* (Oxford: Oxford University Press, 1994), 403.

4.8. Democracy

The existence of multiparty democracy within states can obviously serve the cause of justice of the inhabitants in a variety of ways. The question is: Is it a key component of a Just Peace, and if so, should the promotion of democracy be a concern of the international community? There has been a significant movement of opinion on this matter in the post-1945 era, both regionally and in a UN framework.

The idea that there is a close connection between democracy within states and peace between them has a long history. The view that democracies do not make war on each other is widely, and somewhat confusingly, attributed to Immanuel Kant.[44] Many have supported the 'democratic peace' proposition, and some have gone so far as to call it the most important single generalization in the confusing landscape of international relations.[45] If this claim is correct, then proposals to implement a Just Peace, whether generally, or in specific regions such as the Middle East, may need to have democracy as a central feature.

In the United Nations there has been some thinking along these lines. The early antecedents of this thinking, now largely forgotten, include a Chilean proposal in August 1950 to place on the UN General Assembly agenda the admirably entitled item 'Strengthening of democratic principles as a means of contributing to the maintenance of universal peace'. This was accompanied by a 34-point explanatory memorandum, super-Kantian in tone, calling for the establishment of an 'international democratic pact'.[46] The proposal was withdrawn.

Since the mid-1980s the UN has become more associated than before with the cause of multiparty democracy. It has supported elections as a means of resolving certain internal conflicts; it has become deeply involved in planning,

---

[44] In his *Perpetual Peace: A Philosophical Sketch* (1795–6) Kant actually argued that a *republican* constitutional system could lead to perpetual peace between states. He drew a sharp distinction between republicanism and democracy. He saw republicanism as 'that political principle whereby the executive power (the government) is separated from the legislative power'. By contrast, he criticised democracy as establishing 'an executive power through which all the citizens may make decisions about (and indeed against) the single individual without his consent...', in other words as direct democracy in which the majority may exercise tyranny over the minority. His idea of a republic actually corresponds closely to modern ideas of constitutional democracy. Kant, *Political Writings*, ed. Hans Reiss, 2nd edn. (Cambridge: Cambridge University Press, 1991), 100–1.

[45] For an excellent discussion, see Michael W. Doyle, *Ways of War and Peace: Realism, Liberalism and Socialism* (New York: W. W. Norton, 1997), 258–99.

[46] Point 21 of the Chilean explanatory memorandum of 18 August 1950, *UN General Assembly, Official Records*, Fifth Session, New York, 1950, Agenda item 66, pp. 1–4. See also *Yearbook of the United Nations 1950*, p. 29.

organizing, and monitoring elections in numerous countries; and in at least two cases in the 1990s—Haiti and Sierra Leone—the Security Council gave legitimacy to those who sought to restore a democratically elected government that had been deposed in a military *coup d'état*. The developing association between the UN and democracy confirms the far-reaching implications of the UN's preoccupation with human rights and other justice-related issues. However incomplete, this association appears to be becoming stronger.[47]

Yet there are some difficulties with the idea of encouraging the growth of democracy as a basis of a Just Peace. In some episodes and in some societies the connection between democracy and peace has not been obvious. Democracies are not completely immune from engaging in warlike acts against each other. For example, in 1973 one democracy, the USA, supported a coup in Chile against a democratically-elected President. Even if established democracies are stable, the process of getting there, democratization, can expose deep and explosive problems in a society. For example, in 1990, in all the republics of the Socialist Federal Republic of Yugoslavia, the first genuinely multiparty elections since before the Second World War were held. These elections, in which many parties represented specific ethnic groups and articulated purely national claims, were a prelude to war within and between some of the republics.[48] Multiparty democracy, or at least the transition to it, can be a prelude to war. In 1999, Russia's democratic procedures seem to have tilted the dice in favour of waging a full-scale internal war against the Chechen rebels. In the same year, Indonesia's evolution to a more democratic system was accompanied by the terrible conflict and killings in East Timor. Moreover, there are societies (Haiti is a possible example) where the maintenance of democracy can require at least the threat, and perhaps the reality, of forcible military intervention.[49] Democracy cannot be introduced with equal speed in all societies. There are difficulties in advocating it for, say, China, without considering the very special traditions and characteristics that have impeded its application there. Moreover, the traffic between dictatorship and democracy is far from being one-way. It is not surprising, therefore, that by no means all individuals and states accept that multiparty democracy within states is central to the idea of international justice.

[47] See for example the publication of the UN Development Programme, *Human Development Report 2002: Deepening Democracy in a Fragmented World* (New York: Oxford University Press, 2002). This emphasizes at p. v that democratic participation is a critical end of economic development and not just a means of achieving it.

[48] Lenard J. Cohen, *Broken Bonds: The Disintegration of Yugoslavia* (Boulder, CO: Westview Press, 1993), esp. at p. 146.

[49] See especially David Malone, *Decision-Making in the UN Security Council: The Case of Haiti, 1990–1997* (Oxford: Oxford University Press, 1998).

Despite these complexities, the idea that democracy is a basis for peace has real strength. It corresponds to our experience in Western Europe since 1945: democracy has been seen as a key foundation for the building of a new Europe less war-prone than before, and the model has been so successful that it is being extended eastwards. On a global level, many have seen events since about the mid-1970s as presenting proof that there is a historic trend towards democracy. This view particularly influenced the foreign policy of the Clinton administration. The growth of democracy has been most striking in Europe, both southern and eastern; but has also taken place—however haltingly—in some other parts of the world, including in Latin America and Africa. The international assistance given for democratic development is one of the most remarkable phenomena of our times. The successful holding of free and fair elections in previously war-torn countries is now almost routine. In sum, there is a widely perceived connection between a more democratic world and a more peaceful one.

4.9. Self-Determination

Self-determination is a typical example of a principle of international justice which, depending on how it is interpreted and exploited, can be a basis of Just Peace or a recipe for war. If it means 'national self-determination' in the sense of the right of distinct nations or ethnic groups to establish their own states, then, as the history of Europe up to 1939 suggests, it can cause conflict and war. The UN Charter's framers wisely avoided using the term 'national self-determination', using instead the more cautious and open-ended phrase 'equal rights and self-determination of peoples'. In the post-1945 period the principle of self-determination has had a revival, but its meaning has subtly developed.

Article 1 of both the 1966 UN Human Rights Covenants declares: 'All peoples have the right of self-determination. By virtue of that right they freely determine their political status and freely pursue their economic, social and cultural development.' This reassertion of the UN Charter principle of 'self-determination of peoples' appears to be both emphatic and universal in its application. However, a litany of notoriously difficult questions remains. Which peoples are appropriate candidates for self-determination and which are not? Who decides this? And does 'self-determination' imply a right to separate sovereign statehood? In the 1960s and 1970s the term 'self-determination' was most commonly used in advocacy of a right of statehood for a particularly unprivileged few, including the inhabitants of Israeli-occupied territories and of colonial hangovers in southern Africa. It was not a right for all peoples, since it was implicitly accepted that inhabitants of many existing states, including in the post-colonial world, had already benefited from the exercise of self-determination and had little further need of it. Since the early 1990s the right of self-determination has undergone changes of meaning and nuance—as a right to a degree of self-rule and even a right to democracy, but not necessarily a right to independent statehood.[50] This re-interpretation, still incomplete, could bring self-determination into alignment with the democratic aspect of ideas of Just Peace.

5. 'INDUCTION': A EUROPEAN MODEL FOR PURSUIT OF JUST PEACE?

Efforts to develop a notion of Just Peace are not confined to the United Nations system. Some of the most innovative and important developments are at the regional level. They have taken many different forms in different regions of the world. In Europe in particular, reeling from the experience of two world wars, states have developed innovative methods of cooperation, most notably in the European Union (EU) and North Atlantic Treaty Organization (NATO). In varying degrees they have managed to combine the pursuit of peace with the pursuit of justice.

In the recent history of Europe there have been two episodes which may have something new to contribute to the idea of Just Peace. They involve what is termed here 'induction'—that is to say, assisting change through the magnetic power of successful example, and then, later, through assistance to states preparing for membership of the EU. Both examples are connected with the development of the Organization for Security and Co-operation in Europe (OSCE).

The first example of 'induction' in the pursuit of both justice and peace concerns the significant part played by the 'Helsinki Process'—the precursor of today's more institutionalized OSCE—in the changes in eastern Europe and the Soviet Union in the last two decades of the Cold War. It is true that the pursuit of a policy of détente by Western powers in the period from the 1960s up to the demise of the Soviet Union in December 1991 involved episodes in which justice for individual states and peoples seemed to yield to the requirements of the East–West order. However, the Helsinki process, which began in

---

[50] Discussed further in Adam Roberts, 'Beyond the Flawed Principle of National Self-Determination', in Edward Mortimer and Robert Fine (eds.), *People, Nation and State: The Meaning of Ethnicity and Nationalism* (London and New York: I. B. Tauris, 1999), 77–106.

1972, came to embody a judicious and prudent combination of emphases on both order and justice.

The principal document of the Helsinki process, the Helsinki Final Act of 1975, incorporates a thorough and also subtle balancing of justice and peace.[51] It contained a strong and detailed declaration of principles on interstate relations. This addressed security issues by emphasizing respect for state sovereignty, avoidance of the threat or use of force against states, and the inviolability of frontiers. A range of confidence-building measures such as prior notification of major military manoeuvres was initiated. At the same time the Final Act placed notable emphasis on respect for human rights and fundamental freedoms. After 1975, there were numerous follow-up conferences, which became an important point of contact, and a location for the pursuit of political warfare, between East and West.[52]

There can be no claim that the Helsinki process alone caused the end of the Cold War and the collapse of communist systems. Such great events can seldom be attributed to one cause. Indeed, it is perfectly possible that a number of very different approaches by Western states contributed to the demise of the Soviet Union: not just the Helsinki process, but also the more militantly anti-Soviet approach of Ronald Reagan in the early years of his presidency. Nor can there be any claim that the Helsinki process was free of the moral ambiguities inherent in international relations: in Europe, it involved some unsatisfactory compromises with repressive regimes, while on a global level it coincided with the continuation of super-power rivalry in many regional wars, from Angola to Afghanistan. Yet Helsinki did achieve something. Its security provisions helped to establish expectations of stability, making it easier for the Soviet Union to relax its grip on eastern Europe. At the same time its focus on human rights issues struck a chord in countries in which socialism was already a dying creed, and became the basis for a number of non-governmental movements in eastern Europe—such as Solidarity in Poland and Charter 77 in Czechoslovakia—which demanded greater respect for the rights of ordinary citizens. These movements eventually helped to bring about the collapse of communist regimes in one country after another in eastern and central Europe in 1989. Paradoxically, by recognizing the division of Europe the Helsinki process helped to overcome it.

The Helsinki process that ran from 1972 to 1991 can easily seem to be the supreme example of how order and justice can be pursued in tandem fruitfully, and without a contradiction between the two goals. Perhaps some would

---

[51] *Conference on Security and Co-operation in Europe: Final Act* (London: Her Majesty's Stationery Office, August 1975), Cmnd. 6198.

[52] For different national perspectives on the Helsinki follow-up process, see Richard Davy, (ed.), *European Détente: A Reappraisal* (London: Sage, 1992).

argue that the process operated in easy conditions, since the communist ideology was past its sell-by date. However, the fact that the end of communism was achieved peacefully does owe something to Helsinki. The lesson of the process is that a Just Peace can be achieved by skill and patience, by creating a benevolent framework for change in dictatorial States and by military containment: it does not require military crusading. This lesson, derived from the period when the Cold War ended, is at risk of being forgotten in the post-Cold War world.

The military restraint of the Helsinki process up to 1991 was not, by any stretch of the imagination, pacifism. The 'order' dimension of the Helsinki Final Act, and of the subsequent evolution of the process, was tough-minded. It involved the right of all the participating states to be, or not to be, members of alliances. It implicitly accepted the continuation of systems of military defence and deterrence, and indeed of the general policy of containment. It simply sought to mitigate some points of friction that accompany such systems, and at the same time to uphold the principles of human rights and social progress. In short, Helsinki represented the application of tough thinking to the question of Just Peace.

The second example of 'induction' in Europe in the pursuit of both justice and peace concerns the range of processes and measures involved in assisting certain post-Communist states since 1991. The OSCE has been one leading player in this process, alongside the EU, NATO, the Council of Europe, the UN and numerous other bodies. The forms that such induction have taken include not just the power of successful example—due to the respectable achievements of democratic European states—but also assistance regarding a wide range of specific measures. These have included: addressing issues relating to ethnic minorities; election management, supervision, and monitoring; establishment of parliamentary controls over armed forces and defence policy; cooperation on measures against terrorism; and transition to more market-based economies. Some of these measures have been quite literally 'induction' in the sense of preparations for membership of the EU.

This process of induction has no obvious parallel elsewhere. It is hard to imagine states in the Americas undergoing fundamental adjustments in order to become states of the USA. The explanation for the attraction of the EU may partly lie in the reputation for combining principles of justice with respect for sovereignty that already characterized the Helsinki process before the collapses of communist rule; and it may also lie in the fact that the EU, precisely because it is not a unified superstate, continues to leave ample room for national difference and the maintenance of a significant degree of national independence: important components of any vision of Just Peace.

6. THE SEARCH FOR A JUST PEACE TODAY

Where does this remarkable evolution of ideas and practices bearing on Just Peace leave us today? One thing is certain: the evolution inadequately sketched here cannot be reversed. However, the evolution is not simple. There cannot be a three- or four-part set of criteria for Just Peace comparable to the criteria for what constitutes a just, or at least justifiable, use of force. Some of the numerous elements that contribute to the idea of Just Peace may appeal more to developing states, others to wealthier ones. Some of the elements can only be implemented by consensus, others may require acts of coercion if they are to be achieved. Some may call for implementation at a global level, others may call for regional or local action. In the attempt to further develop and implement the idea of Just Peace, three general questions stand out: (*a*) Is there sufficient international consensus on key principles integral to the idea of a Just Peace? (*b*) To what extent is the state still a necessary part of any vision of a Just Peace? (*c*) In what ways may the use of force be necessary in support of the idea of Just Peace?

6.1. Is there Consensus?

On the face of it, there is a significant degree of international consensus about key principles integral to the idea of Just Peace. No less than 191 states—virtually all—are parties to the UN Charter and the ICJ Statute. The same number of states, 191, are parties to the four 1949 Geneva Conventions, and 161 to their 1977 Additional Protocol I.[53] The two 1966 International Covenants on Civil and Political Rights, and on Economic, Social, and Cultural Rights, have 151 and 148 parties respectively. The 1984 Convention against Torture has 134.[54] In short, states have accepted an impressive range of obligations. Even when states disagree about how they should be interpreted and applied, the principles and language of these treaties is widely accepted as a proper framework for international debate. This situation can be viewed as a foundation, to be built upon in efforts to turn a Just Peace from idea to reality.

However, any international consensus on the many principles of international justice is distinctly patchy in character. The first problem is that certain states are cool, or even hostile, towards some key principles. For example, from Saudi Arabia to Turkmenistan there are governments that

[53] Figures of states parties from ICRC website, 20 March 2004. http://www.icrc.org.
[54] Figures of states parties from UN website, 22 March 2004. http://untreaty.un.org/English/access.asp.

show no signs of changing from an authoritarian system. In addition, many states whether or not democratic, including China, India, Japan, Russia and the USA, reject important parts of the international legal order, including the Rome Statute of the International Criminal Court. A further problem is that even states which do subscribe to many of the key political and legal principles outlined here may not give them priority when they are faced with tough choices. Thus in the military and police operations following the terrorist attacks on the USA on 11 September 2001, the USA established or consolidated alliances with numerous undemocratic regimes. As in the Cold War, so today, the imperious requirements of military alliances and the struggle against a dangerous enemy sometimes take precedence over other legal and political considerations.

Where there is greater consensus is on a regional basis. Europe and Latin America provide two examples of regions in which there is now a high level of agreement on a normative order, which encompasses democracy, human rights, and (especially in Europe) acceptance of regional decision-making in certain issue-areas. The possibility that there might be a Just Peace, just in a region, poses awkward problems. If a group of states develops a Kantian order among themselves, as the EU arguably has, how will it relate to the rougher and tougher world beyond? In particular, will the members of such a regional group be prepared to engage in the military preparations and activities that may be necessary in order to defend a legal order under assault—whether from terrorism, development of weapons of mass destruction, or crimes against humanity in distant lands?

6.2. The State: A Necessary Part of Any Vision of a Just Peace?

It is often suggested that any vision of a Just Peace has to transcend the division of the world into separate sovereign states—an arrangement that is closely associated in many peoples' minds with war and preparations for war. Some enticing visions see a declining role for states as cosmopolitan consciousness and institutions progressively wear away at the narrower institutions and archaic boundaries of states.[55] However, the role of the state as a vehicle for achieving both peace and justice is far from finished. Many states, by avoiding involvement in international war for long periods, have demonstrated that peace and statehood are not incompatible. Often it is not states as such, but rather their breakdown in the face of internal dissension, which

---

[55] One idiosyncratic example of such a prescriptive approach, advocating an international society of the whole human race rather than purely of states, is Philip Allott, *Eunomia: New Order for a New World* (Oxford: Oxford University Press, 1990).

gives rise to civil and international wars. In many cases the state has proven the most effective vehicle for realizing the principles that are essential to a concept of a Just Peace: for example, human rights flourish best in the environment of a strong and legitimate state structure which incorporates the necessary constitutional procedures, legal mechanisms and spirit of tolerance necessary for the realization of human freedoms.

The state can properly be viewed, not as a sovereign entity free to do exactly what its government wants, but rather as a body with rights and duties derived from the larger international society of which it is part. It can be seen as the vehicle whereby the rights of citizens are secured, and effective contributions to their security (and that of international society as a whole) are made. Although the idea of Just Peace may contain some aspects that are subversive of the policies and structures of many states, in principle it is likely to be dependent on states as well as other bodies for its effective implementation.

6.3. The Role of Force in Ideas of Just Peace

Many proposals for a more just order in international relations have had as a key component the idea that the use of force should be limited to the agreed purposes of international society as a whole, and should be essentially collective in character. Thus a study of US liberal internationalism after the First World War consisted almost exclusively of an evaluation of the emerging concept of collective security.[56] The collective use of force has been a key theme in many propositions for a Just Peace, but ideas about it are often flawed, and the flaws may in turn raise doubts about Just Peace.

'Collective security' in its classical sense can be defined as a system, regional or global, in which each participating state accepts that the security of one is the concern of all, and agrees to join in a collective response to any threat to the peace or act of aggression. In this sense it is distinct from, and more ambitious than, systems of alliance security, in which groups of states ally with each other, principally against possible external threats. Typically, a collective security system involves all the states in a given area, and is not necessarily targeted at a specific named adversary state, whereas an alliance involves a more limited group of like-minded states, and is aimed at an actual or potential external adversary.

---

[56] Lloyd E. Ambrosius, *Wilsonian Statecraft: Theory and Practice of Liberal Internationalism during First World War* (Wilmington, Delaware: SR Books, 1991), pp. ix–x.

Proposals for collective security have been in circulation at least since the time of the Peace of Westphalia in 1648. However, no attempt to build a system of collective security has ever succeeded in conforming to the definition outlined earlier. Attractive in theory, ideas of collective security have in practice involved many awkward problems.[57] They depend upon a view of the world as consisting of states all of which have uncontested boundaries and congenial regimes, willing to entrust their security largely to the community as a whole, and to rely on the will and capacity of the major powers to agree on a course of action and follow it. The reality is harsher. States not directly involved do not necessarily see every crisis in terms of aggression versus defence, nor do they rush to take action: like Switzerland, they have often tended towards neutrality regarding other peoples' conflicts. If they favour action, different states may favour different ends, and different means. Even if they do agree on the particular course to be taken, states may still disagree over burden-sharing—with regard to money, military resources, or the risk to their own soldiers' lives—and over command structures. Further, to the extent that groups of states develop a capacity for collective military action, pressures inevitably develop to use it not just for defence, but also for other purposes, including interventions within states to stop gross human rights violations or to restore democratic regimes. Finally, there is a conundrum at the heart of collective security thinking: whether it is best organized on a global level, with attendant risks that the system will be overloaded with commitments to numerous states worldwide, in effect globalizing every conflict; or on a regional level, which involves problems of defining the regions in question, warding off dangers of regional hegemony, and avoiding possible disputes about which particular organization should handle a particular crisis. None of these problems significantly diminished in the course of the twentieth century.

Because of these problems, the idea of Just Peace should not be conceived of as inextricably linked with, and dependent on, the theory of collective security. Collective security in its classical sense is overambitious, and there is no chance of it being implemented on a global scale in the foreseeable future. However, if the well-defined concept of collective security is flawed, its less well-defined relation, cooperative security, may act as a partial substitute. The cooperative use of force by groups of states, often acting with the authorization of the UN Security Council, is one major framework for the employment of coercion in the post-Cold War world. Indeed, it is a positive strength of the

---

[57] For an enumeration of questions relating to collective security systems see Andrew Hurrell, 'Collective Security and International Order Revisited', *International Relations*, 11/1 (1992), 37–55.

idea of Just Peace that it can increase the prospects for the use of force on a cooperative multinational basis.

The idea of Just Peace, with its combined emphasis on cooperative use of force and on human rights, necessarily leads to pressures for humanitarian interventions. How can we claim that we support basic human rights if we are not willing in principle to act militarily to protect them when they are under the most extreme threat? The question is serious, and cannot be evaded by protestations that humanitarian intervention never succeeds in achieving its objects. Certain cases of intervention, including those in East Bengal in 1971, northern Iraq in 1991 and Kosovo in 1999, indicate that interventions can sometimes stop mass killings, enable refugees to return to their homes, and provide at least the beginnings of a more acceptable political order.

To say that humanitarian intervention may occasionally, in exceptional circumstances, be the least objectionable course of action, is not to say that there could or should be any general recognition of a 'right' of states to engage in such intervention. There is a tacit acceptance that the UN Security Council can authorize such interventions. However, mainly because of the obvious concerns about abuse, there is no chance of any formal international legal agreement on a general right of states to engage in humanitarian intervention. It may be for the best that there is no answer in legal principle to the question of whether there is a right of humanitarian intervention: states must bear the burden of making up their minds on the basis of the particular factual and legal issues raised by each case.[58]

Whether intervention forces may be needed for other purposes beside humanitarian intervention is one of the difficult questions that arises from the concept of Just Peace. Ideally such forces would only be used for interventionist purposes in cases where there was authorization from international bodies, including the UN Security Council. However, making any use of force dependent on a single veto is questionable. Such forces might be required to stop such varied activities as gross environmental despoliation, criminal waste of natural resources, major violations of disarmament agreements, and use of territory to prepare terrorist attacks elsewhere in the world. Thus, quite apart from the continuing need for defence, there is likely to be a need for advanced armed forces to have certain interventionist capabilities. However, many European liberal states seem unwilling to provide for such forces, preferring instead to be resentfully dependent on the USA. This produces a strange and paradoxical result: the USA is expected to be the principal provider of armed force to maintain international order, but precisely because of the burden of

---

[58] For a detailed exploration see Adam Roberts, 'The So-Called "Right" of Humanitarian Intervention', in *Yearbook of International Humanitarian Law* 2000, 3 (The Hague: T. M. C. Asser Press, 2002), 3–51.

this expectation it has become intolerant of European and other states which preach internationalist principles but expect the USA to do much of the military dirty work. The Just Peace risks being transformed into a peculiar version of the Pax Americana in which Europeans and others resent what they see as American dominance, while Americans resent the endless demands which a troubled world seems to impose on Washington.

One reason why an intervention capacity needs to be taken seriously by advocates of Just Peace is that if there is a public emphasis on justice, but a failure to take appropriate military action in crises, the very idea of international order may be discredited. In the 1990s, in Bosnia, Rwanda, Sierra Leone, Kosovo, and East Timor, there were times when violent adversaries made a mockery of international expressions of concern about the treatment of civilians: a process that was deeply damaging to any idea that there can be such a thing as justice in international relations. Only belatedly, after much humiliation, was force used to right those wrongs. Its use was of course imperfect, but in all these cases failure to use it at all would have been even more damaging.

Although force may occasionally be needed to defend its core principles, resort to force should never be viewed as routine. The use of non-violent methods, whether of embargoes, constitutional politics or of popular civil resistance, is always the first option, and needs more attention than it has received in international political debate. Also there may be occasions when restraint and patience is needed, as it was in the Helsinki process, even if a price is sometimes paid to tyrants. There are other occasions in which military action is the only way in which to maintain certain international principles and institutions. Choosing when to use force, and when not to do so, is a dilemma inherent in the idea of Just Peace.

The 'War on Terror' announced by the Bush administration in September 2001 is a case in point. The war in Afghanistan initiated by the US and allies on 7 October 2001 was relatively easy to support as a justified response to a serious and long-term terrorist threat. However, in the 'War on Terror' generally, as in other conflicts, there is a risk of excessive zealotry. Any coalition operations, and the treatment of those captured in them, have to be conducted with proper respect to the laws of war. In dealing with terrorism, as with many other problems, only a small part of the response is military. In the overwhelming majority of countries, addressing terrorism will be a matter of slow patient police work, requiring great firmness but not often offering the grand spectacles and occasionally quick results of large-scale military action. Indeed, if an effective international coalition against terrorism is to have any chance of survival, it will have to reflect some idea of justice. It will have to be based on a concern with the fate of Palestinians under Israeli occupation as well as with the casualties of 11 September. Otherwise it will invite only a sceptical response from peoples and states whose support is necessary if it is to succeed.

The 2003 Iraq War reinforced doubts about the use of force in the name of purportedly liberal goals—be they the prevention of terrorism, the implementation of disarmament terms imposed by the UN Security Council, or the spreading of democracy. President Bush sometimes defended the war in terms that suggested that there was nothing wrong with Woodrow Wilson's liberal internationalist vision that could not be put right with a few weapons.[59] This was bound to reinforce scepticism about the idea that force can be used in support of visions of a better order, especially when, as in the case of Iraq, the arguments for the use of force have not been based on rigorous assessment of evidence.

In the past, some conceptions of Just Peace have been undermined by the weakness or excessive simplicity of their proposals regarding the use of force. This analysis has suggested that a Just Peace involves minimizing the use of force wherever possible, but not renouncing it altogether. The cause of Just Peace needs to be complemented by a clear doctrine of 'Justifiable Force'. The fact that Just Peace cannot be imposed by force (except in exceptional circumstances such as the defeat and surrender of Germany and Japan in 1945) still leaves a large number of issues and occasions on which the use of force may be necessary. Working out principles about which uses of force may be appropriate in support of a Just Peace represents one of the most difficult challenges facing the concept. No less difficult is the inevitable requirement, when force is used, to work with allies. The problem is not just that the political systems of many potential allies may fall far short of even basic standards of justice: it is also that, even within an overarching framework of shared values, different states are bound to have different perceptions of events, and to find it difficult to operate under a common leadership.

7. CONCLUSION

This short survey, while suggesting that justice-related issues are central to the conduct of international relations and to the attainment of peace between states, has not concealed the difficulties of the project. Just Peace, whether viewed as an emerging concept or a partially and unevenly established reality,

---

[59] See e.g. President George W. Bush, Speech in London, 19 November 2003. Text available at: http://www.whitehouse.gov/news/releases/2003/11/20031119-1.html

poses severe problems. It can provoke deep resentment in regions of the world racked by poverty, war, and dictatorship; and certain new challenges—especially environmental protection—have yet to be tackled effectively. Perhaps it is a sign of the vitality of the project that it continues today, and will continue in the future, to be the subject of contestation and evolution.

Despite all the difficulties, the notion of a Just Peace is no less necessary to our governments and societies today than was the vision of a just international order that influenced the work of the framers of the UN Charter in the closing months of the Second World War. There is solid substance in the idea of Just Peace. In particular, it has been strengthened by its effective separation from Utopianism, and from schemes for the complete renunciation of force. Both regionally and globally, the idea of Just Peace is not an intellectual pipe dream. Its principles have been developed by states, not least in a large range of treaties and institutions. More importantly, these principles have been applied in practice, most notably in Europe through processes of induction. None of its core ideas—of democracy, human rights, development, support for international institutions, and constraints on the use of force—can be abandoned. It is a useful framework for thinking in realistic and at the same time constructive terms about the improvement of international relations generally. It even has something to offer in the settlement of particular long-standing conflicts around the globe, not least those in the Balkans and the Middle East.

5

Measuring International Ethics: A Moral Scale of War, Peace, Justice, and Global Care

Pierre Allan

Sooner or later in life everyone discovers perfect happiness is unrealizable, but there are few who pause to consider the antithesis: that perfect unhappiness is equally unattainable.[1]

1. INTRODUCTION

An Auschwitz survivor, Primo Levi wrote about the long road to hell and its varied stations. Living in a world of genocide, absolute war, and daily torture, he pondered on the extremes of human experience and their morality. This chapter has a similar goal. It seeks to portray international ethics in its varied appearances and to this end constructs an international moral scale. Besides putting the concept of Just Peace developed in this book in an overall theoretical perspective, such a scale also allows for normative comparison between different international states, that is, measuring international ethics.

I develop an ethical—or moral[2]—scale ranging from perfect happiness for all to absolute misfortune for all. Focusing primarily on the level of the international, not the individual, this scale classifies wrongdoings and good deeds of a nation-state, community, or social group—such as one of the 'peoples' in John Rawls's conception[3] or one of the 'tribes' in Michael Walzer's[4]—not personal grief or happiness. Above all, it is interested in the

---

[1] Primo Levi, *If This is a Man* and *The Truce*, English trans. by Stuart Woolf ([1958] London: Abacus, 1987), 239.

[2] In general, ethics and morality and their adjectives will be used as synonyms.

[3] John Rawls, *The Law of Peoples* (Cambridge, MA: Harvard University Press, 1999), 23–7.

[4] Michael Walzer, *Thick and Thin: Moral Argument at Home and Abroad* (Notre Dame, IN: University of Notre Dame Press, 1994), 63–83.

question of the various kinds of peace and war, and in the often complex relationship between them—as in a Just War.

Better understanding of a concept can come through quite different methods. For example, one can privilege a reading of conceptual break-throughs through the analysis of power relationships governing science in action, or proceed by investigating the change of scientific images analysed through *Gestalt* psychology or more modern cognitive science methods. Or, alternatively, more radical methods such as post-modern deconstruction may be used, deconstructing texts by showing their various interpretations, in particular exhibiting what they presuppose and hide. Another approach is that of the history of concepts or *Begriffsgeschichte*[5] where etymological inquiry is abandoned in favour of the study of meaning and the 'linguistic turn' in order to investigate both change and continuity in the use of specific concepts through a conceptual history.

My method is different. Developing an abstract view of the whole conceptual space of international ethics allows for the identification of boundaries, similarities, and differences of a specific concept with other concepts of a proximate nature. Different kinds of war and peace, and diversity of justice and the 'good' are put into perspective within this general framework. Peace as an absence of war, a 'negative war', a 'non-war', may proceed from an imposed peace, with time needing to flow for generations before might becomes right. Alternatively, peace may stem from indifference or simply geographical distance. A better situation from a moral viewpoint is represented by the concept of stable peace. There, no party considers the possibility of threatening force; war remains only as a logical possibility, since no one envisages the recourse to armed violence.

On the other hand, the concept of Just Peace—while requiring the perception of justice by those affected—is superseded by 'positive peace' that one finds within common values and norms; there, exploitation and 'structural violence' tend to disappear. Finally, I generalize the feminist concept of 'care'[6] at the level of a 'global care' ethic which—because of its deep humane character—supersedes positive peace.

---

[5] Cf. Melvin Richter, *The History of Political and Social Concepts: A Critical Introduction* (Oxford: Oxford University Press, 1995).

[6] See Carol Gilligan, *In a Different Voice: Psychological Theory and Women's Development*, 2nd edn. (Cambridge, MA: Harvard University Press, 1993) whose ideas are extensively discussed and developed by Susan J. Hekman, *Moral Voices, Moral Selves* (University Park, PA: The Pennsylvania University Press, 1995); see also Joan C. Tronto, *Moral Boundaries: A Political Argument for an Ethic of Care* (New York and London: Routledge, 1993); Sara Ruddick, *Maternal Thinking: Toward a Politics of Peace*, 2nd edn. (Boston, MA: Beacon Press, 1995); and Nel Noddings, *Caring: A Feminine Approach to Ethics & Moral Education*, 2nd edn. (Berkeley, CA: University of California Press, 2003).

Table 5.1. An International Ethical Scale

1. Total eradication of humankind
2. Genocide
3. War
4. Non-war
5. Just War
6. Stable peace
7. Just Peace
8. Positive peace
9. Global Care
10. Agape-paradise

All these concepts lie between two extremes. First, an all-encompassing nuclear holocaust completely wiping out humanity. Second, paradise where not only all material wants are satisfied, but where agape—perfect and complete love—reigns, all humans loving each other as if they were saints. Table 5.1 presents the ten categories of the international ethical scale.

The argument is organized as follows: in the next section, the first elements of method are presented. The extreme points of the international ethical scale are then discussed in section three—total destruction of humankind—and in section four—agape-paradise and the resulting vanishing of humankind. In section five, the method is further developed along a scale constituted by the nexus of two separate—and at times contradictory—ethical dimensions, deontological and consequentialist. The eight intermediate steps of the scale—genocide, war, non-war, Just War, stable peace, Just Peace, positive peace, and global care—are then developed and presented in sections six to thirteen, followed by a conclusion.

2. METHOD: CONSTRUCTING AN INTERNATIONAL ETHICAL SCALE—PART 1

My goal: the development of a general scheme to order social action according to universal criteria that, while culturally and historically based,[7] are at the most general level possible. The purpose is not to rank countries, regimes, or groups according to an appreciation of their virtues and 'character' in an

---

[7] Alas, this constraint cannot be fully escaped however hard one tries. Walzer puts it this way: 'A moral equivalent of Esperanto is probably impossible.... There is no neutral (unexpressive) moral language.' Walzer, *Thick and Thin*, 9.

Aristotelician manner, but to evaluate specific acts of goodness and badness in international relations in a comparative normative perspective.

My method: first defining two extremes—of badness and goodness—and two dimensions—a 'quantitative' and a 'qualitative' one; and second, ordering various types of human group action towards other groups. Let me now discuss these various steps in turn, starting with the extremes or end points of the ethical scale, then justifying the moral dimensions, and ending with a presentation of the eight different midpoints on this ten-point scale.

My argument in a nutshell: total war at one extreme and Just Peace at the other cannot constitute the end points of an international moral scale. As Levi reminds us, it is always possible to conceive—and sometimes live through—a greater happiness or a worse hell than previously imagined. Actually, pushing thinking into its logical limits leads us to one conceivable extreme, a nuclear-like holocaust totally eradicating humankind, and to a second conceivable extreme in the form of paradise, pure happiness for all humanity. In a deep sense, the extremes coincide with the disappearance of the human species: should it disappear from the face of the world, then human morality disappears with it. At the other end, if all humans live (forever) in paradise, then they cease being human—and human morality has no place in such a world. Thus morality only exists *between* these two end points. At the two extremes, it ceases being *logically* possible.

While the end points of the scale will hopefully not be too contested, the classification of the intermediary categories will necessarily give rise to multiple critiques. The problem of classifying complex phenomena such as war and peace lies in the proliferation of their defining criteria. These definitions come from different—and often antagonistic—intellectual, cultural, onto-logical, normative, and epistemological traditions. This is only to mention some of the dimensions along which one may envision and classify them. This prevents one from building a true ordinal scale, linking things in a series which has properties which are exhaustive, mutually exclusive, and a unique order of its elements. Nevertheless, it still is useful because of the conceptualization that comes from this exercise. Understanding requires comparison. Both difference and similarity are needed for comprehension.

Let us start from war, the common extreme of international badness. Before the last century witnessed two 'world wars', Thomas Hobbes and Karl von Clausewitz had already imagined what forms a total war could take. When thinking about the state of nature and its relationship to war, Hobbes did not conceptualize the state of war as one with constant bloodshed as a result of constant aggression and everyone trying to kill everyone else. Sadly, the natural worry of mankind stems from an original condition of relative equality among all human beings, which in turn leads to their vulnerability. As a consequence, as Hobbes writes:

For Warre, consisteth not in Battell onely, or the act of fighting; but in a tract of time, wherein the Will to contend by Battell is sufficiently known. . . . So the nature of War, consisteth not in actuall fighting; but in the known disposition thereto, during all the time there is no assurance to the contrary. All other time is PEACE.[8]

Similarly, Clausewitz's 'war as mere continuation of policy by other means', as 'an act of violence intended to compel our opponent to fulfill our will'[9] was, for him, an 'absolute' war. War's objective is to crush the opponent's resistance. Therefore, a military escalation is usually necessary. Since there is no limit to it, the escalation will proceed on both sides till the military forces of one of the parties are crushed and, consequently, the loser will submit to the demands of the victorious party.

Neither Hobbes nor Clausewitz envisaged a total war in the modern twentieth century sense, that is, involving the whole civilian population. It is Erich Ludendorff who put forth this concept immediately after 1918.[10] For the defeated German general, war is total in the sense that it is not armies, but nations that wage war. This requires the complete mobilization of the whole society and economy. Victory means crushing the enemy nation by targeting its civil society and economy.

However, it is when considering a guerrilla war, that Clausewitz—who is the first important thinker to contemplate this kind of unconventional war—anticipates Ludendorff and the twentieth century. In an important sense, guerrilla war is a total war as it requires the mobilization of a whole group or nation against its enemies and thus involves a whole people. It is probably as old as humankind; there was 'war before civilization'.[11] As Mao Zedong—one of Clausewitz's admiring students—put it in one of his famous aphorisms, combatants are 'guerilla fishes in a population sea'. Pushed to the extreme, as in a radical terrorist conception, true non-combatants do not exist, and the *jus in bello* (law of fighting in war) is reduced to the proportionality requirement. In such a view, war not only affects, but truly penetrates the whole of society: all are combatants, no true civilians are left to be protected as such.

---

[8] Thomas Hobbes, *Leviathan*, ed. Richard E. Flathman and David Johnston (New York: Norton, 1997), 70 (capitalization in the original).

[9] Carl von Clausewitz, *On War* ([1832] Harmondsworth: Penguin, 1968), 119; see also Raymond Aron, *Penser la guerre, Clausewitz*, 2 vols. (Paris: Gallimard, 1976), 113, 325.

[10] See Hans Speier, 'Ludendorff: The German Concept of Total War', in Edward Mead Earle (ed.), *Makers of Modern Strategy: Military Thought from Machiavelli to Hitler* (Princeton, NJ: Princeton University Press, 1943), 306–21.

[11] Lawrence H. Keeley, *War Before Civilization* (Oxford: Oxford University Press, 1996).

Thus, while war represents normality for Hobbes, it typically consists only of the possibility of battle or bloodshed. For Clausewitz, a guerilla war extends the circle of those affected and it is left to Ludendorff, Mao Zedong, and their terrorist followers to consider a total war that implicates the whole population. But is that the ultimate 'bad' from an international ethical viewpoint? Certainly not after a twentieth century marked by several genocides. Is then Levi's Auschwitz the absolute horror where man is wolf for man? No, because Levi shows that even there, at the centre of the Holocaust, space for hope, help, and humanity remained.[12] Thinking about gradations of horror leads one to imagine greater abominations than living through the battle of Verdun or walking from the train to the gas chamber. More extreme alternatives need to be considered from a theoretical perspective.

3. ABSOLUTE HELL: TOTAL DESTRUCTION OF HUMANKIND

In his 1962 book, *Thinking about the Unthinkable*, Hermann Kahn tried to make his American contemporaries sensitive to the implications of the possession of nuclear weapons and the nuclear strategies being then contemplated in the Pentagon. His being portrayed as a Dr. Strangelove as a consequence made him bitter and resentful.[13] Actually, we now know that a major nuclear war between the USA and the Soviet Union would have had consequences that were not fully imagined at the time of Kahn's writing, the same year of the extremely dangerous Cuban Missile Crisis. Only thirty years later did the West learn that the USSR considered using tactical nuclear weapons in Cuba in case of a US invasion. As Fidel Castro acknowledged in 1992, he had in fact urged Khrushchev to respond by a nuclear attack on the USA in that event:

Would I have been ready to use nuclear weapons? Yes, I would have agreed to the use of nuclear weapons. Because, in any case, we took it for granted that it would become a nuclear war anyway, and that we were going to disappear.... I wish we had had the tactical nuclear weapons. It would have been wonderful. We wouldn't have rushed to use them, you can be sure of that. The closer to Cuba the decision of using a weapon effective against a landing, the better. Of course, after we had used ours, they would

---

[12] The Austrian psychologist Viktor Frankl makes similar points based on his own experience in German concentration camps. See Viktor E. Frankl, ... *trotzdem Ja zum Leben sagen. Ein Psychologe erlebt das Konzentrationslager* (München: Deutscher Taschenbuch Verlag, 1982).

[13] See Hermann Kahn, *Thinking about the Unthinkable* (New York: Avon Books, 1962), particularly the afterword, 267–90.

have replied with, say, 400 tactical weapons—we don't know how many would have been fired at us. In any case, we were resigned to our fate.[14]

At the same time that Kahn was thinking the unthinkable, Castro was contemplating it concretely. In some sense he wanted to be part of it. Nietzsche would have applauded: no boring peace here![15] The nuclear war Castro envisaged in 1962 would clearly have led to the disappearance of the Cuban people. In fact, as was only learnt in 1992, it could have been much worse since the Soviets did have tactical nuclear weapons already stationed on Cuban territory before the crisis erupted. And, Kennedy did *not* know of this.[16] Even in the comparatively more benign situation as he perceived it at the time, Kennedy estimated the possibility of a nuclear war as 'between 1 out of 3 and even'.[17] And it is only in Gorbachev's times that the full consequences of a large-scale nuclear war were envisaged: a nuclear winter. Thus, the fate of humankind—and not only of one's country—entered the consciousness of decision-makers in the 1980s only.

These considerations remind us that a nuclear doomsday still remains a distinct possibility in our epoch. Would that be the worst that could happen to humankind, from an ethical point of view? In a deep sense, yes. Let us consider the argument proposed by Derek Parfit:

I believe that if we destroy mankind, as we now could, this outcome would be *much* worse than most people think. Compare three outcomes:

(1) Peace.
(2) A nuclear war that kills 99% of the world's existing population.
(3) A nuclear war that kills 100%.

(2) would be worse than (1), and (3) would be worse than (2). Which is the greater of these two differences? Most people believe that the greater difference is between (1) and (2). I believe that the difference between (2) and (3) is *very much* greater.
...Civilization began only a few thousand years ago. If we do not destroy mankind, these few thousand years may be only a tiny fraction of the whole of civilized human history.[18]

---

[14] Fidel Castro responding to Robert McNamara during the Havana conference on the Cuban Missile Crisis, 9–12 January 1992; cf. James J. Blight, Bruce J. Allyn, and David A. Welch, *Cuba on the Brink: Castro, the Missile Crisis, and the Soviet Collapse* (New York: Pantheon Books, 1993), 252–3.

[15] Cf. Francis Fukuyama, *The End of History and the Last Man* (London: Penguin Books, 1992), 330 ff.

[16] Neither did Castro, but at the beginning of the Cuban missile crisis only.

[17] Theodore Sorensen, *Kennedy* (New York: Harper & Row, 1965), 705.

[18] Derek Parfit, *Reasons and Persons* (Oxford: Oxford University Press, 1984), 453–4 (italics in original).

Parfit argues that the classical utilitarians, of whom he is one, would accept his argument because of the vast reduction of the possible sum of happiness. He sees another group that would agree as constituted of all those who emphasize 'the Sciences, the Arts, and moral progress, or the continued advance of mankind towards a wholly just world-wide community'.[19]

His scenario only considers the consequences of a generalized nuclear war, without including the horrors that led to the disappearance of mankind down to its last members, a truly apocalyptic scenario along the lines of the nuclear winter preceding it. Such a doomsday would entail atrocious suffering during this period of human extinction.[20] Unfortunately, this extreme does not appear completely unrealizable: with Prometheus unbound, one can now envision the material possibility of the total destruction of humankind. And with the physical disappearance of humankind, we would have its total extinction. While some species would no doubt survive a nuclear holocaust, the human species as such would most likely be gone forever, and this even considering possible evolutionary mutations in the aftermath.

In sum, I propose the eradication and therefore the disappearance of humankind as the ultimate badness in moral terms.[21] We now turn to the opposite extreme point of the international ethical scale, the ultimate in terms of goodness.

4. THE BEST: AGAPE-PARADISE

Is a Kantian perpetual peace[22] the other moral extreme? Is it a blissful and Just Peace among humankind? While this state of affairs appears at first glance as a perfect one from an international ethical standpoint, it is not: the opposite extreme to the eradication of humankind lies in paradise. Paradise is for two kinds of inhabitants; dead humans and non-humans—gods, angels, and

---

[19] Ibid., 454.

[20] Presumably, all this would be the result of a miscalculation or of an escalatory accident. We may however consider humankind voluntarily proceeding to a complete decimation by way of a universal suicide. We may imagine this decision taken in due consideration of all matters, with the utmost rationality, and following all necessary procedures—such as requiring a universal assent from all living moral agents. But such a suicide would be profoundly selfish and amoral with respect to the possible happiness of future generations, and this not only from a utilitarian perspective.

[21] This is even more extreme than the total disappearance of justice and morality. As Kant wrote: 'If justice perishes, then it is no longer worthwhile for men to live upon the earth.' (Quotation taken from Rawls, *The Law of Peoples*, 128, fn. 7.)

[22] Immanuel Kant, 'Perpetual Peace: A Philosophical Sketch', ed. Hans Reiss, *Kant: Political Writings* (Cambridge: Cambridge University Press, 1991).

other saints. Actually, paradise is an ideal for those who do *not* obey God's wishes—such as Adam and Eve—and who became fully human only after being expelled from it. And they could return only at the price of their death. Whether paradise, this end point of morality in its various conceptions, was reached in a past Golden Age, or is programmed for the end of History—as in Judaism or in Christianity—is immaterial to its nature.

Although Judeo-Christian in inspiration, paradise is posited as a given, a 'primitive'—or ideal—concept. This allows one to escape the necessity of giving it a specific definition and therefore make it vulnerable to criticism coming from different philosophical or theological perspectives. Paradise is an imaginary world without real humans. In Aztec mythology, it is a world of gods. In Eastern philosophies, it comes as rebirth, as an afterlife. There, the experience of a *nirvana* is that of a total peace of mind; all desires are extinguished, thus providing for the highest possible happiness. These various paradisiacal-like situations come about because of the demise of human agents. This has a profound implication: without human presence, no ethical question arises. Should every human thought and act be perfectly moral, nothing would then stay ethical any more. In other words: should perfect morality as a distinguishing feature of the world be always present, then it would simply disappear. Paradise certainly is a place for extraordinary human beings—but they leave the ranks of humankind only once. Even icons such as Mahatma Gandhi, Mother Teresa, or Nelson Mandela remain human beings—at least as long as they are alive.

Thus, the two moral extremes are similar because of their relationship to human agency. No ethics can find a place in situations when there are simply no humans as with the disappearance of humankind or as in paradise. Levi was correct in asserting that both perfect happiness and perfect unhappiness are unattainable on this Earth.

It is important to note here that utopias as developed in the history of thought, although describing social harmony, are still not paradisiacal. Even in Thomas Moore's classic 1516 description of *Utopia*—pointedly, a place of happiness which exists nowhere—crimes nevertheless occur between individuals and wars do not disappear either; Just Wars are allowed in cases of self-defence or to help extend the application of utopia in the colonies. Likewise, Karl Marx's communist ideal for mankind does not represent a perfect society, as it is still filled by men who eventually become—in his conception—fully human and are therefore able to realize their full potential.[23]

Besides paradise posited as being a 'human-free' state is an alternative way of approaching the ultimate in terms of 'goodness' on a moral scale that can

---

[23] Jon Elster, *Making Sense of Marx* (Cambridge: Cambridge University Press, 1985), 82–5.

be envisaged. It is considering situations where love reigns. In the case of pure love, there is no need for morality.[24] The Greeks considered three basic types of love: eros, philia, and agape. Eros, being the love of another person for the pleasure of self is not the kind of love that necessarily leads to the well-being of others. Nor is philia entirely satisfactory in our context, as philia describes the relationship between two friends who enjoy each other's company and see some of their needs satisfied by the other on a regular basis. The ultimate good is agape; the purest type of love, love of the other for the other's sake. A good illustration of agape—though not a perfect one[25]—is the pure love of a mother for her baby. In cases of a true love, of a love for the benefit of the loved one, ethical considerations will tend to evaporate. The perfect mother does not need to consider moral questions; she loves, that is all. For the pure or extreme case of love, we need to turn to the love of a saint for others, the love of a prophet such as Jesus Christ, of a Saint Paul, of God.

The moral extreme in terms of the good lies in felicity. It means the greatest humanity, the most considerate kind of attitude of people with respect to other people, animals, and even things. There, the largest gentleness in its most magnificent kind can be envisioned. In other words, one may extend morality to animal rights for instance, or go further and consider not only the rights of future generations of humans as well as of other species, but see all of this within a holistic ecological ethic. My thesis is that this extreme attitude and action exists also in situations of pure love. That is to say that it is present when there is love simply for the other person's sake or a thoughtful and absolutely selfless consideration of her well-being.[26] Whoever this other person is does not matter. As the Apostle Matthew wrote: 'Love your enemies, bless them that curse you, do good to them that hate you, and pray for them which despitefully use you, and persecute you.'[27] Should all individuals, groups, or nation-states truly love one another and try to do their best for the other—without forgetting their own good, since they are not only moral agents but also moral objects—then morality, being all-present,

---

[24] John, 1st epistle, IV, 8 & 16, *King James Bible.*

[25] The problem of choice is not completely absent, since the lover needs to consider her or his own needs in order to make the other happy, too. In other words, there is a line between love and self-sacrifice. Feminist theorists recognize this issue; see Gilligan, *In a Different Voice*, 149 and Noddings, *Caring: A Feminine Approach*, 105.

[26] Cf. Comte-Sponville's interpretation of agape: André Comte-Sponville, *Petit traité des grandes vertus* (Paris: Presses universitaires de France, 1995), 291–385. I do not follow Joseph Fletcher's *Situation Ethics* ([1966] Westminster: John Knox Press, 1997) which claimed that love was the only absolute rule of morality and that one should attempt to do what love would command in each situation (agapeism).

[27] Jesus Christ according to Matthew, V, 44, *King James Bible.*

simply dissolves in that universal love. This ideal agape situation corresponds to a paradise.

5. METHOD: CONSTRUCTING AN INTERNATIONAL ETHICAL SCALE—PART 2

Theoretical extremes or ideal end points are not too difficult to define. Now comes the more difficult task of developing the scaling—that is, the measurement—of the different ethical categories that lie in between them, the space for true humanity, good as well as bad. So let us continue on our methodological journey.

How does one measure different ethical categories with respect to each other? Let us start from the most basic scale of measurement, the nominal one. There, one simply distinguishes among objects, phenomena, or whatever, allowing each to be put—according to *one* of its characteristics—into one and only one category. Since we normally wish to be able to classify everything that could come about, two requirements are necessary. First, everything needs to find a precise place. Second, *all* phenomena under consideration find their place within the given categories. In more technical terms: the categories have to be mutually exclusive, and the set of all categories need be exhaustive.[28]

This first measurement level is clearly insufficient for our purposes since a nominal scale only allows for distinguishing phenomena, but not for their direct comparison. For that, we need to turn to the next level in terms of the complexity of measurement, or the ordinal scale. This adds a third property to a nominal scale: that of an order placing all categories with respect to each other. This allows us to put them in a sequence according to another characteristic applying to all phenomena that are thus compared. Needless to say, this classification is arbitrary. One may also add that the nominal and ordinal scale are *qualitative* ones and do not require quantitative notions as when using numbers.[29] In this general sense, any language is also measurement. It gives us a necessary differentiation among words and concepts, putting them in relationship one towards the other.

---

[28] On different measurement scales, see the standard work of Brian Ellis, *Basic Concepts of Measurement* (Cambridge: Cambridge University Press, 1968), 52–67.

[29] The two other basic measurement scales, the interval and ratio ones, do not concern us here, given their much more demanding requirements going beyond the possibilities of moral evaluation.

How can we classify international morality? A one-dimensional scale—a characteristic monetary value in economics or physical qualities such as weight or length possess—would make moral evaluation much easier. But then, which ethical dimension to choose? Even in the case where it were possible to be one-dimensional, the central question of how to justify the choice of a specific ethical dimension—and therefore conception—remains. Only those who adhere to a certain ethical tradition will be persuaded by its arguments. And no consensus, not even a partial one, exists presently on which tradition is superior to others. Nor which one is to be followed based on some (universal) grounds. Instead of being monistic in starting from a specific choice of a moral theory, an alternative path to a justifying of morality is to start from moral judgements and determine the theory as a consequence. This is a path followed by Rawls, for example. However, the problem of justification remains because of the variety of ethical theories.

I submit a two-fold approach allowing me nevertheless to move forward in developing a general international ethical scale. First, I define *conflict* as a 'primitive' from a theoretical standpoint. This allows one not to define it specifically and thus enter into all kinds of difficulties due precisely to the truly conflicting nature of various conceptions in this area. All that is claimed is that the absence of harmony, that is, conflict, is 'bad' in ethical terms. The greater the conflict—whatever that term specifically means in a certain context—the less desirable the situation from an ethical standpoint. The more conflict between various social groups, the worse it is ethically on my schematic. Conversely, the less conflict, the more parties agree, collaborate, or are even in harmony, the better in moral terms.[30]

Second, I am using two dimensions to classify various situations from an international ethical point of view. One dimension is consequentialist or teleological, the other deontological. The eminence and centrality of the two ethical theories founding these two dimensions speaks for my conception. Indeed, '[m]any philosophers follow Rawls in supposing that two categories,

---

[30] My perspective is open to criticism. In particular, 'war is the father of all and king of all' (Heracleitus) constitutes an alternative view. In a democratic system for example, conflict is brought out in the open and decided upon using democratic institutions. Both Georg Hegel and his follower Karl Marx saw in conflict the necessary ingredient for progress towards a better world. In social psychology, in psychotherapy, in systemic analyses of society, and in other approaches, conflict performs at times a quintessential function in bettering, in the end, the situation at hand. Still other schools of thought consider the inevitable obstacles that are put in people's and group's path as essential for individual or social satisfaction: too easy paths are not satisfactory ones. These alternative ontologies do not put my perspective into question for two reasons. First, the conflict at hand there is usually a modest one; second, the conflict is/will be overcome if not in the short, then at least in the long term.

teleological and deontological, exhaust the possibilities regarding theories of right action.'[31]

Consequentialism—also known as a teleological approach—evaluates a given action by examining its consequences. This is to say that we should do whatever has the best consequences in terms of the good. For utilitarianism, a consequentialist ethic, we need to consider the greatest happiness for the greatest number of people. This approach is central to several paradigms in international relations theory. Political realism is based on a consequentialist approach to foreign policy in that it is driven by the concept of national interest[32] and, implicitly, the necessity for those who make decisions to consider the interests of the group or state they represent—and not their private interests. Liberalism and especially neo-liberalism, also tend to be consequentialist in their emphasis on interest-based explanations and on mutual advantage. Marxism shares some of the philosophical roots of liberalism and is also consequentialist and utilitarian in its outlook as illustrated in modern neo-Marxist developments such as World-System theory.

The deontological approach concentrates on the correct action, the one following given moral rules, or rules one rationally finds within self. For Immanuel Kant, the greatest thinker espousing this approach, each act should obey the *categorical imperative*: one is acting in such a way as to wish that each act were the exemplification of a universal law. This rational doctrine leads to rights or duties based morality. In particular, a person is always an end and can never be a simple means to an end. Human dignity is at the forefront of morals. This duty/rule-based ethic has influenced liberal idealism after the First World War and its liberal developments after the Second World War. The concept of Just War is an exemplification of such a duty-based international ethic.[33]

Why two dimensions only and not three—or four, or five etc.? Because of Occam's razor: greater complexity may be satisfying for a finer representation of reality, but at the same time it makes the whole classifying experience—and therefore knowledge—more unwieldy, and thus less helpful. An additional argument stems from the fact that other ethical theories have some disadvantages. For instance, in the doctrine of virtues what is morally evaluated is

---

[31] Nancy (Ann) Davis, 'Contemporary deontology', in Peter Singer (ed.), *A Companion to Ethics* (Oxford: Blackwell, 1993), 206.

[32] Cf. Hans J. Morgenthau, *Politics Among Nations: The Struggle for Power and Peace*, 5th rev. edn. ([1948] New York: Knopf, 1978); on the centrality of Morgenthau's work in international ethics, see Robert W. McElroy, *Morality and American Foreign Policy: The Role of Ethics in International Affairs* (Princeton, NJ: Princeton University Press, 1992), 19–27.

[33] Cf. Michael Walzer, *Just and Unjust Wars: A Moral Argument with Historical Illustrations*, 3rd edn. ([1977], New York: Basic Books, 2000). However, some of the elements of the Just War doctrine, such as proportionality, are in the line of consequentialism.

not a specific action, but the moral agent as such. This Aristotelian approach considers what kind of person the agent is, her attitude and general orientation to life, her character. In international relations theory, the thesis that democracies do not wage wars against each other constitutes one example. Since our goal is to develop an international ethical scale to evaluate and compare specific events and deeds, and not to judge international actors per se, Aristotle's virtue ethics and its modern developments[34] are not useful.

With two dimensions, both of which are envisioned as independent of each other, there necessarily appear cases in which one has to compare two acts or situations, for instance one which is 'high' on one dimension and 'low' on the other, while the reverse is true for the second deed. How does one then weigh the first against the second? Is abominably torturing one hundred people for a month worse than keeping one million people under subjugation for years? What about the terrorist who is someone else's freedom fighter? There is no general solution to these dilemmas which run directly against the requirement of good measurement theory since we need categories that are all-inclusive (not too difficult), while mutually exclusive (difficult).

Figure 5.1 represents the international ethical scale. First, the two measuring dimensions are discussed, then the extremes of each are presented, followed by the overall representation in terms of a square,[35] and we end with a discussion of the positioning of eight intermediate international ethical concepts.

The vertical scale is modelled as uni-dimensional, from 'none' to 'many.' Thus the consequentialist and utilitarian dimension—which is arbitrarily represented on the vertical axis—starts from the origin or 'zero' point of no happiness whatsoever for anybody, since no human beings exist at that point. The further one goes away from the origin, the better the situation, that is, the happier people are.[36] Similarly, the deontological dimension on the horizontal starts from no rules obeyed or duties followed at all at the origin, that is, from the morally most reprehensible situation. The further one moves away from the origin—on the horizontal axis—the more respectful of deontological considerations the considered act is. Thus for both dimensions, the zero point of the origin represents the total absence of any moral considerations.

---

[34] Cf. in particular Alasdair MacIntyre, *After Virtue: A Study in Moral Theory*, 2nd edn., (Notre Dame, IN: University of Notre Dame Press, 1984).

[35] The orthogonal depiction of the two axes defines and symbolizes their independence with respect to each other. A square is used on purpose in order to symbolize that none of the dimensions is privileged over the other.

[36] Again, both dimensions are ordinal ones and should be interpreted as such, that is, there is no implicit continuity or interval or ratio scale here.

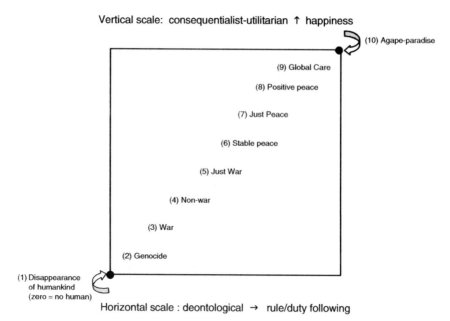

Figure 5.1. An international ethical scale

Conversely, the corner on the upper right-hand side of the graph entitled 'agape-paradise' represents the other extreme—perfect morals followed by all towards all, that is, the dissolution of morality since only gods are capable of reaching this extreme. From the perspective of the vertical axis, agape means perfect happiness for all. Looking at it along the horizontal axis, paradise implies love for all. Both cases imply the disappearance of morality through the disappearance of humankind.

In other words, neither the bottom left nor the upper right corners have any empirical meaning and will never be observed. In fact, the same observation pertains to the other two extreme points of the square. In the upper left-hand corner, all is well in the intentions of everyone and all are happy—while not having any specific moral rules to follow. Likewise, the situation represented by the lower right-hand side corner portrays a situation where everybody perfectly follows her or his duties, but without any consideration whatsoever being accorded to the happiness of anyone; in fact, nobody is happy in such a dry world—but all simply follow the required rules. We can thus observe than none of the four corners describe any real human situation and therefore make any empirical sense. Extending this argument, we further observe that the same is true for all the sides of the square, for all intermediate situations between any of those four ideal points. From a descriptive-empirical point of view, this means that it is *only inside* the square that we have relevant combinations of international situations applying to a world of human beings.

The next sections will be devoted to the presentation of the contents of the ethical square. The discussion will show the necessary fuzziness of the positioning of eight remaining categories with respect to each other. As argued earlier, this stems directly from the fact that two separate dimensions are used to categorize these concepts. The continuum from genocide to care going from the lower left to the upper right in Figure 5.1, while not arbitrary, represents the pure cases of each. In fact, specific historical or hypothetical international acts of one category could well score better than the ideal type representation of other measurement levels. For example, a concrete instance of a brief and relatively bloodless Just War might at times be evaluated as morally better than a stable—but unjust—peace. Having already presented categories one and ten, we can now turn to the second category, genocide.

6. NEXT TO WORST: GENOCIDE

Genocide is a voluntary programme typically supported by a state and intended to eradicate a people or part of a population because of one or several of their individual characteristics as defined collectively—for example, as members of a 'race', a religion, a nation. This is done with no consideration about their acts or intentions, their age, their gender or other such elements, neither at the individual nor at the collective level. It is a war in all senses of the term, but for the fact that the victims usually do not defend themselves. As it often happens within a society and not between societies or nation-states, it is not necessarily an international deed in the narrow sense. From Nazi Germany to the killing fields of Cambodia, from Armenia to Rwanda and Bosnia, the twentieth century has provided us with too many examples of genocide. It is not a modern phenomenon though, if one recalls Gengis Khan, the Crusades, slavery, and quite a few of the chapters of colonization. Compared to the total eradication of humankind, genocide is, in a way, a partial destruction of humankind by extinguishing one of its peoples, and therefore a significant deal of its culture.[37]

---

[37] The UN Genocide Convention of 1948 defines it as any of the following acts committed with intent to destroy, in whole or in part, a national, ethnical, racial or religious group, as such: (*a*) Killing members of the group; (*b*) Causing serious bodily or mental harm to members of the

Whatever the horrors of repeated attempts of holocaust-like dark chapters in human history, a sense of the numerical perspective allows us to say that these are rather the exception than the rule, which explains their prominence in historical writing. The probability of dying in such a situation is very roughly of the same magnitude as losing one's life in one of the more 'normal' forms of war. The central discriminating criterion between the first category, the total destruction of mankind, and an instance of holocaust is precisely that: the first is a unique event, the second constitutes a class. From a consequentialist perspective, one could condone a small genocide in order to prevent a much larger war inducing much more bloodshed. Therefore, some fuzziness in the coding of these two categories remains but I submit that from a deontological perspective, genocide is significantly worse than a typical war.

What then distinguishes the Armenian genocide, the Holocaust, and the Rwanda genocide from a regular war? Genocide is characterized by its completeness in terms of its destructive aims, its organization of the killing for the sake of erasing a people. War, however extreme, bloody, and perverse, is different. Whereas in war, the opponent is to be crushed in order to reach one's war aims, genocide means that the extermination of the opponent is the primary goal of the conflict. Certainly, Hitler and his executioners clearly made that distinction while at the very same time fighting different kinds of wars around the globe. Most interestingly, and showing the real 'badness' of genocide, is the fact that even the Nazis did not propagandize their genocide publicly[38] and did their utmost to hide it.

7. WAR

Why is war bad in moral terms? Precisely because it takes lives and the right to live is a crucial requirement for one's individuality and the enjoyment of life. Thus, from a deontological perspective, each life needs to be preserved. From a utilitarian one, it may depend on consequences, but as the purpose of utilitarianism is the maximization of the happiness of the largest number, the taking of lives in war is morally bad. Walzer reminds us in *Just and Unjust Wars* that '[w]ar is hell whenever men are forced to fight, when-

---

group; (c) Deliberately inflicting on the group conditions of life calculated to bring about its physical destruction in whole or in part; (d) Imposing measures intended to prevent births within the group; (e) Forcibly transferring children of the group to another group.

[38] See excerpts from a speech by Himmler later, in the section on care.

ever the limit of consent is breached. That means, of course, that it is hell most of the time.'[39]

Paradoxically though, war is quite infrequent. Looking from the perspective of single states in the international system—and not forgetting civil wars—war appears as an exception in the intercourse between and within nations. For example, one of the fathers of the systematic study of wars, Lewis Fry Richardson, has calculated that the overwhelming proportion of possible war years of the nations since 1815 have been peaceful ones. Almost all human beings die of other reasons than war. As Richardson put it, '[t]hose who enjoy wars can excuse their taste by saying that wars are after all much less deadly than disease'.[40] On the other hand, there is always conflict somewhere; a systematic study has shown that between 1740 and 1974, war was always present somewhere and thus universal peace has not existed.[41]

The important impact of war on human lives is documented through the different names given to each in order to distinguish it from all the others: the Peloponnesian War, the Crimean one, the Napoleonic Wars, the Vietnam War, the (American or Spanish) Civil War, the 'Football War', the Six Day War, the Seven Years' War, the Thirty Years' War, the Boer War, etc. The list of bloody histories and no less bitter memories is unending and punctuates our rewriting of the past. What then about the absence of war which is a peace of sorts, and the fourth point on the scale?

8. NON-WAR AS PEACE

It is impossible to discuss peace without enquiring into the nature of war. It is as if they were the two sides of the same coin, defining each other by their respective presence. Are they antinomies? To some extent: the presence of peace implies no war, but war may be lurking behind an apparent peace. Spring of 1914 was peaceful though war was on many peoples' minds, from the Kaiser to people on the boulevards of Paris. For the time being, peace was

---

[39] Walzer, *Just and Unjust Wars*, 28.

[40] Lewis Fry Richardson, *Statistics of Deadly Quarrels* (Pittsburgh, PA: Boxwood Press, 1960), 163.

[41] Gaston Bouthoul and René Carrère, *Le défi de la guerre (1740–1974), deux siècles de guerre et de révolutions* (Paris: Presses Universitaires de France, 1976), 57. The following analysts reach similar conclusions based on their data sets: Quincy Wright, *A Study of War*, abridged edn. ([1942] Chicago: The University of Chicago Press, 1964); Melvin Small and J. David Singer, *Resort to Arms: International and Civil Wars, 1816–1980* (Beverly Hills, CA: Sage, 1982); and Jack S. Levy, *War in the Modern Great Power System, 1495–1975* (Lexington, Kentucky, KY: The University Press of Kentucky, 1983).

a choice, but other choices could be made. Reciprocally, a war reaching a Clausewitzean 'absolute' level may pave the way for a permanent peace through the utter defeat—but not the eradication—of a party to it. The vanquished of the Second World War attest to this observation.

In his *Leviathan*, Hobbes argues that it is the mere possibility to pursue one's objectives with the sword that constitutes the state of war. He is right in the sense that 'negative' war—the absence of war—or a sense of insecurity is prevalent throughout history. On the other hand, peace appears much more frequently, in a certain sense. Over the last two centuries, at the interstate level of analysis and taking the year as the counting unit, there were close to one million pairs of states that could have engaged in a war,[42] for example between Liechtenstein and Switzerland, or Columbia and Thailand. But during that period, only around one hundred wars took place.[43] These considerations actually show more concretely how unlikely it is for a war to happen, and that peace is more prevalent in history. So defining peace from a negative stand-point allows one to fill the concept with a nearly unlimited content. Given that war is morally bad, its absence makes for a morally preferable world, both from a deontological and from a consequentialist perspective.[44] The nature of this peace varies greatly. Starting from a situation of large asymmetry in power relationship and moving to increasing symmetry of power, we can identify a few different types of peace.

First, we will discuss peace through *hegemony*. There is a strong asymmetry in power capabilities not compensated by a reverse asymmetry of interests,[45] leading the weak party but to accept peace—no matter how important its interests. This hegemony can be material as well as psychological, such as in the Marxian concept of alienation. This asymmetrical dependence is central to studies for those of the *dependencia* school. It can be exemplified by Columbia versus the USA, or by Monaco versus France.

Second is the classic peace through a *balance of power*. This is a large subject into which we will not meander here. Suffice to say that *Realpolitik* needs to work, and that several moral problems are particularly acute here, such as the

[42] Bruce Bueno de Mesquita, *Principles of International Politics: People's Power, Preferences, and Perceptions* (Washington, DC: CQ Press, 2000), 198.

[43] Cf. Small and Singer, *Resort to Arms*. Of course, wars may last longer than a year and involve more than two parties.

[44] It is interesting to note in this respect that revolutionaries, terrorists, war-loving imperialists, and other such representatives of humankind always justify the necessity of bloodshed by the promise of a better world—that is, in moral consequentialist terms. In other words, war cannot be better than non-war *on its own*.

[45] The case where one party is strongly motivated but weak in power resources while the other one finds itself in the opposite situation is not clear. Such 'compensating' asymmetries are very common in wars of national liberation, ideological battles, terrorism, and guerilla warfare.

primacy accorded to major powers over the smaller ones, and the necessity of certain amorality required to make it work.[46] Niccolo Machiavelli's teachings retain their pertinence and the moral dilemmas between the ethics of convictions and the ethics of responsibility that Max Weber vividly portrayed in his masterly 1918 conference *Politik als Beruf*[47] are constant in situations where the *raison d'Etat* forces decision-makers to choose among conflicting evils.

Third, there is peace by *mutual deterrence*, that is, peace by fear and terror. This is peace by weakness rather than through strength when compared to the other categories above. Unlike the other cases, this distinctive category stems from modernity, that is, from the existence of nuclear weapons.[48]

However, in all these cases, the essence of peace stemming from an absence of war nonetheless remains, in Hobbes's conception, a state of war, because of the mere possibility of war constantly looming in the background of people's minds. In this vein, one could also speak of 'adversarial peace', 'restricted peace', 'precarious peace', or 'conditional peace'.[49]

9. JUST WAR

The clearest evidence for the stability of our values over time is in the unchanging character of the lies soldiers and statesmen tell. They lie in order to justify themselves, and so they describe for us the lineaments of justice. Wherever we find hypocrisy, we also find moral knowledge.[50]

One could say, prolonging this citation of Walzer, that a Just War is one where there are no lies. For deserving the adjective 'just', a war needs to obey all the rules of *jus ad bellum* as well as *jus in bello*: due consideration must be taken of all the elements pertaining first to the right to go to war and, second, to the legitimate ways of fighting it. Transparency, sincerity, honesty—in other words, a good faith effort—are required to evaluate these choices. All rules are

---

[46] Morgenthau, *Politics Among Nations* and McElroy, *Morality and American Foreign Policy*.

[47] *Politics as a Vocation*, cf. http://www.ne.jp/asahi/ moriyuki/abukuma/weber/lecture/politics_vocation.html (consulted 11 November 2004).

[48] See for example the classic work by Alexander L. George and Richard Smoke, *Deterrence in American Foreign Policy: Theory and Practice* (New York: Columbia University Press, 1974).

[49] Cf. Alexander L. George, 'Foreword', p. xi in Arie M. Kacowicz, Yaacov Bar-Siman-Tov, Ole Elgstöm, and Magnus Jerneck (eds.), *Stable Peace Among Nations* (Lanham, MD: Rowman & Littlefield, 2000).

[50] Walzer, *Just and Unjust Wars*, 19.

necessary ones, and only the respect of every single one of them allows for a 'Just War' qualification.

Thus, violence and bloodshed are not outlawed a priori in international affairs—as they are for the doctrine of pacifism. War can be legitimized providing that a series of stringent conditions are met. All are necessary, and none of them, not even a significant subset of them, is sufficient to allow one to wage a war that would be just. The doctrine has attempted— over the centuries from Aristotle and Plato[51] through Saint Augustine and Hugo Grotius—to balance the requirements of humanity with respect to the consequences of acting to defend oneself. International humanitarian law is based upon it. The Just War doctrine can be said to constitute an attempt at synthesizing duties in war without totally forgetting consequentialism.[52] These rules are the following:

Jus ad bellum

1. Just cause (*iusta causa*): war can be fought when it is the best means to restore peace and is acceptable mainly for reasons such as self-defence following aggression.
2. Legitimate authority (*legitima auctoritas*) and public declaration: war is undertaken and waged exclusively by the leaders of the state or community.
3. Right intention (*recta intentio*): a just cause is not enough, the intention needs to be right.
4. Proportionality (*proportionalitas*): the evil and damage of war must be proportionate to the injustice that led to it.
5. Last resort (*ultima ratio*): all plausible non-war solutions to the conflict have first to be attempted.
6. Probability of success: only a reasonable chance of repairing the damage done allows for war.[53]

Jus in bello

1. Non-combatant immunity.
2. Proportionality: all actions taken must be proportionate to their objective.

---

[51] Actually, one can find examples of lineaments of restrictions to war considerably earlier than in ancient Greece in civilizations such as the Egyptian and Mesopotamian ones; see Yves Schemeil, *La politique dans l'Ancien Orient* (Paris: Presses de Sciences Politiques, 1999), 276, 298.

[52] Anthony J. Coates, *The Ethics of War* (Manchester: Manchester University Press, 1997), 114, 171–3, 259–64.

[53] Cf. Walzer, *Just and Unjust Wars* and Brian Orend, *Michael Walzer on War and Justice* (Cardiff: University of Wales Press, 2000); Anthony J. Coates, *The Ethics of War*; and Gordon Graham, *Ethics and International Relations* (Oxford: Basil Blackwell, 1997).

So while there *can* be Just Wars, these stringent conditions imply that the vast majority of them are unjust. Morally, a Just War is to be preferred to a non-war masquerading as peace, both deontologically as well as from a consequentialist viewpoint. Since there is a reasonable chance of repairing the damage, it is superior to such a peace where unjust war is always lurking. But what can one say of a 'real' peace, and not only of non-warlike situations? Is it to be preferred to a Just War? The answer is yes, as we shall see with the concept of a stable peace.

10. STABLE PEACE

'Stable peace is a situation in which the probability of war is so small that it does not really enter into the calculations of any of the people involved' is how Kenneth Boulding defined this concept.[54] Here peace is a negative war, but not simply a war that *does* not happen, but a war that *will* not happen, at least in people's minds, that is, at the cognitive level. It is something that can not be envisaged, and, therefore, it is not. No place for a Just War here! Stable peace leads to a psychological sense of security. Thus, from a utilitarian viewpoint, stable peace is clearly better than an absence of war. From a deontological perspective, no bloodshed being envisaged by anyone is to be preferred, too. However, the question of justice is not at the forefront, as it is with the preceding concept of Just War and the concept of Just Peace which follows in the next section.

This sense of security pertains in different cases where a situation of stable peace constitutes the positive norm. At least six different cases can be defined, ranging from the logical impossibility of war because there is one actor only, to the imposition of peace from the outside, and through intermediary forms whereby the stability of peace is due to mere indifference or to power limitation.

First, there is peace by *universal empire*. If there is one actor only, then it is not possible to have two parties in conflict and warring. Social conflict disappears in a society of one agent only. This is but a logical possibility without any empirical content—up to now. Internal battles and civil wars may rage within, but the central forces would quickly re-establish order in an authentic universal empire.[55]

[54] Kenneth E. Boulding, *Stable Peace* (Austin, TX: University of Texas Press, 1978), 13.

[55] One may envisage, at the level of the empire, internal disorder. Central police forces would however quickly re-establish order. This could mean a situation such as the one of a 'multiple self' with conflict among the various selves of a being, but that conflict would not take a bloody

Second, is a *Carthaginian Peace*: the disappearance of a party—following a genocide for example—that can wage war ironically creates the conditions for stable peace between those who were in conflict up to then. Winning the third Punic War (149–146 BC), the Romans pursued an imperialistic course, destroyed the city, and killed its inhabitants or chained them into slavery.[56] In fact, it was a stable peace precisely because of the utter destruction—in the collective sense—of one of the parties. Although similar to the universal empire, Carthaginian peace is logically distinct, since war remains a possibility between the remaining party and other actors.

Third, would be a state of *indifference*: parties may simply have few interests or identity-forming elements potentially involving them so that there is little room for conflict, and even less for the contemplation of war. The origins of such indifference may stem from geographical—and sometimes socio-logical—distance. For example, the relationship between Poland and Switz-erland would fit this category, as the one between Afghanistan and Nepal.

Fourth, is the *limitation of power projection*, and it constitutes a logically distinct case. The important if not absolute limitation in the projection of power at a distance—that is, a loss of strength gradient—no doubt explains why Nicaragua, Rumania, Burundi, and Malaysia do not go to war against each other. We simply cannot imagine them as being able to do so, for all practical purposes. And it is not only small countries that are presently in this situation, as the contemporary case of China versus Brazil illustrates. Some-times, with air forces in particular, a major power projects its strength far abroad. Usually, though, a mutual lack of these type of power capabilities is correlated with a relative indifference in terms of the interests at hand. The case of the 1982 Falklands/Malvinas war provides for a good counterexample of this category.

Fifth, is the concept of *stable peace* as it has been developed by Arie Kacowicz and Yaacov Bar-Siman-Tov, not as a state of affairs, but as a process between nations that have the capacity to go to war against each other, but which forfeit this possibility.[57] In other words, it is a voluntary limitation of power projection. Once a conflict is resolved, stabilization of peace hinges on

---

turn and would be handled along the various levels of the selves. On the other hand, the mere possibility of this 'multiple social self' could be disputed by those who argue that it is impossible to have a (unique) self without an 'other' which is seen as an absolute necessity for the constitution of the 'self'.

[56] Morgenthau, *Politics Among Nations*, 58–9, 239–40.

[57] See the conceptual framework developed by Kacowicz and Bar-Siman-Tov in Kacowicz *et al.*, *Stable Peace among Nations*, 11–35. They base their framework on analyses of various historical experiences such as the Scandinavian one, Egypt–Israel since 1979, German–Polish relations, the Baltic region, and ASEAN—for those historical examples see Kacowicz *et al.*, *Stable Peace among Nations*.

four cognitive conditions: (*a*) stable political regimes;[58] (*b*) mutual satisfaction with the terms of the peace agreement; (*c*) predictability of behaviour and problem-solving mechanisms; and finally (*d*) open communications channels with initial trust and respect between the leaders.[59] Their approach encompasses classical process-oriented approaches to building confidence and developing a mutually beneficial relationship such as Charles Osgood's 'Graduated and Reciprocated Initiatives in Tension-reduction'.[60] There, states maintain their own security while unilaterally initiating and then inducing reciprocation, all the while demonstrating genuineness. Several of their stable peace factors are akin to Roger Fisher's 'win/win' approach to negotiation which separates specific people from the problem. It focuses on interests, not positions, and generates a variety of possibilities before there is any decision while insisting that the result be based upon some objective standard.[61]

Sixth, is a stable peace as obtained through *imposition*. This is probably among the most frequent kind of stable peace. In this respect, it is ironic to note that the realist principles defining the 'billiard-ball' Westphalian model—non-intervention and territoriality—have in practice been constantly challenged by alternative principles such as the international protection of minorities or human rights, as Stephen Krasner has shown.[62] Actually, stable peace was often obtained by imposition from the outside, typically by major powers. In Europe for example, they imposed their ideology—a religiously tolerant one—after realizing the consequences of the religious wars of the sixteenth and seventeenth centuries. Surprisingly—given the epoch—a choice was made in favour of peace rather than belief, this in a time when nothing seemed more important to people than the salvation of their souls. This amazing fact shows the centrality of peace, even more essential than belief in life after death.[63] The Peace of Augsburg of 1555 set forth the

---

[58] Kacowicz and Bar-Siman-Tov mean something akin to the decent well-ordered peoples in Rawls's terminology. See Rawls, *The Law of Peoples*.

[59] Kacowicz and Bar-Siman-Tov add two favourable, though not necessary, conditions: (*e*) third-party guarantees; and (*f*) spillover effects towards other elites and the population at large with the provision of nonmilitary public goods. For them, if all states involved are democratic, this constitutes a sufficient condition for the consolidation of a stable peace (i.e. the liberal-democratic theory of peace.) They also add normative considerations with the development over time of peace norms according to international standards of peaceful behaviour.

[60] Charles Osgood, *An Alternative to War or Surrender* (Urbana, IL: The University of Illinois Press, 1962).

[61] Roger Fisher and William Ury, *Getting to YES: Negotiating Agreement Without Giving In* (Boston, MA.: Houghton Mifflin, 1981).

[62] Stephen D. Krasner, *Sovereignty: Organized Hypocrisy* (Princeton, NJ: Princeton University Press, 1999).

[63] Aron makes the interesting point that peace was more important than the choice of church for individuals, even though this had implications for the salvation of their souls, something crucial for many at that time. See Raymond Aron, *Paix et guerre entre les nations*, 6th edn. (Paris: Calmann-Lévy, 1968), 393.

post-medieval principle of the prince setting the religion of the people in his territory (*cuius regio, eius religio*), thus allowing for stable peace between Lutheran and Catholic princes.[64] However, dissenters were allowed to emigrate, only public worship could be regulated by the state, and private worship stayed private. In addition, there were some exceptions to the modern principle set in Augsburg, such as the rulers of ecclesiastical states who could not change the religion in their domains. In Westphalia, too, there were exceptions since '[t]erritories were to retain the religious affiliation that they had on January 1, 1624, regardless of the desires of their ruler.'[65] As Krasner writes:

In sum, the Peace of Westphalia, often seen as the beginning or ratification of the modern state system, included extensive provisions for religious toleration that violated the principle of autonomy.... Over time, the principle of toleration that was implied although not explicitly endorsed by the Peace of Westphalia did come to prevail in western Europe.... [I]n Europe religious toleration (and at Vienna even respect for an ethnic minority) was embodied in international agreements that prescribed national law and practices. These accords were usually contractual arrangements among the major powers concluded to end wars. These stipulations, including those found in the Peace of Westphalia, violated the Westphalian model.[66]

The most crucial—and implicit—element for a stable peace conception is security through order. Often, this happens slowly, with the passage of time, as Quincy Wright argues in the conclusion of his monumental *Study of War*: '*The Time Element Must Be Appreciated.*—War might be defined as an attempt to effect political change too rapidly. Social resistance is in proportion to the speed of change.'[67] Extending this line of thought, one could argue that stable peace might be defined as a state of slow political change with little resistance to it. Only the passage of time, the ebb and flow of generations, will in many cases make initial conflicts forgotten and a stable peace possible. But a long duration is not always necessary, and stable peace can come about very rapidly, after a major event. For instance, a traumatic event may dramatically accelerate mutual perceptions and the recomposition of memories, as happened after the Second World War.

But where does justice enter the picture? In fact, stable peace does have a moral worth because of the accepted order that provides everyone with a sense of security. Although its various elements and manifestations are not necessarily just, the very fact that no one is putting this stability in question

---

[64] Krasner, *Sovereignty: Organized Hypocrisy*, 79ff.
[65] Ibid., 79–80.
[66] Ibid., 81–2.
[67] Wright, *A Study of War*, 391 (italics in original).

gives it some legitimacy, and, therefore, some morality. This is what is called in German 'die normative Kraft des Faktischen'—the normative strength of the fact or the reality. As Raymond Aron the realist has reminded us, international law—which is resulting from agreements between states—thus stems from the force that established those states in the first place.[68]

11. JUST PEACE

Just Peace is a stable peace with justice. However, it does not stem from a universal empire or a Carthaginian peace; it does not come from indifference or limitation of power; it is neither what could be called a 'cold' peace of the stable kind as seen earlier, nor is it the result of an outside imposition. Just Peace clearly goes beyond these six kinds of stable peace in the sense that the peace order is seen not only as a 'natural' or normal one, but also as a just one. All parties accept it as regulating their relations in a legitimate way, making all satisfied: this is why it is morally superior to stable peace from a deontological viewpoint. From a consequentialist perspective, it is to be preferred, too, since the feeling of justice is a moral good and contended parties are happier as utilitarians.

Proceeding from a Just War to a Just Peace, one way is to simply extend the *jus ad bellum* and *jus in bello* to a *jus post bellum*. Brian Orend,[69] working in the footsteps of Walzer, proposes the following requirements for this development:

Jus post bellum[70]

1. Just cause for termination: Requires a reasonable vindication of those rights whose violation led to Just War. Most if not all unjust gains from aggression have been eliminated. Cessation of hostilities. Formal renouncement of aggressor. Formal apology from aggressor. Aggressor's submission to reasonable terms of punishment, including compensation, *jus ad bellum* and *jus in bello* war crimes trials, and perhaps rehabilitation.
2. Legitimate authority: Peace terms are publicly proclaimed by the leaders of the state or community of Victim/Vindicator.
3. Right intention: No revenge. *Jus in bello* war crimes trials for the Just War party, too.

---

[68] Aron, *Paix et guerre entre les nations*, 591; he takes that argument from Pierre-Joseph Proudhon.

[69] Orend, *Michael Walzer on War and Justice*, 135–52.

[70] Freely cited and adapted from Orend, ibid., 151.

4. Proportionality: Peace terms are proportional to the end of reasonable rights vindication. The people from the defeated aggressor never forfeit their human rights. No draconian punishments.
5. Discrimination: Punitive measures focused on those most responsible, with proper differentiation between political and military leaders, soldiers, and civilians. No undue and unfair hardship upon civilian population of aggressor.

In Walzer's tradition, a Just War should be followed by a Just Peace. For Rawls, too, '[t]he aim of a Just War waged by a just well-ordered people is a just and lasting peace among peoples, and especially with the people's present enemy.'[71] But this does not imply that a Just Peace needs to be preceded by a Just War. Just Peace can come about for various reasons and may also come after an unjust war. The question for example of whether or not the US Civil War settlement was a just one could be considered in the nineteenth century or even in the beginning of the twentieth century as a pertinent interrogation, at least for some in the South. However, what is sure now is that the citizens of the fifty American States of the twenty-first century consider the peace between them a just one. Time does bring healing, younger generations experience peace as justice, justice as peace. Similarly, the peace between the German states or the one among Swiss cantons originates in provisions of tolerance of the Westphalian Peace treaties.[72] It is this continuous practice that has allowed for stable (and at times just) peace among different social groups within a community.

For some, a Just War is a misnomer if not an oxymoron. Pacifists ask: how can war wrap itself in the noble word of justice, how can spilling blood ever be just? Prima facie, Just Peace should not encounter the same kinds of problems. However, it is vulnerable to some internal difficulties, too: the rightful search for justice may prevent peace. Often, justice is defined a priori, by what constitutes it, such as utility (Bentham, Mill), fairness (Rawls), socialism (Marx), rights (Dworkin), or entitlement (Nozick). The evaluation of a Just Peace outcome will then crucially depend on the specific conception of justice chosen. And we can hardly expect a specific conception pleasing everybody because some may prefer another criterion of justice more

---

[71] Rawls, *The Law of Peoples*, 94.

[72] The formula of an *amicabilis compositio*—that is, the requirement to negotiate—became institutionalized between religions on the basis of a federation, with religious groups partly autonomous from the state and recognized on the basis of parity; see Gerhard Lehmbruch, 'Die korporative Verhandlungsdemokratie in Westmitteleuropa', *Schweizerische Zeitschrift für Politische Wissenschaft*, 2/4 (1996), 19–41.

to their advantage. Therefore, the search for justice may well run against the search for peace.[73]

One solution to this criticism is to consider justice as what parties decree it is, by having found an agreement among them. In their eyes at least, no external justifications are necessary, since they conceive the terms regulating their relationship as being just. This view—which Alexis Keller and I privilege[74]—constitutes an a posteriori approach. It sees the question in terms of a language-oriented process whereby negotiators build a novel shared reality as well as a new common language. Justice then becomes immanent to practice. It does not require any universal ethical justification. It is just, because it is based on four 'conventions' that are negotiated and recognized as common by the parties: *thin recognition, thick recognition, renouncement,* and *rule.* While Just Peace is a desirable state of affairs, it is nevertheless surpassed by positive peace, the eighth category on the international ethical scale.

12. POSITIVE PEACE

Within the 'peace research' tradition, social structures are usually seen as deploying what Johan Galtung has called 'structural violence' because of their unjust social ordering. The equivalent at the international level is imperialism, whether military, political, economic, or cultural.[75] The domination and therefore the exploitation and implicit violence and the resulting alienation need to be uncovered in order to free individuals, groups, and peoples from their chains. Structural violence and oppression should be limited in favour of social justice because even peaceful communities are not free from structural violence. Negative peace is the absence of overt or direct violence, whereas positive peace implies the absence of oppression, structural violence, and social injustice. Therefore, even a Just Peace could be an unjust one from the perspective of the political reformer or the outside moralist. Just Peace may for instance characterize a situation among two imperialist states that are at the same time exploiting their colonies. Positive peace goes beyond this kind of peace which is a just one in an egoistic sense only, because positive peace strives for a more ambitious kind of justice which includes other agents who should also be set free.

[73] See in particular Yossi Beilin's arguments along these lines in this book.

[74] See our concluding chapter in this book.

[75] Cf. Johan Galtung, 'Violence, Peace and Peace Research', *Journal of Peace Research*, 6/3 (1969), 167–91 and Johan Galtung, 'A Structural Theory of Imperialism', *Journal of Peace Research*, 8/3 (1971), 81–117.

Thus, two moral features distinguish a positive peace from a just one. First, Just Peace is a local phenomenon applying only to those directly concerned. Positive peace considers the duties one may have beyond one's 'neighbours': complete strangers should be helped, too. Therefore, positive peace is more utilitarian and, from a consequentialist viewpoint, reaches out to a larger number of people or communities involved. Second, positive peace goes beyond a Just Peace towards a greater justice in redistributive terms. At times, it may even lead to a sense of pity for others whose position is a disadvantaged one with respect to self, with patronizing feelings from the so-called 'top dogs' towards the 'underdogs.'

Rawls's *Law of Peoples* aims at developing an overall positive peace. Continuing in the line of thought of social contract theory starting from Plato through Hobbes and Rousseau, Rawls's international ethics is devised by rational beings for mutual advantage. Political institutions governing the world are constructed by reasonable representatives of the various peoples who agree on rules governing their relations within a 'Society of Peoples'. Whether liberal or non-liberal decent peoples, they all honour a limited list of human rights and 'assist other peoples living under unfavourable conditions that prevent their having a just or decent political and social regime'.[76] This 'realistic utopia' leads to a positive peace between all liberal and decent peoples in a Kantian pacific federation with the important addition of a minimum of distributive justice towards 'burdened' societies.[77]

But positive peace does not apply to interstate or international relations only. One can imagine a world without these entities, as cosmopolitans do. For them, the world is composed of individuals, not of collectivities such as communities, nations, or states.[78] The moral language is the one of universal principles. Values and norms—human rights for instance—are shared among people around the globe. While cosmopolitans do not negate the powerful allegiances to which individuals are bound at different collective levels, they plead for an ethic of globalization where the domain of obligation concerns all human beings within one community only encompassing all humankind, for

---

[76] Rawls, *The Law of Peoples*, 37.

[77] Ibid., 105–20.

[78] Cf. Charles R. Beitz, *Political Theory and International Relations* (Princeton, NJ: Princeton University Press, 1979) and David Held, *Democracy and the Global Order: From the Modern State to Cosmopolitan Governance* (Cambridge: Polity Press, 1995). However, going beyond the nation-state can be criticized and Quincy Wright's point is still well-taken: '*We Must Start from Where We Are*. Neither nations nor international institutions which exist can be ignored, for the fact of their existence gives evidence of loyalties'; cf. Wright, *A Study of War*, 389–90 (italics in original). A prominent cosmopolitan such as Beitz admits to the real challenge to cosmopolitan liberalism posed by John Rawls's constructivist and liberal *Law of Peoples*; see Beitz, 'Rawls's Law of Peoples', *Ethics*, 110 (2000), 669–96.

One World as for example the utilitarian philosopher Peter Singer calls it.[79] And Andrew Linklater, a critical theorist, building upon Jürgen Habermas's work, analyses and defends norms that recognize cultural differences while aiming at reducing material inequalities in order to develop a 'universal dialogic community in which the justice of all modes of exclusion is tested in open dialogue'.[80] In this, he joins communitarians such as Amitai Etzioni[81] who aim for a worldwide community using international institutions developing towards a world government.[82] Walzer, also a communitarian, pleads for a general moral minimalism because '[w]hen identities are multiplied, passions are divided',[83] thus allowing at least for a 'thin' and minimal moral order.

Whatever the criticisms that can be addressed to these alternative views, does positive peace then represent the best or absolute good in international ethical terms? Does in particular Singer's radical utilitarianism represent the most ambitious international ethical position, since it requires—at least in redistributive terms—so much more than Rawls's minimalist positive peace solution and requires greater redistribution than Walzer's moral minimalism? No, because even with universal justice within and between nations, as well as perfect justice among all individuals on this Earth, nevertheless an element of moral goodness that goes beyond justice is still lacking: humane care.

13. GLOBAL CARE

Lying between positive peace and agape-paradise on my international ethical scale, global care, its ninth category, is superior to positive peace from a moral standpoint. Indeed, it goes beyond justice in the abstract—while comprising it in its provisions—by also including an affective dimension in its enactment. Humanity, kindness, mercy, help, tenderness if not love, in short, caring for

[79] Peter Singer, *One World: The Ethics of Globalization* (New Haven, CT: Yale University Press, 2002).

[80] Andrew Linklater, *The Transformation of Political Community: Ethical Foundations of the Post-Westphalian Era* (Cambridge: Polity Press, 1998), 220.

[81] Amitai Etzioni, *From Empire to Community: A New Approach to International Relations* (New York: Palgrave, 2004).

[82] For Kant, the radical defender of individual freedom, such a world government—he called it a 'universal monarchy'—would constitute a despotic nightmare. For him, differences in language and religion have the immense advantage of splitting humankind in different groups. Therefore, this natural differentiation will remain among republics. They will treasure their separateness by being different while, at the same time, remain in 'perpetual peace' because of their internal republican order. See Kant, *Perpetual Peace*, 81–2.

[83] Walzer, *Thick and Thin*.

others, is a deeply human feature of social intercourse. Morally, care is closer to the extreme good on our ethical scale where morality disappears in a non-human world where agape and perfect love reigns. While day to day friendly, maternal, or paternal relations experience the moral dilemmas of consequentialism vs. the deontological, from a moral standpoint, ethical considerations tend to evaporate in the presence of love. It is this proximity to the tenth and final category of our moral scale that elevates care above justice.

While justice and peace are what we strive for, it is injustice and war that attract attention. And when looking at world history, although wars and revolutions are much more studied, peace is much more common. Traditional diplomatic history—or *histoire traités-batailles* as the French *Annales* school historians derogatorily called it—concentrates upon wars and end-of-belligerency treaties precisely because these exceptional 'real-life' dramas appear as 'new,' that is, newsworthy. But this emphasis on the exceptional makes us forget that life goes on for most people outside the stream of history, whether on 14 July 1789, on 1 September 1939, on 9 November 1989 or 11 September 2001. Whether the world is changing or not, features of humanity which are essential keep occurring, no matter what: the amicable relationships among friends, the day-to-day love of parents for their children, the social intercourse in the workplace with fellow workers, the associative activities of all kinds, the common praying and worship as well as innumerable other such activities. All these cannot be subsumed under the heading of care, but from a moral standpoint, these mores—customs, habits, and manners—make for moral attitudes. And it is social relationships—and not considerations of principles of justice—that stand at the centre of people's lives.

The ethic of justice claims to be universal and impartial. It is based on a rational reading of ethical requirements. It seeks to encompass the moral case at hand within a generalized ethical reading. Equity is possible because of the abstract rules that blindly affect everyone. Although it requests interpretation of the specific case at hand—and therefore requires one to morally evaluate particular situations—the universality of its rules guarantees justice. For Rawls, moral development of individuals can be analysed by a sequence of stages. These proceed from the morality of authority to the one of association to the third, and highest, level, the morality of principles.[84] An ethic of justice is based on reason and principles, such as, in a Kantian perspective, his categorical imperatives.

On the other hand, the ethic of care is more particularistic and concrete in its ontology. There, the moral agent seeks to do good around her or himself, taking care of the persons she or he is in a relationship with. These have a face

---

[84] John Rawls, *A Theory of Justice* (Cambridge, MA: Harvard University Press, 1971), 462–79.

and can be identified. Caring implies being responsible for others rather than claiming rights, while stressing the common humanity of all. It is an attitude that seeks to do the good *hic et nunc*, here and now.

Whereas justice is typically associated with the public sphere, care is often seen as belonging to the private one. Without diminishing the essential role of abstract principles of justice, a major problem of theories of justice remains: how are moral agents constituted?

Why have justice theorists neglected the development of the affective capacities underlying our sense of justice? Perhaps because the sense of justice grows out of a sense of care which is learnt within the family. We could not teach children about fairness unless they had already learnt within the family 'certain things about kindness and sensitivity to the aims and interests of others'.[85]

The theoretical problem arises from the fact that modern political thought is permeated by liberalism. General principles of justice can be readily envisaged between rational equals. Whether Kantian, Rawlsian, or Dworkinian, a scheme for setting principles of justice can be readily imagined between free and competent adults. But how is it with children, with unfree, or with incompetent individuals? How can dependents make the responsible choices philosophers assign to liberal agents? Carol Gilligan strongly criticizes this conception:

While an ethic of justice proceeds from the premise of equality—that everyone should be treated the same—an ethic of care rests on the premise of nonviolence—that no one should be hurt. In the representation of maturity, both perspectives converge in the realization that just as inequality adversely affects both parties in an unequal relationship, so too violence is destructive for everyone involved.[86]

But care does not solve all moral questions and there are a number of problems with it, too.[87] Simply caring for people who are close to us is not always satisfactory. It neglects strangers, especially those who are limited in the web of relationships in which they find themselves and have few if any

---

[85] Will Kymlicka, *Contemporary Political Philosophy: An Introduction* (Oxford: Clarendon Press, 1990), 266; he is citing Owen Flanagan and Kathryn Jackson, 'Justice, Care, and Gender: The Kohlberg–Gilligan Debate Revisited', *Ethics*, 97/3 (1987), 622–37 (esp. 625). On this issue, see especially Susan Moller Okin, *Justice, Gender, and the Family* (New York: Basic Books, 1989).

[86] Gilligan, *In a Different Voice*, 174.

[87] The ethic of care has been primarily developed in a feminist perspective by Carol Gilligan (ibid.) who argued that women's moral development led them to speak *In a Different Voice* from men's ethic of justice. Since it comes close to being based on the public–private dichotomy, this leads to at least two problems. First, this dichotomy may in fact explain the differences between the voices of justice and care. Second, making this moral distinction also runs the risk—ironically!— of thus perpetuating patriarchy. See also Hekman who, building upon Gilligan's work, argues for a discursive reconstruction of morality that radically goes beyond the disembodied

people to care for them. Besides that, a sense of justice does not replace justice
per se, since individuals as well as peoples cannot take care of everybody—
priorities are required—and since they need to apportion some of their efforts
for themselves in order to better care for others—a consequentialist requirement. This means that care needs to include at least some general conceptions
of justice in a more encompassing synthesis. Principles of justice are paramount for making the world a better place, as attested by the continuing fight
for human rights. But an ethic of care need not close its eyes to such principles
as will be discussed later. On the contrary, it sees responsibilities for other
human beings in a shared humanity.[88] A good example is Mary Wollstonecraft's 'nurturing liberalism'[89] which synthesizes elements of justice and care.
In her 1792 *A Vindication of the Rights of Woman*,[90] '[s]he embeds justice
within the larger framework of care but demonstrates its importance for
caring relationships.'[91] Her ideal is one of 'mutual sympathy' or friendship,
where natural and pure affection devoid of all coercion exists. It is the duty of
parents to educate their children towards such an autonomy allowing them to
overcome, over time, their dependency situation. The development of private
care throughout society will thus lead to the development of public virtue.
For Wollstonecraft, '[t]he main attribute of a virtuous individual . . . is the
self-conscious fulfillment of one's responsibilities and duties to others.'[92]

   In fact, by putting the humane aspects—consideration, sympathy, or compassion for others—to its forefront, care goes further than justice by demonstrating the lineaments of morality in day-to-day life. The examination of
some extreme moral cases will bolster this claim. First, one can note that even
Auschwitz was not able to eliminate all traces of humanity and morality
between people, as shown by Levi's analysis of *The Lager* which was a gigantic
biological and sociological experience.[93] Among the most interesting features
of his work are the portrayal of the very varied ways that allowed him and a
minority of his fellow prisoners to survive. Humanity and care among

---

general principles of justice—based upon autonomous selves—towards contemporary if not
post-modern subjects who are socially situated. Her epistemological reflections lead her to
'theorize a multiplicity of moral voices constituted by race, class, and culture, as well as gender'.
Susan Hekman, *Moral Voices, Moral Selves*, 163.

   [88] Cf. Kymlicka who criticizes this more expansive way of defining care as in fact adopting a
universalist ethic of justice. Kymlicka, *Contemporary Political Philosophy*, 271.

   [89] Cf. Engster's reading of her work. Daniel Engster, 'Mary Wollstonecraft's Nurturing
Liberalism: Between an Ethic of Justice and Care', *American Political Science Review*, 95/3
(2001), 577–88.

   [90] Mary Wollstonecraft, *A Vindication of the Rights of Woman* ([1792] Oxford: Oxford
University Press, 1993).

   [91] Engster, 'Mary Wollstonecraft's Nurturing Liberalism', 578.

   [92] Ibid., 587.

   [93] Levi, *If This is a Man* and *The Truce*.

prisoners (and at times with some of their jailors, too) constituted essential elements explaining this survival. Second, it is important to remark that even the most ruthless tyrants were not entirely void of some humanity which they displayed to their entourage:

So were Hitler and Stalin capable of caring for others? The answer is a qualified 'Yes'. Hitler sometimes seemed touched by certain kinds of suffering and could show consideration for his staff. He fed birds and tried to reduce the pain of lobsters being boiled alive. Though he could order the extermination of the feeble-minded without compunction, he remembered his secretaries' birthdays and was generous towards those who helped him when he was poor. '*When I think about it,*' he amazingly claimed, '*I realize that I'm extraordinarily humane.*'[94]

The tension between ideological convictions and the requirements of humanity are also made clear in Reichsführer-SS Heinrich Himmler's famous Poznan speech. Talking to top SS officers in a secret meeting, the second most powerful man in Nazi Germany said this about the Holocaust:

I also want to mention a very difficult subject before you here, completely openly. It should be discussed amongst us, and yet, nevertheless, we will never speak about it in public.... I am talking about the 'Jewish evacuation': the extermination (Ausrottung) of the Jewish people. It is one of those things that is easily said. 'The Jewish people is being exterminated,' every Party member will tell you, 'perfectly clear, it's part of our plans, we're eliminating the Jews, exterminating them, ha!, a small matter.' And then along they all come, all the 80 million upright Germans, and each one has his decent Jew. They say: all the others are swine, but here is a first-class Jew. And none of them has seen it, has endured it. Most of you will know what it means when 100 bodies lie together, when there are 500, or when there are 1000. And to have seen this through, and—with the exception of human weaknesses—to have remained decent, has made us hard and is a page of glory mentioned and never to be mentioned.[95]

This shocking admission demonstrates that even people such as Himmler well realized the difficulty of exterminating, concretely and personally, other individuals, be they mortal enemies such as Jews were for the Nazis. The SS leader also realized that every single German wished to protect the individual Jew whom he personally knew. What all this means is that Auschwitz was possible because of the ideology behind it and with the help of institutional strategies dehumanizing the purported 'enemy.'[96] Such was the price for

---

[94] Cf. the book entitled *How Do We Know Who We Are? A Biography of the Self* by the psychiatrist Arnold M. Ludwig (Oxford: Oxford University Press, 1997), 176 (italics in original).

[95] Cf. http://www.holocaust-history.org/himmler-poznan/speech-text.shtml, a speech made on 4 October 1943 (consulted 11 November 2004).

[96] It is significant that learning the trade of soldiering means two things in particular. First, learning to consider the enemy as a barbarian if not a non-human. Second, creating very strong bonds and humane solidarity between the men of the basic combatant unit such as a platoon.

remaining 'decent;' although it made the SS 'hard,' that 'glorious' chapter would nevertheless never be written. And Himmler, too, was one of those Germans who had a 'decent Jew': he helped a Jewish professor to leave a concentration camp and emigrate.[97] And Hitler himself spared many Jews out of sympathy or goodwill, including quite a few who were simple people and whom he did not know personally.[98] He spent a great deal of time, till the end of the war, on carefully studying the files of many such cases and excluding numerous people from the Holocaust—this while simultaneously keeping the final solution as his major goal.

These examples show that *humane*ness persists even in most extreme cases. In this sense, the humane feelings one experiences for other humans with whom one is in touch are universal ones. The problem with Stalin and Hitler lay with their ideology and their fanatic belief in the righteousness of their ideas—which they saw as inextricably linked to their own destiny. The ethical values they espoused were those of communist, respectively Aryan, justice. For these consequentialist moralists, the nobility of the cause permitted everything. This gives another reason why an ethic of care is superior to an ethic of justice: it is better to behave morally at the concrete level than unquestionably follow whatever general principle of justice one is convinced is right. Better to care humanly, in concrete relationships around self, rather than to attempt to bring justice and build Utopia in this world—especially when one uses a sword!

It is through human communication, that is, language—both verbal and non-verbal—that humanity is always expressed. This is why the anthropologist Sarah Blaffer Hrdy can write in *Mother Nature: Maternal Instincts and How They Shape the Human Species*:

Language is integral to the symbolic capacity that allows humans to understand cognitively what others are expressing at the same time as we understand at an emotional level what others are feeling. . . . What makes us humans rather than just apes is this capacity to combine intelligence with articulate empathy. But all humans develop this empathetic component in the first months and years of life as part of a unit that involves at least one other person. . . . To be distinctively human—different

---

Officers well know that soldiers are rarely ready to die for their country, but are willing to take considerable risks of dying for their 'buddies'. In this respect, 'men are made, not born', as Joshua S. Goldstein convincingly shows in *War and Gender: How Gender Shapes the War System and Vice Versa* (Cambridge: Cambridge University Press, 2001), 264.

[97] Bryan M. Rigg, *Hitlers jüdische Soldaten* (Paderborn: Ferdinand Schöningh, 2003), 241. The text in English is Bryan M. Rigg, *Hitler's Jewish Soldiers: The Untold Story of Nazi Racial Laws and Men of Jewish Descent in the German Military* (Lawrence, KS: University Press of Kansas, 2002).

[98] Cf. Rigg, *Hitlers jüdische Soldaten*, 232–57, p. 248 in particular for Hitler's motivations of sympathy.

from, say, a genetically very similar chimpanzee—is to develop this unique empathetic component that is the foundation of all morality.[99]

These arguments coming from evolutionary theory bolster the claim that an ethic of care is primary—in the sense of being internalized by all humans.[100] It is less demanding in terms of reason and autonomy than an ethic of justice. As anyone who has listened to children knows, feelings of justice and fairness come quite early—admittedly under the guise of the denunciation of injustice and unfairness in concrete cases affecting themselves or people in their close surroundings. And it is this empathetic feature of humankind[101] upon which one can build elements of an international ethic that in fact goes beyond simple justice.

Up to now, the discussion on care has centred on its original level of analysis, that of persons in relationship to each other. So how can one move to the international ethical level? One way would be to argue that the Universal Declaration of Human Rights, adopted and proclaimed by the General Assembly of the United Nations on 10 December 1948, sets forth such basic principles along which a global ethic could be founded.[102] However, it is a liberal text foreign to the spirit of an ethic of care. As the theologian Hans Küng cogently argues:

no comprehensive ethic of humanity can be derived from human rights alone, fundamental though these are for human beings; it must also cover the human responsibilities which were there before the law.[103]

Based on Küng's proposals, the Council of the Parliament of the World's Religions, which met in Chicago in 1993, signed a declaration on a global ethic. This declaration was confirmed by the InterAction Council of former

---

[99] Sarah Blaffer Hrdy, *Mother Nature: Maternal Instincts and How They Shape the Human Species* (New York: Ballantine Books, 1999), 392.

[100] Even those who will not be interested in reading Kant and Rawls, if one may write somewhat fatuously. Moral behaviour need not require the lofty principles advocated by those thinkers.

[101] Actually, from an evolutionary point of view, humanity in the sense of belonging to a society of humans already starts in the mother's womb, according to Hrdy: 'By the third trimester a fetus can hear noises beyond the womb, can process affective quality of the speech, and differentiate whether mother or someone else is speaking. This provides the fetus his first clues about the world. It marks the beginning of feeling "embedded" in a social network and the sensation of belonging that gradually develops, after birth, into a capacity to experience feelings for others. The capacity to combine such feelings with our uniquely human ability to guess what someone else must be thinking and feeling is the main difference between humans and other animals.' Hrdy, *Mother Nature*, 527–8.

[102] See also the chapters by Adam Roberts and David Little in this book which extensively discuss the normative importance of this Declaration.

[103] Hans Küng, *A Global Ethic for Global Politics and Economics* (London: SCM Press, 1997), 103.

Presidents of State and Prime Ministers in 1996 and contains 'two basic principles' followed by 'four irrevocable directives':

- Every human being must be treated humanely!
- What you wish done to yourself, do to others
- Commitment to a culture of non-violence and respect for all life
- Commitment to a culture of solidarity and a just economic order
- Commitment to a culture of tolerance and a life of truthfulness
- Commitment to a culture of equal rights and partnership between men and women[104]

I argue that this declaration constitutes one exemplification of a 'global care' ethic. Indeed, these six moral rules are more in line with an ethic of care than one of justice as the Human Rights Declaration. Its first principle goes beyond the right to be treated equally—that is, *humanly*—to the injunction of treating others *humanely*, that is, with a modicum of care. In this sense, it goes further than the liberal tradition of international law by way of a 'principle of recognition'.[105] At the societal level, it is essential that communities are recognized as such. Historically, indigenous peoples obtained the status of an independent 'nation' in this way—this without having had to conform to classic Eurocentric institutions and concepts such as a 'constitution' or being 'civilized'. A dialogue was established between different human communities, none of them superior to the others.

The inclusion of the Golden Rule[106] as the second principle is also central from a care perspective. It implies a universality of humankind whereby every human can empathize with any other because all share the same aspirations. Implicitly, it asserts that every human being has the same basic values. Everyone, by simple introspection, can well realize the essential human wishes

[104] Küng, *A Global Ethic for Global Politics and Economics*, 108–11 (slightly adapted).

[105] Alexis Keller's chapter in this book reappraises this central question historically and therein shows the crucial importance of 'dissident' liberal thinkers, such as Montesquieu, Rousseau, and Chief Justice Marshall.

[106] Küng (*A Global Ethic for Global Politics and Economics*, 98–9) presents 'that Golden Rule of humanity which we find in all the great religions and ethical tradition'. He cites its various formulations by: 'Confucius (c.551–489 BCE): 'What you yourself do not want, do not do to another person' (Analects 15.23); Rabbi Hillel (60 BCE–10 CE): 'Do not do to others what you would not want them to do to you' (Shabbat 31a); Jesus of Nazareth: 'Whatever you want people to do to you, do also to them' (Matthew 7.12; Luke 6.31); Islam: 'None of you is a believer as long as he does not wish his brother what he wishes himself' (Forty Hadith of an-Nawawi, 13); Jainism: 'Human beings should be indifferent to worldly things and treat all creatures in the world as they would want to be treated themselves' (Sutrakrintanga I, 11,33); Buddhism: 'A state which is not pleasant or enjoyable for me will also not be so for him; and how can I impose on another a state which is not pleasant or enjoyable for me?' (Samyutta Nikaya V, 353, 35–342, 2); Hinduism: 'One should not behave towards others in a way which is unpleasant for oneself: that is the essence of morality' (Mahabharata XIII, 114,8).'

of others: survival, security, nourishment, freedom, connectedness to family, group, and culture, and other such basic needs. This Golden Rule principle is a responsibility of all—individuals and communities alike—in the spirit of a global ethic of care.

The commitment to a culture of non-violence is also in line with an ethic of care. It is explicitly argued for by Gilligan for example, for whom the requirement that no one should be hurt is a premise of care.[107] This can be readily extended to the international level, without necessarily leading to pacifism. Just War remains an option there, too. Even Gandhi, the apostle of non-violence, did not object to some forms of violence, in particular when fighting for justice, which is the ultimate duty: 'Gandhi argues that, although non-violence is always the best course of action, it is better to fight with violence for a just cause than not to act because of fear.'[108] Solidarity and tolerance lie in the same vein along an ethic of care. Tolerance means that 'others are like me but since I am unique in certain ways, I accept that they too are unique'. This value therefore leads to mutual toleration of other cultures, groups, peoples, and nations. As for solidarity, it extends to the sympathetic feeling of the others' plight and the willingness to help in a humane way.

An ethic of care thus represents the highest humanly reachable level of an international ethic. Including general principles of justice, it is also demanding obligations from all towards others, individuals and peoples alike, in a responsible and humane way.

One important supplementary argument can be added. Human care does not necessarily spring from a self-interested point of view, contrarily to other species:

Chimps are quite capable of consciously calculating certain kinds of costs and anticipating benefits. They can even anticipate the cost-benefit decisions other animals are likely to make. But humans go a step further. They combine these analytical capacities with new ones—like being able to imagine the future. Even more important, they are able to translate hunches about how another animal will react into full-scale speculation about what others are thinking, and articulate their concerns both to themselves and to others. In this way, humans transform ingenious capacities of observation into the sophisticated capacity to care what happens to others, even those they have never met.[109]

It is this empathy which at times evolves into a quite normal and typical *sym*pathy which allows humans *to care* for others. And this behaviour is readily observed on the international scene, too. The numerous individuals

---

[107] Gilligan, op. cit.; see also Ruddick, *Maternal Thinking*.
[108] R. Rajmohan, 'Gandhi on Violence', *Peace Research*, 28/2 (1996), 35.
[109] Hrdy, *Mother Nature*, 529.

and groups, especially, but not uniquely, non-governmental organizations, who are helping others in concrete instances in many different areas of life, are telling examples of care at the international level. Often based on an ethic of positive peace, they are no less often accompanied by an ethic of care in their day-to-day activities. 'Warm' care is morally superior to a 'colder' positive justice. This superiority also pertains to an ethical Global Care.

14. CONCLUSIONS

To sum up, I present an international ethical scale ranging from war to peace, from Just War to Just Peace, from genocide to global care, and from the absence of war to overall justice as in positive peace. Following Rawls and many philosophers, two at times contradictory approaches, consequentialist and deontological, were used jointly. With their help, different actions were comparatively evaluated and measured—rather than assessing actors *in toto* as in an ethic of virtues. Both ethics are central to international relations theory. Consequentialism, close to utilitarianism, is key to realism, Marxism, and liberalism. The deontological approach leads to a morality based on duties and rights. It influenced Just War theory, liberalism as well, and constructivism.

As I argued, total war at one extreme and Just Peace at the other cannot constitute the end points of an international moral scale. In stating that absolute unhappiness and happiness are not of this world, Levi was correct. Morality ceases to exist when humankind is totally eradicated—category one—as in a nuclear-like holocaust, or in the case of humanity disappearing when everyone is a saint and lives in paradise—and thus ceases to be human (category ten: agape). Between these two extreme points—which by definition have no empirical content—eight intermediary moral situations were then discussed, starting with genocide (category two). The disappearance of a part of humankind clearly represents the worst international crime that can be envisioned. War (category three) is morally superior to genocide. The next category is the absence of war, non-war, that is, peace in a Hobbesian sense, since the possibility of war remains present at all times and with it a basic sense of fear and insecurity. Ethically, non-war is superseded by the old and well-known doctrine of Just War which makes for the fifth category.

After these first four ethical concepts centred on different kinds of war, follow four categories of peace, starting with stable peace (category six) which is a real peace because war is not lurking behind it. From a justice point of view, a stable peace is often based on an imposed and unjust order, and typically comes about after a major war or with the passage of time. However, stable peace does have a moral value because of order that provides everyone with a sense of security. Just Peace—the seventh category—is stable peace with justice. Because it is explicitly accepted as just, it is morally superior. Category eight, positive peace, morally surpasses Just Peace which is typically specific to two directly concerned parties. Positive peace refers to a more generalized justice in international relations which is incompatible with exploitation and structural violence at the global level.

With Global Care, my ninth category, I propose a concept morally superior to positive peace. Caring goes beyond justice in the abstract as it includes a humane, that is, an affective and cultural dimension. Consideration, sympathy, and compassion are at the core of a caring approach. Treating everyone humanely: this first principle goes beyond the liberal right to be treated equally, to the injunction of treating others humanely, that is, with care. A second principle, the Golden Rule, implies a universality of humankind whereby every human can empathize with any other because all share the same fundamental aspirations. The values of non-violence, tolerance, and solidarity complement these principles.

Some methodological weaknesses that are inherent to the theoretical choices made nevertheless remain.[110] I do hope though that this bold attempt at measuring international morality will help to better understand various categories of good and bad. Besides putting the concept of Just Peace developed in this book into an overall perspective, my international ethical scale allows for normative comparison between different concepts of international ethics. Hopefully, it will stimulate further conceptual and theoretical developments.

---

[110] First, the scale is based upon a vision stressing harmony between individuals and groups; alternatively, one could plead for instance for a conflict-prone ethic whereby humankind advances towards the good by struggling. Second, having two independent dimensions for scaling international deeds makes it difficult to always place a concrete international act in one category only. For instance, is Just War with a lot of blood-shedding morally superior—as I posit—to a non-war, that is, peace, but a profoundly unjust one? Or is a stable peace—which may be unjust and result from force and custom—really to be preferred to a Just War—which, after all, should end with a just settlement and prepare a Just Peace? These dilemmas are inherent to my approach and cannot be eliminated. I tried to show however, that the inevitable fuzziness of the positioning of the categories with respect to each other was not as problematic as it appears at a first glance.

6

Just Peace: A Dangerous Objective

Yossi Beilin

1. INTRODUCTION

The term Just Peace has taken root in latter years in international political discussions. Many adjectives are often added to peace: comprehensive, permanent, true, steady, sustainable, and brave. Sometimes separately, sometimes as one, the adjective *just* is added.

If there exists a Just War, might not one also refer to a Just Peace? In practice, this is not so trivial. For a war to be just, one that justifies the heavy cost it encapsulates—the untimely loss of young lives, as well as economic and other damages incurred—it must be unusual. Just War is an oxymoron of sorts, but history has witnessed such wars, especially when fending off an aggressor, and therefore this is a valid concept. The term Just Peace is redundant, but its problem lies not in its redundancy, but in the accompanying concept it introduces onto the stage—'unjust peace'. The existence of a concept such as 'unjust peace' creates a wide margin for resistance to peace, claiming that it is unjust, thus causing injustice to those who pay the price for lack of peace.

I will argue that the concept of Just Peace is not only unnecessary, but may also cause harm, and it is therefore best to avoid using it. An 'unjust peace' is not peace at all, but a different solution. In the past, the concept of peace was used to describe a situation where there was no war, or to define agreements of territorial division among rulers. Peace as a passive concept, that is a situation devoid of violence, much like an imposed peace where territories are partitioned, is not peace. The first is a situation, and the second a solution.

Separating peace and Just Peace greatly diminishes the value of peace, and its consequence is not merely a theoretical and conceptual one. This is a significant political statement, which creates a category that cannot be confirmed in any objective way. While 'comprehensive peace', 'sustainable peace', and 'multilateral peace' are concepts that can be quantified and regulated, the aforementioned Just Peace is an ambiguous concept that is subject to manipulation by each side. As I will show, it is more just to avoid using it.

To demonstrate this, I will address various definitions of peace and justice, give an overview of numerous peaceful situations and peace treaties, as well as present the change in the essence of peace throughout history. I will describe in greater detail the Israeli–Palestinian conflict. Here I wish to show that in various times it may have appeared to the parties that not making peace was justified, whereas in hindsight it becomes clear that greater injustice lay in not making peace. The price paid by both sides for abstaining from making peace at junctions where such an act was possible, because it seemed unjust, was too dear and demonstrated the danger that lies in using the expression 'unjust peace'.

Peace is defined as the absence of war. It is a situation where there is no violence, with emphasis on a lack of inherent, institutional violence between organized groups—nations, states, classes, or religions. The Latin term *pax* is connected to pact—agreement, treaty, contract. However, in comparison with the Roman *pax*, the Greek *eirene*, the Hebrew *shalom*, and the Arab *salaam* seem to approach 'peace with justice, including an absence of direct and structural violence'.[1] In Hebrew, the word *shalom* is connected to the physical level and arises from it. *Shalom* is used upon meeting other people, and it entails integrity and prosperity.[2]

The biblical peace is one of the main human values. Only once is peace mentioned alongside justice, in Psalms 85: 10: 'Mercy and truth are met together; righteousness and peace have kissed.' In the Bible, there are many similarities between the value of peace and the value of justice. Both involve an order of pursuit: 'That which is altogether just shalt thou follow', and 'Seek peace, and pursue it', but at no point do these two values merge. Khanoch Tennen views peace as an intelligent demand made on an individual, in relation to others. In this respect, peace is an obligation, accompanying the right to a life of peace without fearing a compromise of freedom or possessions.

Martin Buber states that God's greatest command to mankind is peace.[3] The most important human task is contributing—where possible—to

---

[1] Joel Krieger, *The Oxford Companion to Politics of the World* (New York and Oxford: Oxford University Press, 1993), 688–9.

[2] Zeev Levi, 'On the Peace Concept in Judaism and in Jewish Thought', *Gesher*, 43 (Summer 2001), 66–71.

[3] Paul A. Schilpp, and Maurice Friedman (eds.), *The Philosophy of Martin Buber*, The Library of Living Philosophers (La Salle: Open Court; London: Cambridge University Press, 1967), vol. XII.

establishing peace all over the world. The struggle for peace is combined with a struggle for justice.[4]

One of history's most important essays on peace is Kant's essay on Eternal Peace.[5] This pretentious concept is in fact a cynical reference to a sign that hung over a pub, which points people to a nearby cemetery. The peace Kant referred to two hundred years ago is also a peace that includes justice, since it is not a consequence of a chess game between kings, and is not artificial or forced. Three basic principles ensure the true peace Kant wrote about, and none of them are easy, at the time of writing or today. The first principle is that civilian law in each country should be republican, that is, it will not be peace between kings, but rather between nations whose representatives are influenced by the citizens. The second is that the world should turn into a federation of free states. This will enable setting universal norms and will naturally lead from states of war to situations of peace. The third is that the right to citizenship of the world should be limited to the characteristic norms of the hosting state in order to prevent unnecessary conflicts driven by normative and cultural differences.

Among the six preliminary conditions Kant makes a statement very important for his time, one which is supposed to prevent injustice towards residents of the state: 'No independent states, large or small, shall come under the dominion of another state by inheritance, exchange, purchase, or donation.' Another preliminary condition is: 'No state shall, during war, permit such acts of hostility which would make mutual confidence in the subsequent peace impossible.'[6]

Kant's basic principles, as well as the preliminary conditions he refers to, present a situation where peace will epitomize values of morality and justice, without his using terms such as Just Peace. Kant's principles are put into practice to a certain extent in the Charter of the United Nations (UN). Article 3 of the first chapter in the UN charter states, 'All members shall settle their international disputes by peaceful means, in such a manner that international peace and security, and justice are not endangered.' Here also, when establishing an institution that realizes to a certain degree Kant's principles, Just Peace is not discussed, but conflict resolution that does not endanger the principle of justice. A resolution of peace encompasses justice and does not part with it.

---

[4] Levi, op. cit.
[5] Immanuel Kant, *Toward an Eternal Peace* (Jerusalem: Magnes, 1976).
[6] Ibid.

2. JUSTICE AND INJUSTICE IN SITUATIONS HISTORICALLY PERCEIVED AS SITUATIONS OF PEACE

The history of the world is very much a history of war and intermediate periods. Many conflicts were resolved using the *winner takes all* principle. Annihilating all the men, capturing women and children, and looting the enemy's possessions were reasonable, acceptable, and even 'just' endings to conflicts. It goes without saying that territories that belonged to the defeated were ceded to the winner.

Once norms of war were set, regardless of the winner, the *winner takes all* principle was not challenged. Thus, for instance, in those economical wars that were resolved by designated representatives, like the battle of David and Goliath, one person's victory determined the fate of the other's camp. It is difficult to locate justice in such a case, but this was a legitimate victory, that was not perceived by the loser—apparently—as criminal injustice, but rather as an inseparable part of a lifestyle he was born into, agreed with, or had come to terms with.

The gates to Janus' Temple would open when war broke out, and lock upon its end. The Romans prayed to Janus, the only god who possessed the ability to see his own back. From 29 BC until the death of Commodus in AD 192, approximately 220 years, the gates remained locked. This period is known as Pax Romana. Rome, the most powerful empire of its time, encountered a period when quiet prevailed in it colonies worldwide. Even if conflicts arose (such as those that arose in and out of Israel), they posed no significant threat to the Roman army. Pax Romana was imposed upon the colonies by means of force, and not as a result of peace treaties. However, its duration was a prosperous time for Rome and its occupied territories. During this period, fewer soldiers were required for draft, economic, judicial and cultural prosperity was evident, agriculture was further developed, and a great momentum of building and prospering of the arts was evident, especially in sculpting.

Pax Romana became a synonym for a future imposed peace, where significant political powers force discipline and stability over much weaker elements. Peoples denied of their freedom and their pride could not have felt justice served, and it therefore cannot be regarded as a time of peace, but rather as a time of stability.

An overview of contracts, understandings and treaties achieved in the Middle Ages and in modern times proves that the term peace was used loosely; in most cases the subject at hand was in fact settlements that put to rest feuds among monarchies. The Treaty of Tordesillas in 1494 is a perfect illustration of this kind of settlement. In this treaty, Portugal and Spain agreed on the partition of the New World between their two countries. This was clearly a real estate contract, discussing the monarchs' personal ownership of lands conquered or discovered. It does not even put up an appearance of just consideration for the people residing in those areas. Justice was only evident in the relations between both courts. Thirty-three years later, in 1529, the Treaty of Saragossa similarly divides the Far East between Spain and Portugal.

In Europe, the Holy League (a coalition of Christian states) separates Turkey from central Europe, and following the eradication of the Turkish army in the Battle of Zenta, The Peace of Karlowitz is signed in 1699, where the territories seized by Turkey are divided among league members. Azov was ceded to Russia, Austria received Turkish lands in Hungary, and Poland seized Podolye.

The Peace of Westphalia, signed in 1648, was different to those before it. It is considered the first agreement to reflect national concerns and not merely those of courts, and therefore is much more just than other peace treaties. It ended a 30-year war between Protestants and Catholics in Germany, which later spread to the rest of Europe. At the end of the war, some German lands were annexed to Sweden, while Holland was declared independent.

Wars were fought by relatively small armies, mercenaries of the kings, and their results show no consideration for those living in the areas so easily turned over from one monarch to the next. These many peace treaties are contracts among monarchs, which reflect their army's balance of power as the battle drew to an end.

Very often the justification for conquering and repartitioning populated areas was the mere existence of an opportunity to do so. The peace dictated after the event shows the winner imposing its norms on the loser. There is no better example of this than the partitioning of Poland during the late eighteenth century. It was a century where this great country was weakened both constitutionally and militarily, primarily during the ongoing battles of leadership among various groups. Russia, Prussia, and Austria gained strength in this period, and were all driven to stir the Polish pot by their Polish dreams.

The civil war that broke out in Paris following battles between Lutherans and Catholics, justified, as far as Russia was concerned, invading Poland. In 1722, one third of Poland's area was torn away and divided among Russia, Prussia, and Austria. The Polish Sejm was forced to convene and authorize the division. Twenty-one years later, when the noblemen of Poland were weary of a reform that might change their privileges, they turned to the empress of Russia, asking her to intervene on their behalf. She gladly did so, cancelling the reform, and together with Prussia seized further Polish land. This was the second time Poland was partitioned. In 1795, Poland was divided a third time ending its sovereignty. Russia and Prussia invaded Poland to suppress the patriot's rebellion in Krakow, led by Kastuszko, and its end was the division of the remainder of Poland. It was justified as maintaining stability in Europe. However, no one gave a second thought as to what the Polish people wanted.

The Versailles Peace Treaty signed in 1783 was unique. Unlike international treaties before it, there was no arbitrary division between rulers, but rather an acknowledgement of sovereignty of North American colonies. Britain, a colonial power, relinquished its hold over a huge colony, and ceded it to the people who rebelled against it.

However, in Europe, peace treaties continued to reflect the shifting balance of power. This was also the case with the second Peace of Paris signed at the Congress of Vienna in 1815. In many ways, this was a true reaction: the victorious monarchs of Europe convened in order to put the continent to rights after Napoleon stormed in, with the intention of preserving the character of their respective regimes and keeping the spirit of the French revolution out of Europe. The success of the Congress of Vienna lay in ensuring relative stability in Europe for close to a hundred years. In this respect, it resembled Pax Romana, though 1800 years before it was one empire which imposed its will upon many, whereas here there were five large king-doms: Austria, represented by Metternich, Prussia, represented by Harden-berg, Russia, represented by the czar Alexander I and Count Nesselrode, England, represented by Lord Castlereagh and France, represented by Lord Talleyrand.

The Congress of Vienna politically took Europe back to the time before the Peace of Westphalia. This is clearly an unjust arrangement, securing the interests of the courts, settling their differences, while ignoring the national liberation movements in Europe and impeding those elements that were acting in the spirit of the French revolution. The three principles of the revolution—liberty, equality, and brotherhood—were challenged by three additional principles—restoration (previous monarchs returning to the throne and restoring kingdom borders that existed before Napoleon's wars), legitimacy, and solidarity (of the European courts).

The small monarchy of Poland established by Napoleon was united as a 'personal unia' with Russia, and the Russian czar presided as king of both. Russia also took over Finland and Bessarabia. Norway was annexed to Swe-den, Austria secured Galicia, a region of Poland, and several regions in northern Italy (Venice, Milan, and Lombardy), the French gained south Italy, and Prussia kept Poznan, Turon, and Gdaum in Poland.

Stability was attained via treaties: the Holy Alliance, established in September 1815 between Russia, Prussia, and Austria, aiming at strengthen-ing monarchy, aristocracy, and the church; the Quadruple Alliance, which included the former three and Britain, established two weeks after the first alliance, whose purpose was to protect by any means necessary the achievements made at the Congress of Vienna for twenty years to come.

The Crimean war in 1854 was the only war that took place between the Congress of Vienna and the First World War, in which most of the European monarchies took part. This conflict between Russia and England stemmed from a disagreement over Russia's right to oversee sacred Christian sites in Palestine. Under Catholic pressure, Turkey refused the Russian demand; the czar conquered the Moldavian and Valerian principalities pending Turkey's submission to his demands. Turkey declared war on Russia, supported by England and France. The war lasted two hard years, and its end was followed by a peace treaty signed in Paris, reflecting Russian defeat. Russia had given up both principalities it held under its power, acknowledged the integrity of the Ottoman Empire, and withdrew its original demand regarding the sacred sites. The Peace of Paris reflected the principles of the Congress of Vienna by demonstrating the collective punishment that follows any digression from the status quo. The end of the war left Europe in the same state it was in at its beginning.

Peace treaties continued to be a characteristic of monarchic interests. The French-German war took place in 1870 over a very typical cause, succession to the Spanish throne. A coup in Spain in 1868 left the throne empty. The Kanzler of the North German Confederation proposed Leopold of the Hohenzollern dynasty for the position. France, ruled by Napoleon III, vetoed this move, and demanded of Wilhelm, king of Prussia, an assurance that no Hohenzollern would rule Spain. Bismarck considered this an outrage, and after war broke out, Germany defeated France. On 2 September 1870 the French army surrendered in Metz and 90,000 Frenchmen were taken as prisoners of war. However, that was not the end of the war. Two days later a republican government was established in Paris, led by opposition head Leon Gambetta and Jules Favre, seeking to sign a peace treaty in order to prevent any territorial losses to Germany. Bismarck was opposed to this, and therefore took the German attack a step further by bombarding Paris for the first time in history, leading to a second surrender by the French in January 1871. In May, following the end of the Paris Commune affair and the French Civil War, Germany and France signed a peace agreement in Frankfurt. France ceded Alsace-Lorraine to Germany, agreed to pay Germany high compensations, and agreed to the situation of German soldiers on its turf until all payments were settled.

The Peace of Frankfurt ignored, obviously, the will of the people whose lives it was determining. Germany was on the receiving end of highly populated French areas, whose opinions were not polled. High compensations further added to the humiliation and hatred. The French did not come to terms with these territorial losses. Alphonse Daudet's story, *The Last Class*, about a school that is to be handed over to the Germans, taught many generations of French nationalists to dream of retrieving that which was lost, despite Gambetta's famous reference to Alsace, 'Think of them always, speak of them never'.

Germany, declared as an independent state in 1871, confronted the defeated France, in a new Europe where united nations replace small principalities, while preparing for greater conflicts. The Peace of Frankfurt was perceived as one of the causes for both world wars in the twentieth century because of the deformities it created. The letter from Jules Favre to the ambassadors of France worldwide on 6 September 1870, while he attempted to achieve peace and preserving the status quo just before the war broke out, and before the French empire collapsed and was replaced by a republican government, is an illuminating document discussing an imposed peace that was to come:

The enemy is at our door, and we are plagued by one thought—expel him from our territories!...The Prussian king has declared war, not against France but against the imperial dynasty. The dynasty has crumbled, free France awakes. Does the Prussian king wish to continue his criminal battle, which may impede him as much as it does us? Does he want to display to this world, in the nineteenth century, a horror show depicting two nations battling each other to oblivion, while with disregard to humane creeds, wisdom and science, they stack their dead? Let him be free to choose whether he wants to take responsibility for that in the eyes of the world and history!

If it is a challenge, we accept it. We do not give so much as an inch of our land, not a stone of our forts. A shameful peace is to become a war of destruction, in a very short while. We will only negotiate for sustainable peace.[7]

In 1873 Bismarck succeeded in bringing three emperors to sign an agreement. Germany, Austria, and Russia all agreed to sign an agreement aiming at protecting the borders of the new Germany as well as suppressing national movements within the German borders. This agreement is greatly reminiscent of the Holy Alliance, and bears no relation to the concerns of the citizens of these European powers.

Following Turkey's adamant attempts to suppress the Balkan rebellion against its rule, Russia lent a hand to the Slavian nations. In 1877 its armies crossed the Danube towards difficult battles with the Turks. Turkey was fended off and sought an agreement with Russia. The agreement was signed in San Stefano in 1878, thus ending Turkey's regime in Europe and greatly

---

[7] Jules Favre, 'Circulaire de M. le ministre des Affaires étrangères aux agents diplomatiques de la France à l'étranger', *Discours parlementaires et écrits divers*, published by Mme. Jules Favre (Paris: Plon, 1870–9), IX, 6–7 (my translation).

diminishing it in Asia. Serbia, Montenegro, and Romania were declared independent and Bulgaria was established. As far as addressing the concerns of the residents of these areas, this was a just agreement.

Nonetheless, conservative Europe could not adhere to the just and reasonable solution sought in San Stefano, and that same year Bismarck convened the congress in Berlin, attended by Germany, Russia, Austria-Hungary, and England. Turkey was ceded back to Europe, followed by a decrease in Bulgaria's territory. Bosnia and Herzegovina were handed over to the care of Austria-Hungary, while Turkey ceded Cyprus to Britain. Bismarck created a new balance between powers to ensure the stability of the monarchies at the expense of European citizens who were forced to accept, again and again, irrelevant sovereignty over their land.

Between the 1870s and the beginning of the First World War, European imperialism thrived, requiring new markets, new materials, and cheap labour. New discoveries are still made today regarding these dark times, where tasteful and diplomatically inclined leaders of Europe went all out in Africa and in east Asia, behaving like outright pirates while misleading the locals, turning some of them into slaves and robbing the rest. Treaties signed during this period were characterized by treating man and land—this time in the colonies—as if they were the monarch's private property. In this respect, it was regression to the fifteenth and sixteenth centuries, only in a much more educated Europe. The only plausible explanation for the part its liberal, advanced leaders played in this imperialistic campaign was a lack of knowledge.

By the end of the nineteenth century, Africa was partitioned in the following way: France and Spain ruled in the northwest; France also ruled central Africa; South West Africa was ruled by Portugal and Germany; Britain ruled in the South; Italy in the North and Belgium ruled over Congo. Leopold II, King of Congo, led a cynical, greedy policy in Africa disguised as scientific research and a desire to help the natives. This was brought to a climax at the Congress of Berlin on Africa in 1885 which was reminiscent of the Congress of Vienna. The Congress aimed at settling demands made by the powers with regards to Africa, and to legislate and thereby legitimize dominating the no-man's land known as Africa. The congress took no notice of the interests of the local population, but it was decided that each European power that ruled over any part of Africa be permitted to seize further areas inland and actively rule them. Order must prevail. Article 34 of the General Act of Berlin says:

Any power which henceforth takes possession of a tract of land on the coasts of the African Continent outside of its present possessions, or which, being hitherto without such possessions, shall acquire them and assume a protectorate... shall accompany either act with a notification thereof, addressed to the other Signatory Powers of the present Act, in order to enable them to protest against the same if there exists any grounds for their doing so.[8]

At the start of the twentieth century, France and Italy signed an agreement by which France would seize Morocco and allow Italy to take over Tripoli. In 1911, France seized Morocco and Italy seized the Balkans. In 1923, Turkey agreed to Italy seizing Tripoli when it signed the Treaty of Lausanne. No one enquired about the opinions of the locals regarding this treaty.

The battle of the powers over land and franchises in China was characteristic of the late nineteenth century and the early twentieth century. Japan, China, Britain, Germany, France, and the USA took advantage of the weaknesses of this large country, and seized its resources. Following a Chinese attempt to fight this phenomenon (the Boxer Rebellion of 1900), mutiny was suppressed by an international army led by Germany and comprised of German, American, French, British, and Japanese soldiers. Peking was conquered. Four years later, war broke out between Japan and Russia over Japan's demand that Russia take its forces out of Manchuria, and acknowledge China's territorial integrity. Russia lost. Its maritime forces were nearly destroyed and, after one and a half years of battle, the Portsmouth Peace Treaty was signed in 1905. Russia ceded half of Sakhalin Island, Port Arthur, and Mukden to Japan, and acknowledged Japan as the dominant power in China and Manchuria.

The West was no different. Following a rebellion in Cuba, the USA declared war against Spain in 1898 and destroyed the Spanish navy in the gulf of Manila. The Spanish surrendered to the Americans in Cuba, and they in turn seized Puerto Rico and the Philippines. In December 1898, a peace agreement was signed by Spain and the USA in Paris, in which Spain sold the Philippines to the USA for 20 million dollars, relinquished its hold over Puerto Rico, and agreed to grant Cuba its independence. Apart from Cuba gaining independence (after only eleven years under American control), in no other territory being handed over did anyone take note of local interests.

In 1904, France and Britain took the world by surprise when they signed the *Entente Cordiale*, addressing the division of their areas of dominance. They divided among them Siam. France retracted its reservations regarding Britain's position in Egypt whereas Britain gave France complete freedom in Morocco. In 1907, Russia also signed an agreement dividing areas of dominance. Russia acknowledged Britain as the dominant power in Afghanistan, provided that Britain would not annex it. Britain also agreed not to invade

---

[8] The Berlin Conference: The General Act of Feb. 26, 1885: http://web.jjay.cuny.edu/~jobrien/reference/ob45.html

Tibet, and Persia was divided between a Russian zone of dominance in the north, a British zone in the south, and a neutral centre.

The Versailles peace conference that took place in 1919 was one of history's greatest failures. It followed the greatest bloodbath in history until that time, taking the lives of 10 million people. Justice was served at the conference, but not wisdom. In attendance were 27 states—those who won the war, their allies, and those countries established after the war. The USA, France, Britain, Italy, and Japan assumed the lead, while the defeated states were not asked to attend. Only after German compensations were settled was Germany invited to sign the treaty, losing in the process 70,000 square kilometres of its European turf, 6.5 million residents—3 million of which were German— 30 per cent of its natural coal resources, 25 per cent of its iron resources, and taking on great military limitations. Germany also took responsibility for the war, and committed to paying a great fortune in damages. Additional treaties were signed with Austria, Hungary, and Bulgaria which were all forced to give up lands and impose limitations on their respective armies.

The Versailles Peace Treaty is an example of an imposed peace treaty that reflected a great measure of justice towards the apparent cause of a war that was unnecessary and cost many lives. However, it unwisely planted the seeds for the next world war twenty years later.

The world's attempt to learn from the Versailles failure led to efforts conducted during the Second World War to establish an international organization that would not exhibit the same weaknesses innate in the League of Nations. In mid-1943, a shift in American public opinion led to the establishment of a movement calling for an organization that would ensure permanent peace. In September of that year, the American Congress embraced the proposal made by Congressman Fulbright to support US participation in an organization aiming to establish and to maintain a just and lasting peace. One month later, the USA, USSR, British, and Chinese foreign ministers met in Moscow to discuss the possibility of maintaining lasting peace after the war. At the Yalta conference convened in 1945, the allies decided to meet in San Francisco two months later to draft a UN charter. However, the conference itself addressed the old idea of world partition, still overlooking those who were defeated in the war and the true will of those residing in the areas whose future was determined by the winners. Stalin decided to keep all territories seized by the Soviet army. The British were guaranteed dominance in Greece, and the Soviets were guaranteed dominance in Bulgaria and Romania. Hungary and Yugoslavia were each divided into two zones of dominance and Germany was partitioned among the victorious powers. However, a decision had not been made regarding Poland and Czechoslovakia. In July 1946 an international peace conference took place in Paris. Twenty-one countries that fought against the axis powers were in attendance. Within three months, peace treaties were signed with Italy, Bulgaria, Romania, Hungary, and Finland. This time, humiliating the defeated was not a priority and the American Marshall Plan proposed to the European countries included winners and losers alike. The lesson of Versailles was well taken. A historical Just Peace may bring forth disaster if it does nothing to uproot the seeds of the next war.

3. RELATIVITY OF JUSTICE: THE ISRAELI–PALESTINIAN CONFLICT

Following the European Jews' departure from the ghetto in the nineteenth century and their accelerated process of education, they then faced the need to be integrated into the intellectual, economic, and political élites of Europe. The fear that they would become the élite increased the levels of anti-Semitism, and inflicted grave limitations on Jewish businesses. Many of them, who now considered religion an irrelevant issue, became Christians so they would not be subjected to discrimination in their professional activities, as were Heine, Mendelssohn, and Marx. However, this was not enough to prevent anti-Semitism. Educated and secular Jews were becoming increasingly sure that they could no longer live in Europe and realize their potential as people. They then proposed the idea of Zionism which advocated establishing a state, in which the citizens would be mostly Jewish, in the land of Israel where a Jewish state existed 2000 years earlier. This was a land that had been the object of yearning for the Jewish people since they were exiled from it. It was also a land where Jews, albeit in small numbers, lived throughout an exile that lasted thousands of years.

The Jewish immigration to Palestine, coupled with the Balfour Declaration (made by the British colonial secretary), which stated that Britain would look favourably on the establishment of a national home for the Jews in Palestine, created a fear of Jewish invasion among the Arabs residing in Palestine. In 1920, at San Remo, Britain was assigned the mandate for Israel, and in 1921 the territory east of the Jordan River was ceded to the Amir Abdullah. In March 1921, after the Palestinian mandate was assigned to the Colonial Ministry and was no longer under the foreign ministry's responsibility, the British colonial secretary, Winston Churchill, visited Palestine. At a meeting held on 28 March, attended by the head of the Arab High Committee, he refused to revoke the Balfour statement, saying that it was just for the Jews scattered all over the world to have a national home. He added that it could be only Palestine as the Jews had been bound to this land for 3000 years. He assumed that this arrangement would be in the best interest of the world, the Jews, and the British Empire. He also hoped that it would be in the best interest of the Arabs residing in Palestine.

Since the beginning of the twentieth century, the Arab–Jewish tale is one of mutual fear, both physically and demographically. The Jews sought a country, but realized one would require a Jewish majority, and to that end a massive immigration to Israel was vital. The Arabs feared an invasion of Jews to Palestine, and preferred a joint state where they would be a majority and thus able to prevent further Jewish immigration. The Jews preferred a smaller state established on a portion of the territory, if by doing so they would gain total sovereignty and ensure unlimited immigration.

The Jewish dream was reflected in a map sent to the peace conference in Paris in 1919 by the Zionist organization. It included all of western Palestine, spanning Sinai in the south, Sidon in the north, the Golan Heights in Syria, and a large chunk of today's Jordan up to Amman in the east. This plan was rejected by the conference, and within a few years the Zionist leadership realized this was a case of 'too many irons in the fire', since in this area there lived four times as many Arabs as there were Jews. The realistic faction within the Zionist movement understood it would have to settle for much less if it wanted to achieve an independent, democratic state. Eighteen years later, after years of violence and killings, it agreed to the recommendation made by the British commission, headed by Lord Peel, that a Jewish state be established on a portion of land less than 20 per cent of Palestine's total area. The Arab High Committee was opposed to this plan, and the idea of partitioning the country was held off for another ten years, during which the Second World War and the Jewish holocaust took place.

Had both sides agreed to the Peel proposal, two states would have been established two years before the Second World War, and eleven years before the British mandate expired. In 1937 there could have been peace between a Jewish state, spanning one-fifth of Palestine, and an Arab or Palestinian State, spanning four-fifths of it. Many Jews might have been spared the awful fate that befell them in the holocaust, when nearly every country closed its gates to them. The Palestinians would have gained self-determination for the first time in their history and would have avoided the refugee problem that arose in 1948. Both sides had their own reasons for regarding Peel's solution as an unjust one. The Palestinians regarded themselves a majority in Palestine, and were prepared to live with a Jewish minority, provided that this minority would not grow through immigration. They thought it unjust for a minority to establish a state, not even a mini-state, to be crowded with an increasing number of Jews. A significant minority of the Jews believed that after east Jordan was torn away from Israel, it would be unjust to settle for only a portion of the remaining land, and unfair to those Jews the world over who wish to make Israel their home, and who had no say in the decision over this compromise.

In hindsight, one cannot find a more just solution. This is one of the most distinct examples in the twentieth century of a settlement lost. There could not have been a settlement more just and in keeping with the existential concerns of both peoples, and it was easiest at that point of time to claim it was an 'unjust peace'. Many years later, Golda Meir, who was adamantly opposed to the Peel proposal of division, said that had it not been the Arabs who turned down the offer, she could never forgive herself for being in the opposition when Ben Gurion accepted the offer on behalf of the Jews. However, being smart in retrospect can only assist in avoiding similar mistakes in the future. To be wise is to recognize the existence of a political opportunity when one presents itself, and to understand the meaning of justice at that point in time when weighed against the injustice of turning the opportunity down. If one agrees to the term Just Peace, then what appeared to be an 'unjust peace' in 1937 was in fact the most Just Peace on earth when compared with what the next eleven years held in store.

Ten years later, on 29 November 1947, the UN approved the proposed division of Palestine in resolution 181. Israel accepted the proposal, while the Palestinians objected, with the support of the Arab world. The holocaust and the locked gates the Jews encountered just before the war played a significant part in raising world support for the proposal. The UN Special Committee on Palestine, in its recommendations for the country's future, said:

The basic conflict in Palestine is a clash of two intense nationalisms. Regardless of the historical origins of the conflict, the rights and wrongs of the promises and counter-promises, and the international intervention incident to the Mandate, there are now in Palestine some 650,000 Jews and some 1,200,000 Arabs who are dissimilar in their ways of living and, for the time being, separated by political interests which render difficult, full and effective political cooperation among themselves, whether voluntary or induced by constitutional arrangements.[9]

The majority of the committee supported the establishment of an Arab state spanning 38 per cent of the mandate area west of the Jordan River, and 62 per cent for the Jewish State. The final proposal was 45 per cent for the Arab State and 55 per cent for the Jewish State. In rejecting the UN

---

[9] Meir Avizohar and Yeshayahu Friedman, *Partition Plans' Studies* (Ben Gurion University Press, 1984), 280.

resolution, the Palestinians claimed that they have been a majority in Palestine for centuries, and that the UN's support of the people's right to self determination entitles them to determining their own future. They further claimed that the Balfour declaration and the mandate were null and void, since Britain did not have the authority to offer the Jews land that was not theirs to give. However, the principles of the mandate had already been implemented, and the 'safe refuge' the Jews strove for had been established, and should not be enlarged.[10]

What would have happened had both sides agreed to the resolution, and lived peacefully in economic cooperation? Would that have been 'unjust peace'? The Palestinians felt that the world was demanding they pay for a holocaust that was not their doing, and settle for less than half the area when only a few years earlier they refused to settle for the 80 per cent that was proposed to them. The Jews would have seen injustice in a resolution forcing them to give up settlements, even cities, built during the first half of the twentieth century, and to settle for little over half the mandate area, when it was clear to all that hundreds of thousands of Jews, most of them European refugees of the holocaust, wished to immigrate to Israel and needed room.

In hindsight, it is clear how 'just' this peace might have been. On the one hand, it provided a partial solution to the terrible distress of the European Jews, having made it clear to all that their lives could have been saved had they been permitted to immigrate to Israel. On the other hand, the war in 1948, and its many dead, could have been avoided. This war witnessed the burial of holocaust survivors who lived through the camps, came to Israel, found themselves forced to bear arms and fight the Arab armies, and were killed. Israel buried 1 per cent of its population during the war in 1948–9. Thousands of Palestinians were killed, and 700,000 became refugees; some for fear, some due to their leaders' propaganda, and some were deported by the Jews who felt that nothing they would do could measure up to the dire conditions their people had to endure during the war. The Palestinian feeling that this was an 'unjust peace' in 1947 stood in their way of getting a greater measure of justice for themselves and for the Israelis alike.

On 19 June 1967, a week after the Six Day War ended, the Israeli government was willing to make peace with Syria and Egypt on the basis of international borders and Israeli security needs, although this was kept secret at the time. The proposal was submitted to these countries' representatives via the US representative in the UN, Arthur Goldberg. Two negative responses were received shortly thereafter. Two and a half months later, at the Arab

---

[10] Shmuel Dothan, *The Struggle For Eretz Israel* (Tel-Aviv: Ministry of Defense, 1981), 365.

summit convened in Khartoum in Sudan and the famed 'three no's' were decided upon: no peace, no negotiation, and no recognition of Israel.

The prevailing feeling in Egypt and Syria must have been that this was an 'unjust peace', that would help them gain what they had lost in the war but would in turn force them to agree to peace with Israel, a move they were not prepared for before to the war. Had they agreed to peace, the deaths of 1973 would have been avoided. Both countries attempted using force to gain this land, to no avail.

On 9 February, the Egyptian president, Anwar al-Sadat, agreed to a proposal made by the UN envoy, Gunnar Jarring, to make peace with Israel on the basis of international borders. This proposal bore great resemblance to the peace treaty eventually signed by Israel and Egypt in 1979. However, the Israeli Prime Minister, Golda Meir, turned it down, refusing to believe Sadat was acting in good faith. Moshe Dayan, then minister of defence, chose Israeli control in Sharm el-Sheikh in Sinai over peace.

Had a peace agreement been signed between Egypt and Israel at the time, it would have been perceived as 'unjust'. Egypt would have broken the Arab ban on Israel in making bilateral peace, without resolving the Palestinian problem, only to regain Sinai. Israel was willing to risk letting go of territory it seized in battle while defending itself against Egypt. Israel and Egypt paid in blood for not signing this treaty in 1973.

In 1978, Sadat tried to convince Syria and Jordan to join him in making peace with Israel. Both refused, breaking off diplomatic relations with Egypt. Sixteen years later Jordan and Israel signed a peace treaty in which Jordan was not ceded (and did not demand) any land Israel seized in 1967. Syria has not got the Golan Heights at the time of writing.

On 11 April 1987, King Hussein and Shimon Peres, the Israeli foreign minister, reached an unsigned understanding regarding an international summit that would lead to negotiations between Israel and a Jordanian–Palestinian delegation. Prime Minister Shamir rejected this agreement. He considered the world's involvement in the Israeli–Palestinian conflict unjust. In his viewpoint, the world proved its lack of decency when it turned its back on the European Jews in the Second World War, when it repeatedly made decisions that damaged Israel, leading to the lowest point when Zionism was declared a racist movement in a UN resolution. The Palestinians regarded the Hussein–Peres understanding as unjust because of Hussein's attempt to lure them to the discussion table under his umbrella merely a year after the discussions between Jordan and the Palestine Liberation Organisation (PLO) on establishing a future confederation failed. However, the PLO was not asked and Shamir did his work when he stopped this move in its tracks. The 'unjust peace', as many believed it to be, was not achieved. Within months, the Intifada took the lives of many on both sides. Four years later, the Gulf War led to the Madrid summit where Shamir found himself in the very same international conference he had previously refused. The Palestinians found themselves attending as part of a joint delegation led by Jordan. What appeared unjust to both sides in 1987, later appeared to be the right thing to do after further bloodshed.

The missed opportunity for a peace treaty between Israel and the Palestinians in 2000, was widely regarded as unjust, on both sides. This was true although it may have ended a long and difficult conflict between both peoples. The Palestinians, now willing to settle for the territories seized by Jordan and Egypt in 1948—22 per cent of western Israel—claimed that any further compromise would be unfair. Furthermore, they claimed that a peace treaty that did not permit the return of 1948 refugees and their exclusive sovereignty over Palestine would be an injustice. Israel stated that modifications to the borders were in order, as the situation changed since 1967. They pointed to the fact that letting the refugees return would make the Jews a minority in their national home just when a Palestinian nation is established at its side. They further claimed that Temple Mount is the place where the Temple stood, and therefore called for no less than joint sovereignty.

Had the Palestinians agreed to President Clinton's proposals at the Camp David summit, the Israeli Prime Minister, Ehud Barak, would have faced the difficult task of convincing his constituents that this was a just move. However, the Palestinians spared him this test by turning the proposals down. On their part it seemed a just decision, while Ariel Sharon's victory in the election implies that many on the Israeli side regarded this peace as unjust as well. The Intifada, which began in September 2000, may greatly increase the cost in blood before both sides rejoin the negotiating table. When the Palestinians pull up a chair, they will find that the most practical common ground is Clinton's plan of 2000. Should both parties be strong enough to sign such an agreement, great justice will be served on both sides.

4. CONCLUSIONS

According to the Western tradition of international law, peace is an agreed-upon contract. The peace we are discussing is a peace among peoples, or the sovereign states that represent them. In this context, Pax Romana or the numerous divisions of Poland do not come under this definition. Imposed peace must also be excluded for the same reason an imposed contract cannot be regarded as a contract. Such peace is a result of a sovereign and legitimate decision on both sides, acting on what they perceive as correct community interests.

A peace treaty is usually signed following a war and addresses mainly the definition of borders, regulation of diplomatic relations and many other settlements setting the nature of relations between both states in the future. For such an agreement to work it is imperative to create a 'win-win' situation through careful balance of interests, and to prevent a situation where one party signs it due to weakness or lack of alternative. The agreement must, where possible, avoid leaving open issues from which future conflicts may arise, as well as providing mechanisms for resolving these conflicts in a non-violent way (joint committee, mediators, arbitration, etc.).

Peace can only be defined as such if it is not unjust. It is an agreement that does no more wrong than right, and one in which the wrongs done are within the acceptable framework of the times. For example, a peace agreement between Israelis and Palestinians whereby Israeli settlers should leave occupied territories could be perceived as an unjust agreement from the settlers' point of view. Yet we must weigh this injustice against the injustice in taking resources such as land and water from the Palestinians, and additional killing on both sides if a solution is not found. Since justice is always relative, a balance of justice must lead to the eviction of settlers.

The proposed use of the term Just Peace is based on the commonly used Just War, suggesting one cannot refer to a Just War while refraining from use of Just Peace. To justify war, the parties try to portray it as just, an act of necessity and a result of circumstances. Just War is usually portrayed as imperative in preventing severe damage or destruction, by pre-emptive blow. The justice of war stems from the fact that the party taking action is convinced that abstaining from it would lead to national disaster whose cost would far exceed that of a war. The clearer the threat, the more present the danger, the more justified is the war. I doubt there's such a parallel for peace.

War only requires justifying in the eyes of 'warmongers', and therefore the concept of Just Peace is not only redundant, but also harmful. Some adjectives restrain peace, for example, cold peace, partial peace. However, since there is no greater justice than peace, when peace is unjust there is no reconciliation, and if there is no reconciliation there is no peace.

Logically, if peace brings forth reconciliation and prevents the loss of lives and possessions, it is just by definition. It may, of course, be imperfect. It may even damage someone and wrong him, but that does not make an 'unjust peace'. An unjust solution is possible, but as of that moment it can no longer be termed peace.

The great danger in the term Just Peace is, naturally, legitimizing the term 'unjust peace'. It is not a big stretch from its academic use to a political one, and may justify opposition to peace by claiming that it is unjust. Since no peace treaty can address the needs of both sides in their entirety, a newly legitimized excuse may be provided for those opposing it.

Peace is a situation where (mostly young) people need not be killed by each other. They are able to dedicate their lives to realizing their potential in their community while contributing to their own development, their community and even the world, instead of living in constant fear and tension. They can dedicate their lives and their resources of time and finance to defending themselves and preparing for the next Just War.

The least Just Peace is that signed too late. Unwillingness to sign an agreement may delay it for too long, leading to many additional graves before to its finalization. What can be less just than taking young lives under the excuse that Just Peace has yet to be achieved?

7

Peace, Justice, and Religion

David Little

1. ORIENTATION

In responding to the question, 'What is a Just Peace?', we may attempt to defend three propositions. First, the bearing of religion on the subject is at once important and complicated. Important because, for better or worse, religion is very much a fact of contemporary international life, and, consequently, will have to be accounted for. Complicated because religious traditions say different and sometimes conflicting things about justice and peace. The diversity of doctrine within and among religions requires sensitive analysis.

Second, the most adequate approach is to conceive of the idea of Just Peace as an 'umbrella term', one that covers a multitude of sub-problems. That is, there appears to be no one simple answer to the question, 'What is a Just Peace?'. Rather, there are several answers relating to the various sub-parts of the concept that need to be sorted out and elaborated in any comprehensive examination.

Third, despite the complexities, there is one important unifying theme: the persistent relevance of internationally recognized human rights. The Preamble to the Universal Declaration of Human Rights makes the point elegantly: 'the equal and inalienable rights of all members of the human family is the foundation of freedom, justice and peace in the world.' Accordingly, the task before us is to break the idea of peace down into its component parts, sketch them out, analyse and exemplify them in relation to issues of justice, and especially human rights, and (adding an additional layer of difficulty) show how religion ties in.

In face of possible objections, we may add a preliminary word in defence of the idea of Just Peace. While it may be true, as some would argue, that the only 'real' peace (read: lasting, truly secure peace) is a Just Peace, and that, as a consequence, the idea of Just Peace is redundant, there are two problems with that assumption. One is that in the real world, the ideas of justice and peace often pull against each other. The impulse to mitigate violent conflict frequently inspires a willingness to sacrifice considerations of justice for one reason or another. Thus, peace understood simply as *the absence of violence* competes, in everyday reality, with the idea of a Just Peace.[1] The other problem is that the idea of 'justice' is itself hardly self-explanatory. The standard definition of justice as 'allocating to everyone what is due', obviously begs large questions about what it is exactly that is every person's due. Philosophical and theological tomes are filled with disputations over the meaning of justice.

Starting with the first term in our triad, we begin by enumerating four activities that pertain to the general pursuit of peace: *peace enforcing, peacekeeping, peacemaking,* and *peacebuilding,*[2] and then showing, by way of example, how justice and religion fit in. Though these categories have rather porous borders (as we shall see), they are coming to be understood, in current discussion, as identifying more or less discrete subject areas relevant to the achievement of peace.

2. PEACE ENFORCING

Peace enforcing refers to efforts to achieve the reduction of violent conflict, or the imminent threat thereof, in what is known (somewhat euphemistically) as a 'non-consensual environment'. That is, the various parties in a conflict have not as yet consented to common terms of peace, and a use of force or other forms of 'coercive diplomacy' are contemplated or undertaken by outside parties in order to compel such consensus among the belligerents. Recent examples are the military response by the North Atlantic Treaty Organization (NATO) to the conflicts in Bosnia and Kosovo, as well as the use of force and other coercive instruments now being employed by the USA and its allies in

---

[1] Kant begins his essay, *To Eternal Peace* [*Zum Ewigen Frieden*], with the following comment: 'Whether the above satirical inscription, which once appeared above the picture of a graveyard on the signboard of a certain Dutch innkeeper, applies to all human beings, or particularly to the heads of state, who can't get enough of war, or perhaps only to those philosophers who dream their sweet dreams of peace, remains an open question.' Carl J. Friedrich (ed.), *Philosophy of Kant* (New York: Modern Library, 1949), 430. I have somewhat altered Friedrich's translation.

[2] I am afraid that my treatment of these categories is going to be rather unbalanced in favour of 'peace enforcement'. That is mainly because of the limitations of time, and because I have recently been thinking most actively about questions related to this category. I also think, especially with the crisis precipitated by the September 11 events, that the questions of peace enforcement are most immediate.

the campaign against 'worldwide terrorism', all undertaken with the ultimate objective of 'enforcing peace'.

How justice applies is not far to seek. There are, for one thing, strictly legal questions concerning the validity, according to existing international standards, of the use of force in Bosnia, Kosovo, or, currently, in Afghanistan. In the case of Bosnia, there was eventual United Nations (UN) Security Council authorization for NATO bombing, which helped to terminate hostilities and lead to the adoption of the Dayton Peace Accords in 1995. On the other hand, considerable controversy continues over whether the UN, and especially the Security Council, properly fulfilled its responsibilities by adequately protecting war victims during the course of the war, and by bringing an end to violence with sufficient dispatch and resolution.

Kosovo represents an even more tangled case so far as legal validity goes. The 1999 NATO bombing campaign against targets in Kosovo and Serbia was undertaken without any authorization by the Security Council. Since it was assumed that China and Russia would veto any such proposal, no effort to gain Security Council authority was undertaken. Moreover, no explicit provision exists in the UN Charter for using force in the name of 'humanitarian' causes, such as attempting to thwart extensive human rights violations. In its present form, the charter contains a very strong 'status quo' bias. It does pay homage in a vague way to the advancement of human rights and social and economic development, but pursing these objectives in no way justifies the use of force between states. For the authors of the charter, '*peace was more important... than justice*'[3] (speaking of the tensions between justice and peace!). Finally, legal proceedings have been initiated against NATO for bombing targets allegedly protected from direct attack by the rules of humanitarian law.[4] In short, there remains intense controversy over the question of whether the Kosovo campaign was 'legally just'.

In some respects, the question of the legal validity of the current use of force in Afghanistan by the USA and its allies is (at least so far) clearer and more consistent than was the case in either Bosnia or Kosovo. A day after September 11, the UN Security Council unanimously passed Resolution 1368, condemning 'in the strongest terms the horrifying terrorist attacks' and describing 'such acts as well as any act of terrorism as criminal and unjustifiable, regardless of their motivation'. The resolution designates the attacks as a 'threat to international peace and security', and affirms 'the inherent right of

---

[3] Louis Henkin (ed.), *Right Versus Might: International Law and the Use of Force*, 2nd edn. (New York: Council on Foreign Relations, 1991), 38 (emphasis added).

[4] Specifically, NATO is being sued for disobeying the laws of armed combat by bombing what are taken to be civilian targets, such as radio transmitters accused of broadcasting hate propaganda.

individual or collective self-defence in accordance with the Charter'. It calls upon all states 'to work together urgently to *bring to justice* the perpetrators, organizers, and sponsors of these terrorist attacks, and stresses that *those responsible for aiding, supporting or harbouring* [*them*] *will be held accountable....*'[5] Both the UN Secretary-General[6] and the president of the Security Council[7] publicly reaffirmed the right of the USA to take military action against the terrorists and their Taliban supporters in Afghanistan.

In addition, Mary Robinson, the former UN High Commissioner for Human Rights, has described the September 11 events as 'an attack on the rule of law, democracy and human rights' that constitute a 'crime against humanity', and she emphasized that 'you cannot, in the name of any religion, much less in the name of Islam, commit a crime against humanity'. Along with references to the UN War Crimes Tribunals for the Former Yugoslavia and Rwanda, she invoked the Security Council's counterterrorism resolution of September 28, which criminalizes terrorists and their supporters, and declared the responsibility of 'all governments to seek out the perpetrators and hand them over to justice'. Once apprehended, they might be tried, she suggested, in domestic courts (including US courts), or perhaps in an international tribunal yet to be worked out.[8]

Incidentally, Ms Robinson subsequently criticized President Bush's military order of 13 November 2001 authorizing the prosecution of terrorists in irregular US military tribunals. Along with many other legal experts, she objected that the tribunals denied fundamental rights of due process,[9] and such criticism eventually caused the Bush administration to modify some of the more obvious deficiencies of the original proposal.[10] Furthermore, Ms Robinson, again in company with others,[11] challenged the Bush administration's decision to classify prisoners detained in connection with the

[5] 'UN Security Council Condemns Terrorist Attacks on U.S.', *International Information Programs* www.usinfo.state.gov, 12 September 2001 (emphasis added).

[6] 'U.N. Secretary-General Affirms U.S. Right to Self-Defense', ibid., 8 October 2001.

[7] 'UN Resolution Gives U.S. Right to Use Force, Envoy Says', ibid., 24 September 2001. The president of the Security Council was Jean-David Levitte of France.

[8] 'September 11 Attacks Were Crimes Against Humanity, Says UNHCR's Robinson', ibid., 17 October 2001. Harvard international law professor, Anne-Marie Slaughter, advocates setting up an 'ad hoc international tribunal with jurisdiction over all terrorist acts on or after September 11, wherever committed. It should be composed of justices from high courts around the world and co-chaired by a US Supreme Court Justice and a distinguished Islamic jurist of similar rank.' *Financial Times*, 19 October 2001, 23.

[9] 'Rights Official Criticizes U.S. Tribunal Plan', *New York Times*, 8 December 2001. Cf. 'Critics' Attack on Tribunals Turns to Law Among Nations', *New York Times*, 26 December 2001, p. B1.

[10] 'Draft Rules for Tribunals Ease Worries, but Not All', *New York Times*, 29 December 2001, p. B7.

[11] William F. Schulz, 'The Fate of Quaeda Prisoners', *New York Times*, 19 January 2002, p. A3.

military operation in Afghanistan as 'unlawful combatants', thereby reserving to the US government the authority to accord prisoners rights under international law it might see fit.[12]

Legal questions regarding the use of military force, including the terms of due process for those detained or imprisoned in connection with such action, are, then, an important part of determining whether a campaign aimed at enforcing peace is 'just' or not. However, there are, in addition, moral and religious questions, which must also be factored in and evaluated.

Mary Robinson's comment that a crime against humanity cannot be committed in the name of religion focuses the issue, for one of the most striking features of the September 11 attacks is that they *were* justified by religious appeals. The heart of the justification expressed by Osama bin Laden and his followers is a religious variation of an *emergency defence*.[13] The same defence on behalf of 'irregular wartime practices' was expressed by some Serbian Orthodox and Croatian Catholic officials during the Bosnian and Kosovo conflicts. The essential claim is that one's religion—all it means and all it stands for—is catastrophically threatened by hostile forces, and adherents are therefore justified in responding in extreme and extraordinary ways, even to the point of disregarding, if necessary, the most fundamental laws of armed combat.

Osama bin Laden invokes Qur'anic authority for retaliating against what he believes is a severe threat to Islam represented by the West and especially the USA. For him that threat has come in the form of an intrusive and corrupting presence in Islamic 'sacred lands', especially Saudi Arabia, but also Egypt and other Muslim states, ever since the overthrow of the Ottoman Empire, eighty years ago. Added to that is US support for anti-Islamic forces such as Israel and the Sudanese People's Liberation Army waging war against the Muslim government of Sudan. Moreover, the US record in the Islamic world is, he claims, one of gross and consistent violation of humanitarian standards, as in the enduring effects of allied military activity in the Gulf War on Iraqi civilians, and the effects of Israel's military policies towards the Palestinians, which are taken to be fully underwritten by the USA. Attacks of the sort launched on September 11 are fair reprisals for what the USA has done to the Islamic world.

In the case of the Serbian Orthodox and Croatian Catholics in the Bosnian conflict, with resonances in Kosovo, the argument made by some leaders, ironically, turned the tables on bin Laden. It was, church officials claimed, because these two Christian communities and the 'sacred territories' they

---

[12] *New York Times*, 12 January 2002.
[13] See John Kelsay, 'Bin Laden's Reasons', *Christian Century*, 27 Feb–6 Mar 2002, 26–9.

inhabit, were under dire threat in part from Islamic fundamentalism, that they were required to fight for their very cultural and religious identity with everything at their disposal. If that required ethnic cleansing and worse, that is the price of survival.

By 1992, the charges against Albanians, Croats, and Slavic Muslims had been woven together into a claim of both actual and imminent genocide against Serbs by a worldwide Islamic conspiracy aided by Germany and the Vatican. The charges were repeated by Serb Church leaders.... No account of Bosnia can be complete without an examination of the role of Croatian Christoslavism [the idea that authentic Croatians are Roman Catholics] in supporting the destruction of the Bosnian [Muslims].[14]

As we hinted at the beginning, religious and moral authorities disagree among themselves over these questions. Not all Muslims accede to bin Laden's claims, just as not all members of the Balkan Orthodox and Catholic communities agree with the more extreme formulations mentioned earlier. Numerous Muslim authorities have strongly rejected bin Laden's arguments, claiming that normative Islam allows no exceptions to the Qur'anic prohibition against direct and intentional attacks on non-combatant civilians. And religious authorities from other traditions have joined the chorus against bin Laden, invoking similar rules from their respective traditions. For example, religious publicists have, of late, called attention to the 'just war tradition',[15] which, among other things, would rule out direct and intentional attacks on non-combatant civilians as a fundamental and unconditional moral principle.

In an important sense, September 11 represented a fundamental point of decision in respect to what it means to enforce a Just Peace. On the one side, there is existing international law, together with extensive moral and religious support, in favour of the inviolability of civilian protection against direct and intentional attack. On the other side, there is a vociferous body of opinion prepared to modify, if not altogether reject, the provisions and grounds of existing international law, including what we may call the antiterror rule.

---

[14] Michael Sells, *A Bridge Betrayed: Religion and Genocide in Bosnia* (Berkeley, CA: University of California Press, 1996), 65 and 92. See also 89: 'The goal here is to demonstrate what has so often been denied concerning the genocide in Bosnia: That it was religiously motivated and religiously justified.'

[15] For example, see J. Bryan Hehir, 'What Can and Should Be Done?', *Harvard Divinity Bulletin*, 30/2 (2001), 18–19. Hehir is a Roman Catholic priest, currently head of Catholic Charities, and a former professor of ethics and international affairs at Harvard University. Considerable interesting work is currently being done on 'just war thinking' outside the Christian tradition as well. See, for example, John Kelsay, *Islam and War: A Study in Comparative Ethics* (Louisville, KY: John Knox Press, 1993); and Teresa Bartholomeusz, *In Defense of Dharma: Just-War Ideology in Buddhist Sri Lanka* (London: RoutledgeCourzon, 2002).

The law of armed conflict is succinct and unmistakable: 'The civilian population... shall not be the object of attack. Acts or threats of violence the primary purpose of which is to spread terror among the civilian population are prohibited';[16] what is more, '[such] attacks against... civilians by way of reprisals are prohibited'.[17] In short, the antiterror rule[18] permits of *no exceptions or excuses*, including the emergency excuse, religious or not. The idea of 'a systematic attack against any civilian population' is basic to the notion of a 'crime against humanity', extensively elaborated in the Rome Statute, which is the founding document of the International Criminal Court.[19] The rule lies at the foundation of what a Just Peace is taken to mean, and as such undergirds everything else that is held to be worthy of defence and protection in regard to human rights and humanitarian law. That conclusion illuminates Mary Robinson's claim that the attacks of September 11 amounted to a full-scale attack on 'the rule of law, democracy, and human rights', and were thus 'crimes against humanity'.

There is good reason to accept Mary Robinson's characterization. For one thing, the attacks themselves stood out as an indubitable and pristine violation of the antiterror rule. It is just because what happened on September 11 was so easy a case that it could come to constitute, as it has, an important defining moment in world affairs. For another thing, the way of life Osama bin Laden believes to be imperilled, and in defence of which the acts of September 11 were apparently performed, is best signified by the two countries he has specifically identified with, helped to support, and from which he has received sanctuary: the National Islamic Front government of Sudan, and the Taliban government of Afghanistan. It would be hard to find two more

---

[16] 1977 Protocols to the Geneva Conventions, Protocol I, art. 51, para. 2. Technically, this definition does not apply to the acts of September 11 since the Protocols pertain to states and 'organized armed groups' engaged in 'sustained and concerted military operations'. Still, in the absence of a comprehensive convention on international terrorism, this is the clearest legal definition we have. It is the only place, so far as I know, where the term 'terror' occurs in the international humanitarian legal documents, and it is important that al-Qaeda has, it appears, deliberately committed acts prohibited by the laws of war.

[17] Ibid., para. 6.

[18] The term 'terrorism' is a controversial one, and there is debate as to whether it should be used. My view is that direct and intentional attacks on civilians, 'the primary purpose of which is to spread terror among the civilian population'—what I am calling the 'antiterror rule'—is an important and useful definition and should be retained. I admit this definition somewhat restricts the notion of terrorism. However, it is not clear to me, for example, that a surprise attack on a military target, such as the assault on the USS *Cole* in Yemen or on the US military barracks in Saudi Arabia, should be classified as 'terrorism'. Such examples do not conform to the terms of the antiterror rule, and there is good reason, in my view, to press for precision in these matters. (Attacks like those in Yemen and Saudi Arabia are, no doubt, some other kind of offence.)

[19] See Adam Roberts and Richard Guelff (eds.), *Documents on the Laws of War*, 3rd edn. (Oxford: Oxford University Press, 2000), 667–97.

egregious violators of the rule of law, democracy, and human rights than these two regimes.

It is worth remarking, in passing, that the whole edifice of human rights and humanitarian law, including the antiterror rule, may be seen as a reaction by the international community after the Second World War to what was perceived as a massive abuse of the emergency defence by Adolf Hitler and the fascist system he led. It was, after all, article 48—the virtually unrestricted emergency provision of the Weimar Constitution—by which Hitler took power. In his writings and speeches, Hitler went out of his way to claim the overriding right of the 'Herrenvolk' to defend itself against its mortal enemies without and within, and to do that by retaliating for what he claimed was vicious mistreatment suffered at their hands. All 'necessary' action—prominently including systematic and comprehensive violation of the antiterror rule—was for him unquestionably justified.[20]

But if September 11 represents a critical decision point in regard to what it means to achieve a Just Peace in a 'non-consensual environment', there are important implications for those who are prepared, with Mary Robinson, to conceive of the 'war on terrorism' in terms of the enforcement of human rights and humanitarian law. One implication, obviously, is that the peace enforcers—in this case, the USA and its allies—behave in accord with, and in a way that continues to protect and promote, the rule of law, democracy, and human rights. To invoke the antiterror rule, and to make it the foundation of the present campaign, self-evidently entails taking responsibility for the strictest compliance with humanitarian and human rights norms, together with the traditional 'just war' standards lying behind them,[21] in regard to the use of force, as well as related activities. (This clearly calls for the most careful scrutiny and monitoring by an open media, the non-governmental community, and an alert citizenry. So far as the current conduct of armed combat in Afghanistan goes, there is already cause for concern as to whether 'superfluous suffering' on the part of Afghani civilians has been stringently enough guarded against.)

---

[20] The last chapter of Hitler's *Mein Kampf* is entitled, 'Notwehr als Recht' ('the Necessity or Emergency Defense as Right'). I have developed these ideas in an unfinished ms., 'Rights and Emergencies: Protecting Human Rights in the Midst of Armed Conflict'.

[21] As Richard Falk puts it, 'any use of force should be consistent with international law and with the "just war tradition" governing the use of force—that is, it should discriminate between civilian and military targets, be proportionate to the challenge and be necessary to achieve a military objective, avoiding superfluous suffering. If retaliatory action fails to abide by these guidelines, with due allowance for flexibility depending on the circumstances, then it will be seen by most as replicating the fundamental evil of terrorism.' See Richard Falk, 'A Just Response', *Nation*, 8 October 2001, 3.

An additional implication is that the USA and the international community review the bombing policy in the Gulf War, together with the subsequent sanctions policy towards Iraq, in the light of the continuing charges that those policies may have violated restrictions against civilian targets.[22] The same kind of reassessment would seem to be called for in regard to the NATO bombing policy in Kosovo.[23]

Beyond these implications, there is need for a thorough and careful review and re-evaluation of the foreign and domestic policies of the peace enforcers and their allies to determine how scrupulous existing policies are in respect to observing the antiterror rule, and, more broadly, the enforcement of the rule of law, democracy, and human rights. This kind of review will need to be applied with intensified scrutiny to nations like Israel and Sri Lanka, which are engaged in fighting local forms of terrorism, as well as to Saudi Arabia and Pakistan, which are accused of condoning and encouraging groups disposed to terrorism.

At the same time, the antiterror rule will also have to be applied with equal rigour and consistency against those—whether Palestinians, Northern Irish or Tamil Tigers—who excuse their acts by appealing to a right of reprisal against oppression or to a struggle for national liberation. As we saw, the antiterror rule permits no exceptions. It goes without saying, of course, that consistent denunciation and punishment of terrorism will need to be accompanied by policies that also address the resentment and hostility upon which terrorism feeds.

There is one more implication of embracing a human rights approach to Just Peace enforcement that we may mention. That is the need to confront the problem, mentioned earlier, of authorizing armed humanitarian intervention, such as occurred in Kosovo. To repeat, the UN Charter does not now provide for outside armed intervention within the 'domestic jurisdiction of any state' that is aimed at restraining and correcting extensive human rights violations or other humanitarian disasters.

No less an authority than UN Secretary-General Kofi Annan has expressly criticized what he calls the 'old orthodoxy' of prevailing interpretations of the UN Charter, according to which the use of force is restricted to protecting states from outside interference, and maintaining international peace and

---

[22] See summary of comments by Fr. John Langan, S. J., that raise the question as to whether allied bombing during the Gulf War was sufficiently attentive to the requirement of noncombatant protection, in David Smock, *Religious Perspectives on War: Christian, Muslim, and Jewish Attitudes toward Force after the Gulf War* (Washington, DC: United States Institute of Peace, 1992), 5–7.

[23] See David Little, 'Force and Humanitarian Intervention: The Case of Kosovo', in William Joseph Buckley (ed.), *Kosovo: Contending Voices on Balkan Interventions* (Grand Rapids, MI: William B. Eerdmans, 2000), 359.

stability.[24] Such a 'status quo bias', he has argued, improperly excludes the
defence and promotion of human rights as a central and unavoidable objective of the UN, and ignores the need for authorizing armed humanitarian
intervention in extreme cases. Accordingly, the Secretary-General has gone so
far as to indicate his specific support for the 1998 NATO military operation in
Kosovo, where at the time, of course, violations of the antiterror rule and
other human rights standards were extensively reported.

It is of interest that among the traditional 'just causes' contained within the
'just war tradition' we alluded to above, is *the punishment and restraint of
wrongdoing* in support of armed humanitarian intervention. Hugo Grotius, a
seventeenth-century Dutch Protestant and legal philosopher whose influence
on the 'just war tradition' and modern international law was immense, left no
doubt about his sentiments on this question:

> If, however, the wrong is obvious, in case [a leader] should inflict upon his subjects
> such treatment as no one is warranted in inflicting, the exercise of the right [to
> intervene] vested in human society is not precluded.... If, further, it should be
> granted that even in extreme need subjects cannot justifiably take up arms...,
> nevertheless it will not follow that others may not take up arms on their behalf....
> Hence,... *I may make war upon one who is not one of my people but oppresses his own*,
> as we said when dealing with *the infliction of punishment, a procedure which is often
> connected with the protection of innocent persons.*[25]

Grotius summarizes his position concerning the fundamental purpose of war
in the following way: 'war ought not to be undertaken except for the enforcement of rights.'[26]

There is, in other words, strong support within the 'just war tradition' for
reform of existing legal norms governing the international use of force that
Kofi Annan and others are currently advocating. The implications are quite
radical, and it is not yet clear just how or whether the kind of reform Kofi
Annan and his supporters call for will be realized. But what is most important
for our purposes is that the *legal* definition of Just Peace enforcement is itself
at present being seriously re-evaluated in the light of urgent new concerns,
reinforced by insistent moral and religious appeals, for 'the protection of
innocent persons' and 'the enforcement of [their] rights'.

Before leaving our examination of peace enforcement, we must refer to the
non-violence tradition, which has its own strong religious and moral proponents. Indeed, when the pacifist alternative is figured in, the debate over

---

[24] Ditchley Lecture, 26 June 1998, 2.
[25] Hugo Grotius, *Law of War and Peace*, trans. Francis W. Kelsey (New York: Bobbs-Merrill
Co., 1925), II.XXV.iii.2, p. 584 (emphasis added).
[26] Grotius, *Prolegomena to the Law of War and Peace*, trans. by Francis W. Kelsey (New York:
Liberal Arts Press, 1957), 18.

peace enforcement is even more complicated than the foregoing discussion suggests.

Religious proponents of non-violence are especially active these days making proposals in regard to non-violence and peace, including peace enforcement. Some of these proposals represent a radical challenge to conventional thinking, and for that reason must be considered and appraised. Theorist-practitioners like the Mennonite pacifist, John Paul Lederach, is a particularly good example. In 1993 Lederach applied some of his ideas about non-violent peace enforcement to the war in Bosnia, which was then in full swing.[27] He expressed strong reservations about the effectiveness and moral justifiability of military intervention in contemporary international conflicts. On his account, force works against justice in the pursuit of peace, since force has a way of defying and subverting limits and restraints placed upon it.

In place of military intervention, Lederach advocated the idea of an international 'Peaceforce', designed, trained and dedicated to non-violent intervention, and to be developed under UN auspices. It should consist of a large standby force so that thirty thousand or so operatives could be promptly dispatched where needed. The corps would, of course, require strong dedication based on 'rigorous non-violent discipline', but with the appropriate preparation and motivation, it could, according to Lederach, be as effective in the short term as a military force, and 'it would prove far more effective than the military approach over the long term',[28] presumably, because the proliferating effects of force would be forestalled.

Lederach's bold proposal usefully sharpens debate as to whether there is, after all, any place for 'legitimate force' in seeking a Just Peace. The case in favour is by no means open and shut. Of late, non-violence has gained a new respectability as a way of mitigating conflict in part because of the impressive record of non-violent transition in places like Eastern Europe, South Africa, and the Philippines. Incidentally, the role of non-violent religious actors was very important in some of those cases.

Moreover, resort to arms as a way to resolve conflict has lost much of its lustre, especially among industrialized democracies. There is a new sobriety about what we may call 'the pathology of force', that self-sustaining cycle of revenge and retaliation that frequently attends the use of force, and that is especially ominous under modern conditions. This pervasive new mood is largely responsible for the growing popularity of innovative non-violent

---

[27] David R. Smock, *Perspectives on Pacifism: Christian, Jewish, and Muslim Views on Nonviolence and International Conflict* (Washington, DC: United States Institute of Peace, 1995), 41–60.
[28] Ibid., 46.

methods in the effort to reduce conflict and achieve peace and justice, a cause strongly influenced by religious proponents like John Paul Lederach.[29]

However, Lederach's proposals are not altogether convincing in the case of Bosnia. Certainly much else might have been done diplomatically and in other ways to avert violence in the first place. Also, who can say conclusively that imaginative and disciplined non-violent efforts at various stages of the war might not have helped. It is only that a careful review of the course of the war supports the conclusion that, other things having failed, an appropriate use of force was by no means as ill-advised or as ineffective, both in the short term, and probably in the long term, as Lederach and other pacifists claim.

There is a growing consensus that the failure of the UN and NATO to intervene militarily to deter the Serbs early in the war, or later to protect the 'safe areas' like Srebrenica and Zepa from mass slaughter (see later), contributed neither to justice or to peace. The same is true of the arms embargo against the Muslims, which put them at a severe disadvantage. Michael Sells passionately denounces such inaction as 'passive violence', or moral negligence that is responsible for unspeakable human suffering.[30]

Moreover, the decision by NATO eventually and at long last to use decisive force in bringing hostilities to an end, and thereafter to provide military support for the Dayton Peace Accords, and for reconstruction and institution-building, has proved indispensable. There is, of course, no certainty about the ultimate outcome. However, there is good reason to believe that continuing, if diminishing, military presence is absolutely necessary (though admittedly not sufficient) if Bosnia is to have any hope of developing into a stable, tolerant society.[31]

---

[29] See his recent book, *Building Peace: Sustainable Reconciliation in Divided Societies* (Washington, DC: United States Institute of Peace, 1997).

[30] Sells, *A Bridge Betrayed*, 128–45; Stanley Hoffmann, 'Humanitarian Intervention in the Former Yugoslavia', in Stanley Hoffmann *et al.*, *The Ethics and Politics of Humanitarian Intervention* (Notre Dame: University of Notre Dame, 1996), seems to have gotten the story exactly right as to why the United States eventually (and grudgingly) favoured a serious use of force in Bosnia: it was, says Hoffmann, that in the summer of 1995 'the alternative to a resort to force aimed at a genuine cease-fire and embryonic settlement was far worse: an American military intervention aimed at helping UNPROFOR extricate itself ignominiously from a war-ravaged Bosnia', 52. Cf. the review of Richard Holbrooke's new account, *To End a War*, by Mark Danner, 'Slouching Toward Dayton', *New York Review of Books*, 23 April 1998, 59–65, in which Holbrooke came close to trapping Clinton into adopting a new policy towards Bosnia. According to Danner, 'the performance [Holbrooke describes] on the part of President Clinton and his advisers amounts almost to criminal incompetence'.

[31] One must certainly take seriously Robert C. Johansen's non-violent alternatives to military intervention, which he counterposes to Stanley Hoffmann's advocacy of a measured use of force under appropriate conditions. See Johansen's 'Limits and Opportunities in Humanitarian Intervention', in Hoffmann *et al.*, *The Ethics and Politics of Humanitarian Intervention*, 61–80. Still, I find myself in agreement with Hoffmann: 'I share', he says, 'many of [Johansen's]

3. PEACEKEEPING

Peacekeeping has conventionally been understood as the 'stationing [of] military personnel, with the consent of warring [parties], to monitor cease-fires and dissuade violations through interposition between competing [armed groups]'.[32] In other words, in contrast to peace enforcement, peace-keeping typically takes place in a 'consensual environment' in that it is the attempt to implement and sustain the terms of a peace settlement based on the prior agreement of the contesting parties.

The UN has been far and away the principal administrator of international peacekeeping operations, and the preceding understanding has applied, more or less aptly, to what are known as the 'first generation' of UN peacekeeping activities. Examples would be the UN Truce Supervision Organization and the two UN Emergency Forces, mandated respectively to oversee the truces between Israel and the Arabs in 1948 and the truce between Israel and Egypt in the Sinai, 1956–67 and 1973–9. Another example is the UN Military Observer Group in India and Pakistan delegated for the purpose of monitoring the India-Pakistan truce in Kashmir.

Generally speaking, the record of the fifteen or so peacekeeping missions of the so-called first generation is not altogether positive. With a few exceptions, 'none succeeded in doing more than freezing conflicts in place, although that itself represented an accomplishment given the tensions between the belligerents. And rather than "keeping" that peace, they limited their role to observing it.' While the missions were intended to create the conditions of peace, that rarely happened. 'Indeed, the UN's presence may well have prolonged the underlying conflict by removing any incentives to settle it.'[33]

Gradually, the conception of UN peacekeeping missions has altered and broadened somewhat, partly in response to the perceived inadequacies of first-generation efforts. Typically, those efforts involved the interposition of a UN military force between two or more armies, with their consent, for the purpose of monitoring and stabilizing peace agreements, such as truces and ceasefires, by minimizing violence, but lacking, as yet, a full political settlement. By contrast, second-generation operations, or the 'new peacekeeping', are understood as 'UN operations, authorized by political organs or the

---

reservations. Force is a blunt and often counterproductive instrument. And yet it is sometime— when prevention fails—the only realistic one....', 98.

[32] This definition is adapted from Steven R. Ratner, *The New UN Peacekeeping* (New York: St Martin's Press, 1995), 10. It is modified to make it applicable beyond UN examples (e.g. NATO peacekeepers in Bosnia and Kosovo).

[33] Ibid.

Secretary-General', and as 'responsible for overseeing or executing the political solution of an interstate or internal conflict, with the consent of the parties'.[34] Moreover, peacekeeping missions are coming to be seen in more than military terms.

In regard to second-generation missions, a peace agreement is usually still part of the picture, but, in addition, broader political and humanitarian objectives are also agreed upon by the rival parties, and thereby become included in the mandate of the peacekeepers. Examples are the UN Observer Group for the Verification of Elections in Haiti, 1990, and the International Civilian Mission in Haiti, 1993—for the purpose of monitoring human rights conditions, the UN Observer Mission in El Salvador, 1991–5 to supervise the peace accords including human rights monitoring, and the UN Transitional Authority in Cambodia, 1992–3 with responsibilites for supervising the peace accords, and implementing democracy and human rights.

In addition, there are a few examples of recent UN peacekeeping missions that share the features of the second-generation, and yet deviate in some ways. These usually have a very expansive humanitarian mandate, undertake their responsibilities well in advance of any peace agreement, and are invited at least to consider expanding the use of force beyond self-defence. These were the sort of conditions attached to the UN Protection Force (UNPROFOR) in Croatia and Bosnia-Herzegovina of 1992–5. Alas, the record of achievement of such missions, at least in the case of UNPROFOR, is little short of disastrous, as we shall shortly reveal.

Questions of justice are directly relevant to the development of peace-keeping operations. Assuming that the terms of a given peace treaty are just, if peacekeepers are in a position to inhibit the implementation of those terms, as appears to be true of many of the first-generation attempts, then such behaviour hardly qualifies as advancing a Just Peace. But beyond that obvious point, it has more and more occurred to those responsible for peacekeeping that human rights and humanitarian concerns are crucial to achieving a stable peace. As we have mentioned, this new emphasis is very much at the heart of the second-generation missions. Accordingly, human rights and humanitarian standards are, sometimes implicitly, sometimes explicitly, coming to define the 'necessary just conditions' for the implementation of any peace agreement. In some cases, human rights concerns are central to the peace terms themselves, and to their implementation.

---

[34] Ratner, *The New UN Peacekeeping*, 17.

As one example, we may cite the following revealing and appreciative observation regarding the work of the UN Observer Mission to El Salvador, 1991–5:

The case of El Salvador shows both the feasibility and the importance of a more energetic human rights agenda. Because of the sophistication of the Salvadorans themselves and the vision of the UN officials involved, human rights played a central role in the UN-sponsored peace process. Even before the peace accord, one hundred UN Human Rights Monitors were deployed in the country to deter abuses and to build a climate of confidence in which both sides could make compromises necessary for ending the war.... The peace accord, signed in 1992, provided for continuing UN monitoring. It also established a Truth Commission to provide an official accounting of the abuses of the prior twelve years, a restructuring of the security forces to neutralize some of the most abusive agencies, and a purging from the army of those who had been responsible for gross abuses.[35]

The record of the UNPROFOR in Croatia and Bosnia-Herzegovina, 1992–5 stands in sharp contrast to the achievements of the El Salvador mission, and illustrates how catastrophic the failure can be to coordinate justice and peace.[36]

The basic problem is well-summarized by the title of a document dedicated to appraising the record of UNPROFOR: *With No Peace to Keep....*[37] The mission was to involve an international and neutral group of ground troops under UN auspices with several open-ended humanitarian and human rights objectives. Its mandate was based on specific consensual arrangements worked out among the belligerents, but in a setting where no overall peace agreement had been accepted. On the one hand, the mission reflected some of the features of second-generation missions, in particular the commitment to providing minimal justice, especially for the victims of war. On the other hand, the absence of a general political settlement, together with the fact that the mission had to function in the midst of ongoing and intensely violent conflict without any clear indication of where or under what terms it might employ force, or how it might contribute to overall peace, condemned the operation from the beginning.

The sad story of Tadeusz Mazowiecki, Poland's first post-communist Prime Minister, and UN Special Rapporteur for Human Rights in former

---

[35] *Improvising History: A Critical Evaluation of the UN Observer Mission in El Salvador: A Report of the Lawyers Committee for Human Rights* (New York, Dec. 1995), 2.

[36] See David Little, 'Protecting Human Rights During and After Conflict: The Role of the United Nations', *Tulsa Journal of Comparative and International Law*, 4/1 (1996), 87–97, for a comparative discussion of UN peacekeeping operations in El Salvador and Bosnia.

[37] Ben Cohen and George Stamkowski (eds.), *With No Peace to Keep* (London: Greenpress, 1995).

Yugosalvia, illustrates the problem. He was a dedicated, conscientious, and honourable figure, thoroughly committed to upholding human rights. Mazowiecki produced forthright, unflinching reports, and as early as August 1992, and repeatedly thereafter, he demanded forceful, effective measures for protecting the victims of the war. Some of these were eventually adopted as Security Council Resolutions, but several of them were never implemented. They were all, we should take special note, related in one way or another to enforcing what we referred to earlier as the antiterror rule.

One proposal was that pressure be put on military authorities to discontinue the policies of ethnic cleansing; another was that detention camps be dismantled, prisoners freed, and perpetrators of atrocities brought to justice. A third was that 'safe areas' be created for protecting refugees, which culminated in Security Council Resolution 836, issued in June 1993. The wording of the Resolution to so designate Srebrenica, Zepa, and other now-famous centres is arresting: 'to enable UNPROFOR to take all necessary measures, including the use of force, to deter attacks, monitor ceasefire, [and] promote withdrawal of military units... in and around the safe areas'. As it began to appear, to Mazowiecki's horror, that safe areas might be transformed from protected locations into slaughterhouses, he appealed urgently to the Secretary-General to send troops—to no avail, as we know. What was intended to provide protection from terror became instead a vehicle for terror.

4. PEACEMAKING

Peacemaking may generally be defined as the process of sustained interaction by which hostile parties are brought to agree upon a peace settlement. Conventionally understood, the process of interaction is a diplomatic one, in the sense that it is undertaken by official representatives of the relevant parties, perhaps in the presence and with the assistance of third party officials, whether of other governments or international institutions. This process has become known as Track I peacemaking.

Nevertheless, particularly in recent years, Track II peacemaking, which may in a variety of ways create a supportive and encouraging environment in which Track I diplomacy may effectively proceed. It is particularly in this second setting where religious individuals and groups have begun to play a significant role in facilitating peace settlements. In a comprehensive treatment, we would need to review some important examples of Track II diplomacy, including cases involving religious influence, in order to illustrate the importance of this new element among the effective instruments in the pursuit of peace.[38] Here, however, we may simply summarize the conclusions of some recent studies regarding the conditions of what are essentially successful Track I peace settlements. Of special interest to us is the significant connection that appears to obtain between justice and peace in the process of crafting peace agreements. At the end of this section, we shall give one example of a distinctive religious contribution to accommodating justice and peace in the context of official peacemaking.

The first such study is written by Fen Osler Hampson, *Nurturing Peace: Why Peace Settlements Succeed or Fail.*[39] Having reviewed five peace agreements—Cyprus, Namibia, Angola, El Salvador, and Cambodia—Hampson admits that 'peace and justice do not always work in tandem'.[40] Efforts to develop 'power-sharing structures that accommodate rival factions and interests' do not necessarily coincide with strong commitments, also evident, 'to root out the perpetrators of human rights abuses'. Similarly, provisions for reforming the police and the military in a peacemaking setting may conflict with need to attract to the negotiating table officials, or their representatives, who have a strong vested interest in those very institutions. 'The evidence suggests that a concern for justice must be tempered by the realities of negotiation and the parties' interests in reaching a political settlement.'[41]

Still, Hampson also concludes that while compromise is always part of the picture, considerations of justice may never altogether be excluded from a successful peacemaking process. Two of the specific requirements for a peace settlement he recommends make that clear. Both point to the indispensability of *procedural justice*: 'First,' he says, 'it is absolutely essential that all the warring parties have a seat at the negotiating table and are directly involved in discussions about the new constitutional and political order that will be created after the fighting stops. A "good" agreement is one that has been crafted by all parties to the conflict.'[42] If this rule is ignored, excluded parties will be disposed to undermine the agreement, in some cases by resorting to violence. As an example, Hampson cites the unhappy consequences of excluding the Greek and Turkish Cypriots from the 1960 Cyprus Constitutional Accords.

---

[38] See Douglas Johnston and Cynthia Sampson (eds.), *The Missing Dimension of Statecraft* (New York: Oxford University Press, 1994), which contains several examples of the role of religious actors in making peace.
[39] Fen O. Hampson, *Nurturing Peace: Why Peace Settlements Succeed or Fail* (Washington, DC: United States Institute of Peace, 1996).
[40] Ibid., 230.
[41] Ibid.
[42] Ibid., 213.

According to Hampson, a second feature of a good agreement is assuring that after elections both winners and losers share power. Failure of that score is one reason, he says, that the 1992 Angola agreements collapsed. In the case of the Cambodian agreements, by contrast, the parties understood from the beginning that it would be necessary to include rival factions in a coalition government if national reconciliation were to be achieved.[43] If power-sharing arrangements cannot be worked out, there must at a minimum be provision for equal access to the political process by groups formerly excluded. 'The new rules about political competition must...be seen as fair and just.'[44]

A third requirement is providing for third-party participation, especially during the implementation phase of the settlement process. Third parties can play a number of crucial supporting roles, but one to which Hampson gives special emphasis is a contribution to 'promoting new norms and codes of conduct, particularly in the area of human rights'.[45] Despite all the interim problems of adjusting vested interests with the claims of human rights, 'if a social order based on the rule of law and accepted principles of justice is to be fashioned, respect for human rights and due process must be nurtured.'[46] In short, 'without justice, democratic institutions, and the development of the rule of law, the peace itself will not last.'[47]

A second work of importance for the tasks of peacemaking is *Peoples versus States: Minorities at Risk in the New Century* by Ted Robert Gurr.[48] The conclusions of Gurr and his associates are rather surprising.[49] Globally considered, the conventional belief that ethnonational conflict is on the rise, and that governments at both national and international level are losing control of civil violence, appears to be mistaken. Since around 1995, 'more effective international and domestic strategies for managing ethnopolitical conflict' and majority–minority relations have been developed. This trend, extensively documented throughout the volume, is described as a 'global shift from ethnic warfare to the politics of accommodation'. Among the 275 minorities studied, more and more of them are turning to participatory politics and abandoning armed violence, thereby reversing a long-standing pattern.

Although the decline in the number of groups engaged in violent conflict was not particularly striking during the 1990s, there was a significant decrease

[43] Hampson, *Nurturing Peace*, 218.
[44] Ibid.
[45] Ibid., 229.
[46] Ibid.
[47] Ibid., 230.
[48] Ted R. Gurr, *Peoples versus States: Minorities at Risk in the New Century* (Washington, DC: United States Institute of Peace Press, 2000).
[49] Ibid., 275–7.

in the level of violence in a large number of cases. Moreover, very few new ethnopolitical conflicts occurred after 1994, and secessionist wars declined sharply. On the basis of this encouraging news, Gurr states that it is 'not only ethnic conflict that spreads by example; the successes of conflict management also are contagious....'

Of special interest is the conclusion that during the 1990s new, more accommodating state policies had the effect of reducing cultural and political discrimination against minorities, particularly in Europe, Asia, and Latin America. In this regard, Gurr identifies three principles that comprise what he calls an 'emerging regime of managed heterogeneity':

'The first and most basic' is 'the recognition and active protection of the rights of minority peoples: freedom from discrimination based on race, national origin, language, or religion, complemented by institutional means to protect and promote collective interests'. This principle implies 'the right of national peoples to exercise some degree of autonomy within existing states to govern their own affairs',[50] and, according to Gurr, it has been signalled by the recent movement in human-rights thinking from exclusive concern with individual rights to the protection of group rights, enunciated with special force in the documents of the Organization of Security and Cooperation in Europe.[51]

Gurr admits it is easier to implement the principle of non-discrimination on a national basis than it is a scheme of 'substate autonomy', both because central authorities tend to resist devolution of power, and because of the difficulties of working out mutually-agreeable arrangements. Still, armed rebellions in a large number of cases have been significantly modified or pacified by autonomy agreements, mainly concluded in the 1990s, as, for example, in Northern Ireland, Moldova, Nicaragua, Burma, Bosnia, Ethiopia, and Bangladesh.[52]

Second, political democracy, 'in one of its European variants', is 'widely recognized as the most reliable guarantee of minority rights'. 'It is inherent in the logic of democratic politics that all peoples in heterogeneous societies should have equal civil and political rights. Democratic governance also implies acceptance of peaceful means for resolving civil conflicts.'[53] By a

---

[50] Ibid., 278.

[51] See, in particular, 'Document of the Copenhagen Meeting of the Conference on the Human Dimension of the CSCE' (Copenhagen, 29 June 1990), arts. 30–41, in *Documents of the Human Dimension of the OSCE*, prepared by Dominick McGoldrick (Warsaw, 1995).

[52] Gurr, op. cit., 196–206.

[53] Ibid., 279. Gurr's discussion of political democracy in regard to the tasks of peacemaking turns out to contain some inconsistencies and perplexities. That is, some of the details of Gurr's discussion of the role of democracy in peacemaking, would lead one to modify, though not reject, this second principle. We shall not take up these complexities here. See David Little, 'State Structure and Conflict in Multiethnic Societies: Reflections on Recent Data', unpublished paper. Cf. Jack Snyder, *From Voting to Violence* (New York W.W. Norton, 2000).

ratio of 20 to 7, according to Gurr, democratic governments have been particularly successful in working out negotiated settlements.[54]

Third, 'disputes between [ethnic] groups and states are best settled by negotiation and mutual accommodation'.[55] In the chapter entitled, 'Challenge of Resolving Ethnonational Conflicts', Gurr concludes:

Two-thirds of negotiated settlements of ethnopolitical wars in the past forty years have been concluded since the end of the Cold War. . . . Since 1990, . . . settlements have ended or led to de-escalation of sixteen wars. This remarkable post-Cold War shift towards reliance on negotiations to settle separatist conflicts is consistent with other researchers' findings that ever-larger numbers of civil wars of all kinds are being terminated at the negotiating table.[56]

One of the most interesting features of the growing attraction of nego-tiated settlements is, according to Gurr, the international connection. The findings indicate that major powers, as well as international and regional organizations, by employing various combinations of diplomacy, medi-ation, inducements, and threats, have contributed significantly to the reso-lution or management of ethnic conflict.[57] International actors also make an important contribution, according to Gurr, to strengthening the other two principles, the protection of collective rights, and the promotion of political democracy.[58]

Despite the overall positive tone of *Peoples versus States*, Gurr is sensitive to the remaining challenges and obstacles to promoting the peaceful manage-ment of ethnic heterogeneity. He points to 'a number of protracted ethno-political conflicts' that are 'highly resistant to regional and international influence', such as Afghanistan and Sudan, or the conflict between the Kurds and Turkey and Iraq, or the containment of the tension between the Hutus and Tutsis in Rwanda and Burundi.[59] While the best prospects for diminishing risk are in much of Europe, and in Latin and North America, places like the Balkans, Nagorno-Karabakh, and Chechnya continue to be high-risk areas, as do parts of the Middle East and South Asia, including Kashmir, Pakistan, and Sri Lanka.[60] Also, 'Africa's situation is most grave'. Twenty African groups are, says Gurr, 'at medium to high risk of future rebellion', including Nigeria.[61] But in his last words, Gurr offers a prescription based on his overall positive reading: 'No one strategy is likely to contain deep-rooted communal conflicts in Central Africa or any other high-risk regions. What is needed is coordinated effort by international actors and major powers to facilitate negotiated settlements, guarantee local and

---

[54] Gurr, op. cit., 204.   [55] Ibid., 279.
[56] Ibid., 204; see Table 6.1, 198–202, for examples.   [57] Ibid., 287.
[58] Ibid., 176, 177, 280.   [59] Ibid., 282.   [60] Ibid., 286.   [61] Ibid.

regional security, promote democratic power-sharing, and assist economic development.'[62]

Along with other international actors, both governmental and non-governmental, mentioned by Gurr, it is evident that religious individuals and groups can also play an important supplementary role in official peace-making. A striking example is the important contribution to the resolution of the civil war in Mozambique in 1992 by the Rome-based lay Catholic group known as St Egidio.[63] Working with a leading Mozambican Catholic official, who was able to establish his bona fides with warring parties, and eventually help to mediate the dispute, members of St Egidio provided, over a two-year period, a setting of trust, respect, and dependability, in which the parties gradually came to reduce their mutual hostility and suspicion. They also helped the negotiations to move towards and sustain a rather remarkable degree of 'forgiveness and reconciliation' on the part of participants and the groups they represented. '[T]he political character of the peace process was not transformed by the presence of religious elements, but simply enriched by them. A religious contribution made the political discourse more flexible and able to respond to the increased complexity of the process.' On the basis of this example, it appears that religious peacemaking 'needs to be conceived as a contribution to a larger political process to which both religious and non-religious elements contribute'.[64]

5. PEACEBUILDING

It is clear from the Hampson and Gurr books that peacemaking, the process of sustained interaction by which hostile parties are brought to a peace settlement, is interconnected in an important way with what is called peace-building, the design and creation over time of practices and institutions capable of replacing the conditions of hostility and violence with social harmony and civil unity. Their books lay special emphasis on the cultivation of human rights practices and institutions as crucial for the achievement of

---

[62] Ibid., 288.

[63] See Andrea Bartoli, 'Forgiveness and Reconciliation in the Mozambique Peace Process', in Raymond G. Helmick, S. J. and Rodney L. Petersen (eds.), *Forgiveness and Reconciliation* (Philadelphia PA: Templeton Foundation Press, 2001), 361–81. Cf. Cameron Hume, *Ending Mozambique's War: The Role of Mediation and Good Offices* (Washington, DC: United States Institute of Peace Press, 1994), for a discussion of the role of the lay Catholic group, St Egidio, in facilitating peace in Mozambique.

[64] Ibid., 262.

successful and lasting peace treaties. Another book that elaborates on the interconnection of peacemaking and peacebuilding, particularly in connection with the development of human rights institutions, is Christine Bell's recent study, *Peace Agreements and Human Rights.*[65]

Bell's study arrives at a number of important conclusions as regards peacemaking and peacebuilding, including new thinking concerning the idea of self-determination, and the role of international law and the international community in the achievement of peace. For our purposes, however, her reflections on human rights and peace are especially interesting.

She provides a comparative analysis of recent efforts at peacemaking in four cases of ethnically based conflict: South Africa, Northern Ireland, Bosnia-Herzegovina, and Israel–Palestine. While, according to Bell, the agreement worked out in each case is far from perfect or free from continuing difficulty, she nevertheless believes they can be ranked as to their relative success, and that in the order just listed. Generally speaking, what turns out to be a critical determinant of success, on Bell's account, is the kind of provision made for human rights considerations.

First, the relation between individuals and groups, and how their respective rights and interests are articulated and guaranteed, appears as a key factor in achieving a successful 'deal' (in Bell's language).[66] In all four of the cases, the arrangements incorporate both the mechanisms and language of both democracy and group rights, but they coordinate and balance them in different ways. In South Africa and Northern Ireland, individual rights, guaranteed equally to all members of the political community, precede concessions to group interest. In Bosnia and Israel–Palestine, group interest outweighs individual protections, and comprehensive individual rights guarantees are either ignored, as with Israel–Palestine, or are 'left to the feeble institutions of an emaciated common sphere, whose power to enforce rights within autonomous spheres is negligible (as in Bosnia)'.[67]

In other words, individual rights, understood to extend equally to the entire population, provide common values in which all have a stake, assuming of course they are impartially enforced. Such arrangements provide a stable framework within which to accommodate special group interests and needs, as with South Africa and Northern Ireland. On the other hand, Bell suggests that the agreement between Israel and Palestine failed completely in that respect. The Oslo accord and subsequent proposals, premised as they are on separating Israelis and Palestinians territorially and politically, provide 'no

---

[65] Christine Bell, *Peace Agreements and Human Rights* (Oxford: Oxford University Press, 2000).

[66] Ibid., 189.   [67] Ibid.

reciprocal interest to see human rights [for all] instituted as part of the deal. Indeed, quite the opposite: the focus on separation provided a distinct disincentive to incorporate human rights protections within the deal'.[68]

There is, in effect, no vested interest in peacebuilding on either side, because there is no common commitment, expressed in the form of common institutions, to the enforcement of shared values applied equally to both populations. Bell concludes that the entire peace process between Israel and the Palestinians needs to be 'reimagined' so as to make it subject to 'overarching international law constraints', which would centrally include mutual human rights provisions.[69]

The case of Bosnia–Herzegovina stands somewhere in between South Africa and Northern Ireland, on the one side, and Israel–Palestine, on the other. It is an example of 'a compromise between opposing demands of separation and sharing'.[70] To an important extent, it is by means of national human rights guarantees and institutions that the Dayton Accords attempted to reverse the effects of ethnic cleansing, and thus to modify, if not eventually eliminate, the ethnic entities into which Bosnia is at present divided. The problem is that the 'formal powers of the [central] government are extremely limited'. '[T]he territorial concessions... through the devolution of power to the Entities create difficulties for the implementation and effectiveness of those human rights protections.'[71]

Second, those agreements that give attention to the role of civil society, and are in part the product of civil society participation, are more successful. This factor underscores, in Bell's mind, the importance of local or domestic involvement in peacemaking and peacebuilding, alongside international participation.

In a divided community civic society plays a crucial role in mediating the positions of political elites. It provides a space for creative thinking.... It provides an agenda which goes beyond the traditional political divisions, and so enables those traditions to be reconceived. Civic society can supplement an impoverished political sector with a narrow focus.... The peace agreements in Northern Ireland and South Africa not only deal with a broad range of rights issues,... but use the agreements to provide specific space for civic society. In so doing, they acknowledge the importance of civic society to implementation.[72]

Bell emphasizes the importance of 'internally driven' civil society efforts in regard to peacebuilding, because such efforts tend to 'preserve the link between politicians and their constituents'. In contrast to agreements

---

[68] Ibid., 196.   [69] Ibid., 205.   [70] Ibid.; cf. 203ff.

[71] Ibid., 196.   [72] Ibid., 316.

primarily arranged by international actors, domestic efforts engage 'the skills of those who have waged peace through churches, voluntary associations, women's groups, and trade unions...[thereby mobilizing] key experience and expertise in how to fashion workable mechanisms for achieving social goals....'[73]

Third, Bell characterizes the peace process in cases like the four under consideration as governed by a 'jurisprudence of transition' which requires that attention be paid simultaneously to the past and the future. The notions of justice, according to which the conditions of peace are worked out, are invariably shaped by the need both to rectify past violations, and to avoid such violations in the future.

The plight of refugees dislocated or driven from their homes by the conflict, the loss of land, possessions, and means of support, arrangement for the release of and provision for prisoners, redress for acts of abuse and mistreatment, including terrorist tactics, ethnic cleansing, torture and other grave breaches of human rights and humanitarian law, are the sorts of condition and behaviour that must be confronted and dealt with by the mechanisms of 'transitional justice'. Beyond that, legal, political, economic, and cultural institutions must eventually be 'built' that help to restore justice and discourage further injustice.

Nevertheless, this area, especially as regards to the past, is, according to Bell, particularly sensitive and difficult. It is particularly hard for post-conflict societies to confront and cope with their past. Among the case studies, South Africa made an attempt by means of its Truth and Reconciliation Commission, and Bosnia participated in the International Criminal Tribunal for the Former Yugoslavia as a way of addressing, at least in part, the violations associated with the war. On the other hand, neither Northern Ireland nor Israel–Palestine have set up any 'comprehensive "past-oriented" mechanisms', though there are some ad hoc efforts in that direction.[74]

Bell's comments, particularly her statement that without substantial consensus concerning the causes of conflict, the past can neither adequately be accounted for, nor many crucial details of a peace agreement properly implemented, points to an essential, yet highly complex, feature of peacebuilding. Is the record of past violations best addressed, and appropriate amends made, by the application of criminal, or retributive, justice, in the form of an international tribunal, as in Bosnia, or domestic proceedings, as used elsewhere? Or, should criminal proceedings be supplemented, or perhaps replaced with, other mechanisms, such as the South African Truth and

---

[73] Bell, *Peace Agreements and Human Rights*, 231.
[74] Ibid., 273.

Reconciliation Commission, which attempt to confront past violations and develop consensus regarding what happened, in a non-judicial setting. Here non-retributive measures are emphasized, such as public encounter of perpetrator and victim accompanied by acts of confession and forgiveness, the possibility of amnesty and/or reparation, all of which are sometimes defined as 'restorative justice'. Or, as another alternative, should some combination of 'retributive' and 'restorative' justice be worked out?

Though in the four cases considered, these questions were handled outside of the specific terms of the original peace agreement (South Africa and Bosnia), were dealt with in a piecemeal manner (Northern Ireland), or were virtually neglected altogether (Israel–Palestine), Bell leaves no doubt that the process of peacebuilding critically requires taking up these questions and working out a sustained and thoughtful response to them.[75]

Bell concludes her study by emphasizing the centrality of human rights provisions as a condition for the success or failure of the transition from conflict to peace in each of her four cases.

What is clear is that the ability or not of the deal to deliver on human rights commitments will significantly affect, and even determine, the nature of the transition [from violence to peace]. . . . [Even] in South Africa majority power without majority social and economic justice is unlikely to lead to stability. In Northern Ireland power-sharing without the human rights agenda is likely merely to transfer ethno-nationalist struggles to the capsule of the devolved Assembly, leaving root causes of conflicts unaddressed. In [Bosnia] the (current) failure of human rights institutions seems to point to either prolonged international involvement, or international exit and concurrent moves towards partition and instability. In Israel–Palestine the absence of human rights constraints means that it looks increasingly as if, while the actors might change, the lives of ordinary Palestinians will not.[76]

It should be added that religion has played an important role in the areas of peacemaking and peacebuilding, as is made clear in a growing literature on the subject. Religious individuals and groups, such as the Moravians, the Quakers, the Catholic Church, Moral Rearmament, along with the (Christian) Community of St Egidio, mentioned earlier, have substantially aided the process of reducing conflict and reaching agreements in places like Nicaragua, Nigeria, the Philippines, South Africa, Zimbabwe, as is detailed in *Religion: The Missing Dimension of Statecraft*.[77]

---

[75] Ibid., 285–91.   [76] Ibid., 312.

[77] Douglas Johnston and Cynthia Sampson (eds.), *Religion: The Missing Dimension of Statecraft* (New York: Oxford University Press, 1994).

The activities of religious peacebuilders, especially in advancing human rights, in promoting interfaith dialogue and collaboration in conflict settings, and in developing truth and reconciliation commissions, as, for example, in South Africa, have been documented and examined in Scott Appleby's recent volume, *The Ambivalence of the Sacred: Religion, Violence and Reconciliation.*[78] Appleby's book elaborates on themes, suggested by Christine Bell, regarding the role of religious communities (and other non-governmental organizations) in the cultivation of civil society, and of various experiments in 'reconciliation' and 'restorative justice', in South Africa and elsewhere, all as important antidotes to violent conflict.

A concrete example of the potential contribution religious communities (among others) may make to peacebuilding is the expansion of interreligious endeavours in post-war Bosnia-Herzegovina.[79] In 1997, not long after the Bosnian war ended, a new Bosnia-wide Interreligious Council was formed, consisting of leading officials from the Serbian Orthodox, Roman Catholic, Muslim, and Jewish communities. That has been followed by the creation of a widening group of local interfaith councils.

Among other things, these groups are beginning to deal in various ways, and with varying degrees of commitment, with some urgent problems such as the right of minority return, the right of property restitution, including, prominently, the rebuilding of destroyed sacred sites, and the rights of religious freedom and equality. The solution of these problems is essential to the creation of a just and peaceful society in Bosnia.

It is clear the religious communities of Bosnia-Herzegovina are not capable by themselves of building a Bosnia that is unified and tolerant of ethnic and religious difference. Local, national, and international political, and other institutions bear a huge responsibility for that task, as well. Still, there are three reasons why the subject of religion and peacebuilding in Bosnia is an important one.

First, consistent and unmistakable evidence that the religious communities, especially the Orthodox, Catholics, and Muslims, now stand resolutely on the side of interfaith cooperation and national unity based on human rights and constitutional democracy, would reverse patterns of religious nationalism that, under political and other pressures, have in recent times stimulated rather than retarded ethnocentrism, and still less have encouraged tolerance.

Second, as the result of a heritage that, under the Europeans and Ottomans, entwined religion and nation too closely or, under the Communists, set out to

---

[78] Scott Appleby, *The Ambivalence of the Sacred: Religion, Violence and Reconciliation* (New York: Rowman & Littlefield, 2000).

[79] See David Little and Kate McCann, 'Religion and Peacebuilding in Bosnia', unpublished paper.

destroy the connection altogether, there is a weak tradition of associations and organizations independent of the state of the sort that is essential for entrenching democracy and respect for human rights. The religious communities are in a unique position to help fill that void if they are able to expand and intensify the initial steps, and exploit the new opportunities.

Third, as Christine Bell has stressed, nation-building requires indigenous effort, however important international assistance may be. There is some evidence that the religious communities of Bosnia-Herzegovina are beginning to provide that effort, and that they may be capable of offsetting to some degree the spirit of ethnic nationalism that continues to retard forward motion in Bosnia-Herzegovina.

6. CONCLUSION

On inspection, the idea of Just Peace turns out to be a complex affair. Any comprehensive account will need, as we have tried to demonstrate, to take account of at least four constitutive facets of the idea, peace enforcing, peacekeeping, peacemaking, and peacebuilding. So far as the question of justice goes, each of these facets exhibits distinctive (if sometimes overlapping) characteristics of both an empirical and normative sort. It is, presumably, only when each of the distinctive problems posed by these four categories is addressed, and the responses consistently connected, that a satisfactory answer to the question, What is a Just Peace?, can be achieved.

As a step in the direction of a comprehensive answer, we have tried to show—albeit in a rather sketchy and suggestive manner—that the promotion of internationally recognized human rights provides a unifying theme, and thereby serves to connect justice and peace in a particularly compelling way.

As what we hope is an additional contribution to the discussion, we have endeavoured to hint at the pertinence as well as the diversity of religious reflection on the question of Just Peace. An implication is, that religious commentary on the various aspects of the pursuit of peace will need to be taken account of in any complete examination of the subject.

8

A Method for Thinking about Just Peace

Edward W. Said

In my opinion this is a subject that requires a series of reflections rather than a string of assertions or affirmations. I do not therefore believe that we can or should even try to produce a formula for Just Peace, in the form of the sentence 'a Just Peace is so and so'. What I propose instead is a method for thinking about Just Peace as a way of getting beyond the usually bipolar oppositions that lock collective antagonists together in conflicts that may or not be actual war. I shall assume that conflict and/or war between at least two such antagonists is what we must start with in order to think about Just Peace. At the same time, and perhaps paradoxically, I shall assume that if the conflict is profound and long enough in time—the Palestinian–Israeli one proposes itself immediately, but there are several others, many of them hitherto addressed by solutions that have offered partition as the answer (Ireland, Cyprus, India–Pakistan, the Balkans, several African states)—one should concentrate on those elements in the antagonism that are irreconcilable, basic, irremediably concrete. In other words, I think it is futile to look for a Just Peace in transcendence, synthesis, and ultimate reconciliation.

And, finally, a most important disclaimer on my part: I write these things not as a practical politician in search of results nor as a policy expert looking for new proposals to present to the parties nor as a philosopher trying to define the terms analytically, but rather as a cultural and literary historian concerned with secular ways of articulating and re-presenting experience that defy ordinary patchwork solutions because that experience by its nature is so extreme, intractable, and intransigent at its core. Most of my work has been concerned both with the history of conquest and dispossession, mostly through imperialism, and the various strategies for national, as well as cultural, emancipation and liberation that opposed empire and successfully brought about re-possession and the enfranchisement of the peoples who had been the objects of empire. In particular I have been interested in the kind of knowledge and cultural forms that have risen by these struggles, for and against conquest.

This concern I believe requires a particular care with the rhetoric and style one uses when trying to come to terms with these subjects, which because they stretch out well beyond the here and now, well beyond so-called pragmatic frameworks that underpin discussions of the what-is-to-be-done kind, well beyond the highly limited histories of the sort that create convenient narratives for action and choice based on simple binary oppositions (us-versus-them), require more deliberation, more care in rendering different views together. Elsewhere, in *Culture and Imperialism*, mainly, I have discussed this style and called it contrapuntal, that is, trying to render some sense both of a longer and wider view and also the reality of simultaneous voices.[1] This is not so much a matter of hesitation and qualification as it is of trying to break out of the mould maintaining the classic oppositions that provoke war and, alas, have underwritten notions of what peace is possible, notions in which a Just Peace is simply the mirror image of what 'we' think a just war is. Can one break out of that instrumental style of thought which, in my opinion, was one of the flaws in the America–Israeli vision of peace via the Oslo process?

Justice and peace are inherently, indeed irreducibly positive in what they suggest separately and of course even more so when they are used together. It would be hard to imagine anyone for whom the notion of Just Peace in a world where injustice and conflict are so prevalent is not in itself desirable. And yet the questions how and in what circumstances a Just Peace could take hold surround the notion forbiddingly with such a number of qualifications and circumstances as to make the phrase 'Just Peace' nearly impossible to use with any kind of universal consistency. At closer range, however, there is no doubt, for instance, that a people whose basic rights to self-determination have not been realized because they are under military or imperial occupation and who have struggled to achieve self-determination for many years, have a right in principle to the peace that comes as a result of liberation. It is hard to fault that as a statement of what a Just Peace might entail. But what is also entailed is perhaps greater suffering, more destruction, more distortion and a whole lot of problems associated with an aggrieved nationalism ready to exact a very high price from its enemy and its internal opponents in order to achieve justice and peace. The cases of Algeria and the Congo are stark evidence of what I mean, the colonial distortion giving rise to later post-colonial distortions that multiply the horror of the initial situation. These too must be figured out.

Still, concrete circumstances, and the historical setting are very important here, especially since, as I use the word secular, I am referring neither to an

---

[1] Edward W. Said, *Culture and Imperialism* (New York: Vintage Books, 1994).

ultimate condition that develops redemptively or because of revelation, nor to miraculous conversions of swords into ploughshares. These may be wonderfully attractive to long for, but they pertain to another realm entirely, that of revelation, divine or sacred truth against which, following Vico, the historical, secular world made by human labour is set. It is this historical world that I am talking about, not the mysterious or inaccessible (to me, at least) one of religion or that of nature. To try to establish an order in which, as Blake put it, the lion and the lamb shall lie down together, and to try to impose on it a real conflict, seems to me a form of what Adorno sarcastically once called a kind of extorted reconciliation that is very much what religious politics (Judaic, Christian, Islamic, Sikh, Hindu, etc.) has always been propagating. For all sorts of reasons, many of them obvious enough now, my inclination is to shun the blandishments of religious solutions particularly in cases where religion already plays a role in fomenting and deepening conflict. I do not say that religion is not important, but I do say that it must be treated as a special exacerbated aspect of secularism.

On the other hand it must be underlined that, as Edward Thompson once argued when in the late 1920s he set about describing why Indians took offence at the tone and content of such monuments of scholarship as the *Oxford History of India*, great and disproportionate power inflects, imprints, conditions any thought about peace and justice usually in very insidious and sometimes invisible ways.[2] Contrast for example writings about the Irish troubles in nineteenth-century British prose and that of Irish writers. There is in the former instance a loftiness, even an Olympian quality to the tone that derives from a history of holding power, and that allows in the prose of Lloyd George during the negotiations of 1921–2 a sense in his Irish antagonists of an outraged feeling that he was 'playing with phrases' while they were desperately pressing their case for liberation.

This disparity in arguing about the terms of a Just Peace is not surprising at all: England had invaded Ireland in 1172 and for those 750 years had accustomed itself to seeing Irish people as savages deserving death or permanent servitude. Literature, philosophy, history, political theory took it for granted that Ireland's place was subordinate, a view that was supported by all sorts of ideas about the Irish nature, the language and temperament of its people, the character of the British overlords, the community of settlement (the so-called ascendancy), and so on. When as a result of years of insurrection and great emancipatory achievements by the Irish liberation movement that undermined British rule in Ireland, negotiations for peace finally took place between Sinn Fein and the British Government in 1921 (described memorably

---

[2] Edward Thompson, *The Other Side of the Medal* (Westport, CT: Greenwood Press, 1974).

in Frank Pakenham's book *Peace by Ordeal*[3]) the position of each side varied accordingly. The British were all principle and tradition and administration, the Irish were negotiating with passionate urgency over the recovery of their land, an actuality behind which lay years of suffering, poverty, dispossession, forced settlement, famine, and the like.

A Just Peace must necessarily reflect these differences, all of them based on actual but widely divergent experiences, and this is one reason why a Just Peace which in its meaning suggests the stability of something finally achieved is a contradictory or at least a very fluid, rather than a stable, concept. A Just Peace does not bring quiet and the end of history at all, but rather a new dynamic which I want to discuss later. For the time being I would like to stress that all modern wars are fought over territory, not ideas or values or civilizational projects, as has been quite incredibly argued by recent policymakers in the USA and Europe. So I want to suggest that the geographical element is basic in that claims for sovereignty, ownership, dominance, hegemony made by one side against another, both before and after the Peace of Westphalia, run through the conflicts that concern me here, even though it is also true first that such claims are not always pressed in those terms alone, and second, that in many instances (Ireland's being one) imperial partition postpones peace as the ownership of land remains unsettled.

In the Irish case, for example, British politicians from the seventeenth century on conceived of the British role in Ireland as bringing civility to the place by way of plantation, and a return to the old English way of doing things that had been stopped by a barbaric Gaelic wave. For Irish nationalists the land was to be regained from all sorts of entailments placed on it, whether by usurpation, conquest, or economic exploitation: the best image for the experience is Maria Edgeworth's remarkable early nineteenth century short novel *Castle Rackrent*.[4] By the end of the nineteenth-century Irish republicanism had evolved an entire culture of reconquest, whereby the Anglicization of the land (dramatized in Brian Friel's play *Translations*[5]) was to be reversed, and a new Ireland, depicted in the great works of the Irish literary renaissance, brought forth a new post-imperial geography. It is not surprising therefore that in its opening sentences the Irish constitution of 1919 speaks of ownership of all the land of Ireland by the Irish people, at the very moment that Ireland is being partitioned into Eire and Northern Ireland.

To recapitulate briefly: a Just Peace pertains to the secular historical domain, that is, it is the result of human labour. Second, the process for peace

---

[3] Frank Pakenham, *Peace by Ordeal: An Account from First Hand Sources, of the Negociation and Signature of the Anglo-Irish Treaty, 1921* (Cork: The Mercier Press, 1951).

[4] Maria Edgeworth, *Castle Rackrent* (Oxford: Oxford University Press, 1969).

[5] Brian Friel, *Translations* (London and Boston: Faber & Faber, 1981).

takes place on and over the ownership and disposition of territory which—
and this is very important, I think—is imagined in different ways by the
antagonists. Why? Because territory is depicted as the culmination or the
stage for the enactment of collective histories. During the era of high imperialism, for instance, Britain's destiny as a nation was imagined as the result of a
native genius for overseas colonial expansion, in which education, trade,
administration and even scholarship were seen as taking place in distant
locations, over and above the wishes of the native inhabitants. Hence the
colonization of South (and Southeast) Asia—India, West, and South Africa,
the Middle East, North America, Australia, Ireland. And this in turn produces
counternarratives of nationalist resistance, that I have described in my book
Culture and Imperialism,[6] narratives whose logic was intended to dislodge one
presence with another. The various processes of handing over from the British
to the local nationalist authority, as in India on August 14, 1947, do not
necessarily fall into the category of a Just Peace because the partition of India,
the subsequent disturbances, the feelings of loss and betrayal all round
detracted from universal feelings of satisfaction and fulfilment, although
retrospectively—as in post-apartheid South Africa—the emergence of a
multicultural Indian society, and the emergence also of new discourses in
revisionary historiographies of Britain and India (e.g. the rise of cultural and
post-colonial studies in Britain, in India of Subaltern Studies) seems to have
mitigated the damage of partition and colonial failure and produced currents
of thought that have escaped the old binary oppositions, but at the same time
introduced new ones. This may be inevitable.

In all sorts of ways, the Palestinian–Israeli impasse is in part a confirmation,
in part an exception to what I have been saying. I might as well begin with my
own experience of 1948, and what it meant for many of the people around me,
since the *actual* experience of real Palestinians is at the very core of what I am
trying to discuss here. I talk about this at some length in my memoir *Out of
Place*.[7] My own immediate family was spared the worst ravages of the catastrophe: we had a house and my father a business in Cairo, so even though we
were in Palestine during most of 1947 when we left in December of that year,
the wrenching, cataclysmic quality of the collective experience (when 780,000
civilian Palestinians, literally two-thirds of the country's population, were
driven out by Zionist troops and design) was not one we had to go through. I
was twelve at the time so had only a somewhat attenuated and certainly no
more than a semi-conscious awareness of what was happening; only this
narrow awareness was available to me, but I do distinctly recall some things

---

[6] Said, op. cit.
[7] Edward W. Said, *Out of Place: A Memoir* (New York: A. A. Knopf, 1999).

with special lucidity. One was that every member of my family on both sides became a refugee during the period; no one remained in our Palestine, that is, that part of the territory (controlled by the British Mandate) that did not include the West Bank which was annexed to Jordan. Therefore, those of my relatives who lived in Jaffa, Safad, Haifa, and West Jerusalem were suddenly made homeless, in many instances penniless, disoriented, and scarred forever.

I saw most of them again after the fall of Palestine but all were greatly reduced in circumstances, their faces stark with worry, ill health, despair. My extended family lost all its property and residences, and like so many Palestinians of the time bore the travail not so much as a political but as a natural tragedy. This etched itself on my memory with lasting results, mostly because of the faces which I had once remembered as content and at ease, but which were now lined with the cares of exile and homelessness. Many families and individuals had their lives broken, their spirits drained, their composure destroyed forever in the context of seemingly unending, serial dislocation: this was and still is for me of the greatest poignancy. One of my maternal uncles went from Palestine to Alexandria to Cairo to Baghdad to Beirut and now in his eighties lives, a sad, silent man, in Seattle. Neither he nor his immediate family ever fully recovered. This is emblematic of the larger story of loss and dispossession, which continues today.

The second thing I recall was that for the one person in my family who somehow managed to pull herself together in the aftermath of the *nakba*, my paternal aunt, a middle-aged widow with some financial means, Palestine meant service to the unfortunate refugees, many thousands of whom ended up penniless, jobless, destitute and disoriented in Egypt. She devoted her life to them in the face of government obduracy and sadistic indifference. I have described her more fully in my memoir *Out of Place*.[8] From her I learnt that everyone was willing to pay lip service to the cause, but only very few were willing to do anything about it. As a Palestinian, therefore, she took it as her lifelong duty to set about helping the refugees—getting their children into schools, cajoling doctors and pharmacists into giving them treatment and medicine, finding the men jobs, and above all, being there for them, a willing, sympathetic, and above all selfless presence. Without administrative or financial assistance of any kind, she remains an exemplary figure for me from my early adolescence, a person against whom my own terribly modest efforts are always measured and, alas, always found lacking. The job for us in my lifetime was to be literally unending, and because it derived from a human tragedy so profound, so unacknowledged, so extraordinary in saturating both the formal

---

[8] Ibid.

as well as the informal life of its people down to the smallest detail, it has been and will continue to need to be recalled, testified to, remedied.

For Palestinians, a vast collective feeling of injustice continues to hang over our lives with undiminished weight. If there has been one thing, one particular delinquency committed by the present group of Palestinian leaders for me, it is their supernally gifted power of forgetting: when one of them was asked recently what he felt about Ariel Sharon's accession to Israel's Foreign Ministry (well before he became prime minister), given that he was responsible for the shedding of so much Palestinian blood, this leader said blithely, 'we are prepared to forget history'—and this is a sentiment I neither can share nor, I hasten to add, easily forgive. One needs to recall by comparison Moshe Dayan's statement in 1969:

We came to this country which was already populated by Arabs, and we are establishing a Hebrew, that is a Jewish state here. In considerable areas of the country [the total area was about 6 per cent] we bought the lands from the Arabs. Jewish villages were built in the place of Arab villages, and I do not even know the names of these Arab villages, and I do not blame you, because these geography books no longer exist; not only do the books not exist, the Arab villages are not there either. Nahalal [Dayan's own village] arose in the place of Mahalul, Gevat in the place of Jibta, [Kibbutz] Sarid in the place of Haneifs and Kefar Yehoshua in the place of Tel Shaman. There is not one place built in this country that did not have a former Arab population.[9]

What also strikes me about these early Palestinian reactions is how largely unpolitical they were. For twenty years after 1948 Palestinians were immersed in the problems of everyday life with little time left over for organizing, analysing, and planning, although there were some attempts to infiltrate Israel, try some military action, write, and agitate. With the exception of the kind of work produced in Mohammed Hassanein Haykal's *Ahram* Strategic Institute, Israel to most Arabs and even to Palestinians was a cipher, its language unknown, its society unexplored, its people and the history of their movement largely confined to slogans, catch-all phrases, negation. We saw and experienced its behaviour towards us but it took us a long while to understand what we saw or what we experienced.

The overall tendency throughout the Arab world was to think of military solutions to that scarcely imaginable country, with the result that a vast militarization overtook every society almost without exception in the Arab world; coups succeeded each other more or less unceasingly and, worse yet, every advance in the military idea brought an equal and opposite diminution in social, political, and economic democracy. Looking back on it now, the rise to hegemony of Arab nationalism allowed for very little in the way of

[9] Haaretz, 4 April 1969.

democratic civil institutions, mainly because the language and concepts of that nationalism itself devoted little attention to the role of democracy in the evolution of those societies. Until now, the presence of a putative danger to the Arab world has engendered a permanent deferral of such things as an open press, or unpoliticized universities, or freedoms to research, travel in, and explore new realms of knowledge. No massive investment was ever made in the quality of education, despite largely successful attempts on the part of the Nasser government in Egypt as well as other Arab governments to lower the rate of illiteracy. It was thought that given the perpetual state of emergency caused by Israel, such matters, which could only be the result of long-range planning and reflection, were ill-afforded luxuries. Instead, arms procurement on a huge scale took the place of genuine human development with negative results that we live with until today. Thirty per cent of the world's arms are still bought by Arab countries today.

Along with the militarization went the wholesale persecution of communities, pre-eminently but not exclusively the Jewish ones, whose presence in our midst for generations was suddenly thought to be dangerous. Similar abuses were visited on Palestinians inside Israel, who until 1996 were ruled by the Emergency Defence Regulations first codified and applied by the British; they remain a discriminated against community, without even the status of a national minority (they exist juridically as 'non-Jews'), even though they constitute 20 per cent of Israel's population. In terms of land, budgetary support, and social status, they are woefully underprivileged and underrepresented. I know that there was an active Zionist role in stimulating unrest between the Jews of Iraq, Egypt, and elsewhere on the one hand, and the governments of those Arab countries were scarcely democratic on the other, but it seems to me to be incontestable that there was a xenophobic enthusiasm officially decreeing that these and other designated 'alien' communities had to be extracted by force from our midst. Nor was this all. In the name of military security in countries like Egypt there was a bloody minded, imponderably wasteful campaign against dissenters, mostly on the Left, but independent-minded people too whose vocation as critics and skilled men and women was brutally terminated in prisons, by fatal torture and summary executions. As one looks back at these things in the context of today, it is the immense panorama of waste and cruelty that stands out as the immediate result of the war of 1948 itself.

Along with that went a scandalously poor treatment of the refugees themselves. It is still the case, for example, that the thousands of Palestinian refugees still resident in Egypt must report to a local police station every month; vocational, educational, and social opportunities for them are curtailed, and the general sense of not belonging adheres to them despite their Arab nationality and language. In Lebanon the situation is direr still.

Almost 400,000 Palestinian refugees have had to endure not only the massacres of Sabra, Shatila, Tell el Zaatar, Dbaye and elsewhere, but have remained confined in hideous quarantine for almost two generations. They have no legal right to work in at least sixty occupations, they are not adequately covered by medical insurance, they cannot travel and return, they are objects of suspicion and dislike. In part—and I shall return to this later—they have inherited the mantle of opprobrium draped around them by the Palestinian Liberation Organization's (PLO) presence (and since 1982 its unlamented absence) there, and thus they remain in the eyes of many ordinary Lebanese a sort of house enemy to be warded off and/or punished from time to time.

A similar situation in kind, if not in degree, exists in Syria; as for Jordan, though it was (to its credit) the only country where Palestinians were given naturalized status, a visible fault line exists between the disadvantaged majority of that very large community and the Jordanian establishment for reasons that scarcely need to be spelled out here. I might add, however, that for most of these situations where Palestinian refugees exist in large groups within one or another Arab country—all of them as a direct consequence of 1948—no simple, much less elegant or just, solution exists in the foreseeable future. It is also worth asking, why it is that a destiny of confinement and isolation has been imposed on a people who quite naturally flocked to neighbouring countries when driven out of theirs, countries which everyone thought would welcome and sustain them. More or less the opposite took place, no welcome was given to them (except in Jordan) another unpleasant consequence of the original dispossession in 1948.

This now brings me to a specially significant point, namely the emergence since 1948 in both Israel and the Arab countries of a new rhetoric and political culture. For the Arabs this was heralded in such landmark books as Constantine Zurayk's *Ma 'nat al-Nakba*, the idea that because of 1948 an entirely unprecedented situation had arisen for which, again, an unprecedented state of alertness and revival was to be necessary. What I find more interesting than the emergence of a new political rhetoric or discourse—with all its formulas, prohibitions, circumlocutions, euphemisms, and sometimes empty blasts—is its total water-tightness (to coin a phrase) with regard to its opposite number. Perhaps it is true to say that this occlusion of the other has its origin in the fundamental *irreconcilability of Zionist conquest* with *Palestinian dispossession*, two antithetically opposed secular experiences related to each other, however, as cause and effect, but the developments out of that fundamental antinomy led to a separation between the two on the official level that was never absolutely real even though on a popular level there was a great deal of enthusiasm for it.

Thus we now know that Nasser, whose rhetoric was next to none in implacability and determination, was in contact with Israel through various intermediaries, as was Sadat, and of course Mubarak. This was even more true of Jordan's rulers, somewhat less so (but nevertheless the case) with Syria. I am not advancing a simple value judgement here since such disparities between rhetoric and reality are common enough in all politics, although they were cruelly wide between the negotiating and the actual on-the-ground environments of the Oslo peace process. But what I am suggesting is that a sort of orthodoxy of hypocrisy developed inside the Arab and Israeli camps that in effect fuelled and capitalized the worst aspect of each society. The tendency towards orthodoxy, uncritical repetition of received ideas, fear of innovation, one or more types of double-speak, etc. has had an extremely rich life.

I mean, in the general Arab case, that the rhetorical and military hostility towards Israel led to more, not less ignorance about it, and ultimately to the disastrous politico-military performances of the 1960s and 1970s. The cult of the army which implied that there were only military solutions to political problems was so prevalent that it overshadowed the axiom that successful military action had to derive from a motivated, bravely led, and politically integrated and educated force, and this could only issue from a citizens' society. Such a desideratum was never the case in the Arab world, and it was rarely practised or articulated. In addition, there was consolidated a nationalist culture that encouraged, rather than mitigated Arab isolation from the rest of the modern world. Israel was soon perceived not only as a Jewish but as a Western state, and as such was completely rejected even as a suitable intellectual pursuit for those who were interested in finding out about the enemy.

From that premise a number of horrendous mistakes flowed. Among those was the proposition that Israel was not a real society but a makeshift quasi-state; its citizens were there only long enough to be scared into leaving; Israel was a total chimera, a 'presumed' or 'alleged' entity, not a real state. Propaganda to this effect was crude, uninformed, ineffective. The rhetorical and cultural conflict—a real one—was displaced from the field so to speak to the world stage, and there too with the exception of the Third World, we were routed. We never mastered (or were permitted) the art of putting our case against Israel in human terms, no effective narrative was fashioned, no statistics were marshalled and employed, no spokespersons trained and refined in their work emerged. We never learnt to speak one, as opposed to several contradictory languages. Consider the very early days before and after the 1948 debacle when people like Musa al-Alami, Charles Issawi, Walid Khalidi, Albert and I think Cecil Hourani, and others like them undertook a campaign to inform the Western world, which is where Israel's main support derived from, about the Palestinian case. Now contrast those early efforts, which were soon dissipated by infighting and jealousy, with the official rhetoric of the Arab League or of any one or combination of Arab countries. These were (and alas continue to be) primitive, badly organized, and diffused, insufficiently thought through. In short, embarrassingly clumsy, especially since the human content itself, the Palestinian tragedy, was so potent, and the Zionist argument and plan vis-à-vis the Palestinians so outrageous. I do not want to waste any time here giving examples of what those from my generation already know too well.

By impressive contrast, the Israeli system of information was for the most part successful, professional, and in the West, more or less all-conquering. It was buttressed in parts of the world like Africa and Asia with the export of agricultural, technological, and academic expertise, something the Arabs never really got into. That what the Israelis put out was a tissue of ideological, incomplete, or half-truths is less important than that as a confection it served the purpose of promoting a cause, an image, and an idea about Israel that both shut out the Arabs and in many ways disgraced them.

Looking back on it now, the rhetorical conflict that derived from and was a consequence of 1948 was amplified well beyond anything like it anywhere else in the world. To forget or ban it from consideration of what a Just Peace might be is a mistake, because even in 2001, most of the developed world sees Arabs through Israel's eyes. For part of the time, the rhetorical conflict took on some of the vehemence and prominence of the Cold War which framed it for almost thirty years. What was strange about it is that like the events of 1948 themselves there was no real Palestinian representation at all until 1967, and the subsequent emergence and prominence of the PLO. Until then we were simply known as the Arab refugees who fled because their leaders told them to. Even after the research of Erskine Childers and Walid Khalidi utterly disputed the validity of those claims and proved the existence of Plan Dalet thirty-eight years ago, we were not to be believed.[10] Worse yet, those Palestinians who remained in Israel after 1948 acquired a singularly solitary status as Israeli Arabs, shunned by other Arabs, treated by Israeli Jews under a whip, by the military administration and, until 1966 as I said earlier, by stringent emergency laws applied and assigned to them as non-Jews. The lopsidedness of this rhetorical conflict in comparison, say, with the war between American and Japanese propagandists during the Second World War as chronicled by John Dower in his book *War Without Mercy*[11] is that Israeli misinformation,

---

[10] Erskine Childers, 'The Other Exodus', in Walid Khalidi (ed.), *From Haven to Conquest: Readings in Zionism and the Palestine Problem until 1948* (Beirut: Institute for Palestine Studies, 1971); Walid Khalidi, 'Why did the Palestinians Leave?', ibid.

[11] John Dower, *War Without Mercy: Race and Power in the Pacific War* (New York: Pantheon Books, 1986).

like the Zionist movement itself, allowed no room for an indigenous opponent, someone on the ground whose land, society, and history were simply
taken from him/her. We were largely invisible, except occasionally as *fedayin*
and terrorists or as part of the menacing Arab hordes who wanted to throttle
the young Jewish state, as the expression had it.

One of the most unfortunate aspects of this state of affairs (and this
brings me back to what I said earlier about rhetoric) is that even the word
'peace' acquired a sinister, uncomfortable meaning for many Arabs, at just
the time that Israeli publicists used it at every opportunity. We want peace
with the Arabs, they would say, and, sure enough, the echo went around that
Israel fervently desired peace, while the Arabs—who were represented as
ferocious, vengeful, gratuitously bent on violence—did not. In fact, what
was at issue between Israelis and Palestinians was never a real or a Just Peace
but the possibility for Palestinians of restitution of property, nationhood,
identity—all of them blotted out by the new Jewish state, and this was never
even talked about. Moreover, it appeared to Palestinians that peace with
Israel was a form of exterminism that left us without political existence: it
meant accepting as definitive and unappealable the events of 1948, the loss
of our society and homeland. So even more alienated from Israel and
everything it stood for, the whole idea of separation between the two peoples
acquired a life of its own, though it meant different things for each. Israelis
wanted it in order to live in a purely Jewish state, freed from its non-Jewish
residents both in memory and in actuality. Palestinians wanted it as a
method for getting back to their original existence as the Arab possessors
of Palestine. The logic of separation has operated since 1948 as a persistent
motif and has now reached its apogee and its logical conclusion in the
hopelessly skewed, unworkable and—now since 29 September 2000—the
terminated Oslo accords. At only the very rarest of moments did either
Palestinians or Israelis try to think their histories and cultures—inextricably
linked for better or for worse—together, contrapuntally, in symbiotic, rather
than mutually exclusive terms. The sheer distortion in views both of history
and of the future that has resulted is breathtaking and requires some
example and analysis here.

I do not think that anyone can honestly disagree that since 1948 the
Palestinians have been the victims, Israelis the victors. No matter how much
one tries to dress up or prettify this rather bleak formulation, its truth shines
through the murk just the same. The general argument from Israel and its
supporters has been that the Palestinians brought it on themselves: why did
they leave? Why did the Arabs declare war? Why did they not accept the 1947
plan of partition? And so on and so forth. None of this, it should be clear,
justifies Israel's subsequent official behaviour both towards itself and its

Palestinian victims, where a hard cruelty, a dehumanizing attitude, and an almost sadistic severity in putting down the Palestinians has prevailed over all the years, rarely more so than in recent months. The frequently expressed Israeli and general Jewish feeling, that Israel is in serious peril and that Jews will always be targets of anti-Semitic opportunity, is often buttressed by appeals to the Holocaust, to centuries of Christian anti-Semitism, and to Jewish exile. This is a potent and in many ways justifiable sentiment.

I have gone on record in the Arab world as saying that *it is* justified for Jews—even for American Jews whose experiences have been nowhere near as traumatic as their European counterparts—to feel the agonies of the holocaust as their own, even unto the present, but I keep asking myself whether the use of that feeling to keep Palestinians in more or less permanent submission can repeatedly be justified on those grounds alone. And are the official and intemperate (to say the least) harangues about Israeli security justified, given what a miserable lot has been the Palestinians'? Are the huge numbers of soldiers, the obsessive, excessive measures about terrorism (the meandering and profligate significations of which require a treatise of their own), the endless fencing in, the interrogations, the legal justification of torture for many years, the nuclear, biological, and chemical options, the discriminations against Israeli Palestinians, the fear and contempt, the bellicosity—one could go on and on—are all these things not a sort of massive distortion in perception and mode of life, all of them premised on and fuelled by the extreme separatist, not to say xenophobic sentiment that Israel must be, must remain at all costs an endangered, isolated, unloved Jewish state? And that its strength is derived falsely from its unwillingness to examine or reflect candidly on its past and to accord Palestinians the right to remember *their* catastrophe as the essential feature of their collective experience. Does not one have the impression that the language and discourse of Israel—there are exceptions of course—generally signify a refusal to engage with the common regional history except on these extreme separatist terms?

Here is Adorno discussing in the *Minima Moralia* distortions of language in the dominated and the dominating:

The language of the dominant turns against the masters, who misuse it to command, by seeking to command them, and refuses to serve their interests. The language of the subjected, on the other hand, domination alone has stamped, so robbing them further of the justice promised by the unmutilated, autonomous word to all those free enough to pronounce it without rancour. Proletarian language is dictated by hunger. The poor chew words to fill their bellies. From the objective spirit of language they expect the sustenance refused them by society; those whose mouths are full of words have nothing else between their teeth. So they take revenge on language. Being forbidden to love it, they maim the body of language, and so repeat in impotent strength the disfigurement inflicted on them.[12]

The compelling quality of this passage is the imagery of distortion inflicted on language, repeated, reproduced, turning inwards, unable to provide sustenance. And so it seems to me has been the interplay since 1948 between the official discourses of Zionism and Palestinian nationalism, the former dominating but in the process twisting language to serve as an endless series of misrepresentations organized around the basic binary opposition which does not serve their interests (Israel is *more* insecure today, less accepted by Arabs, more disliked and resented), the latter using language as a compensatory medium for the unfulfillment of a desperate political self-realization. For years after 1948 the Palestinians are still an absence, a desired and willed negativity in Israeli discourse, on whom various images of absence have been heaped—the nomad, the terrorist, the fellah, the Arab, the Islamic fanatic, the killer, and so forth. For Palestinians their official discourse has been full of the affirmation of presence, yet a presence mostly dialectically annulled in the terms of power politics and hence affirmed in a language like that of Darwish's poem *Sajjil Ana 'Arabi*—'I am here, take note of me'—or in the ludicrous trappings including honour guard and bagpipes of a head of state allowed himself by Yasir Arafat. Over time it is the distortions that are increased, not the amount of reality in the language.

This is a difficult point but, for my argument, central to try to express, so let me give it another formulation. The modern history of the struggle for Palestinian self-determination can be regarded as an attempt to set right the distortions in life and language inscribed so traumatically as a consequence of 1948. Certainly in religious terms, this is what Hamas and Jihad Islami promise. There has never been any shortage of secular Palestinian resistance, and while it is true that there have been some advances here and there in Palestinian struggle—the first Intifada and the invigorations provided by the PLO before 1991 being two of the most notable—the general movement either has been much slower than that of Zionism, or it has been regressive. Where the struggle over land has been concerned there has been a net loss, as Israel through belligerent as well as pacific means has asserted its actual hold on more and more of Palestinian land. I speak here of course of sovereignty, military power, actual settlement. I contrast that with what I shall call Palestinian symptoms of response, such as the multiple rhetorical attempts to assert the existence of a Palestinian state, to bargain with Israel over conditions of Israeli (and not Palestinian) security, and the general untidiness,

---

[12] Theodor Adorno, *Minima Moralia: Reflections from a Damaged Life*, trans. E. F. N. Jephcott (London: New Left, 1974), 102.

sloppiness, and carelessness—absence of preparations, maps, files, facts and figures among Palestinian negotiators in the Oslo process—that have characterized what can only be called a lack of ultimate seriousness in dealing with the real, as opposed to the rhetorical, conditions of dispossession. These, as I said earlier, multiply the distortions stemming from the original condition of loss and dispossession: rather than rectifications they offer additional dislocations and the reproduction of distortions whose widening effects extent the whole range, from war, to increasing numbers of refugees, more property abandoned and taken, more frustration, more anger, more humiliation, more corruption and cruelty, and so on. From all this derives the force of Rosemary Sayigh's startlingly appropriate, and even shattering phrase, 'too many enemies'[13]—the poignancy is that Palestinians, by a further dialectical transformation, have even become their own enemies through unsuccessful and self-inflicted violence.

For Israel and its supporters—especially its Western liberal supporters—none of this has mattered very much, even though the encomia to Israel and/ or a generalized embarrassed silence when Israel has indulged itself in ways normally not permitted any other country have been unrelenting. One of the main consequences of 1948 is an ironic one: as the effects of that highly productive dispossession have increased, so too the tendency has been to overlook their source, to concentrate on pragmatic, realistic, tactical responses to 'the problem' in the present. The present peace process is unthinkable without an amnesiac official abandonment, which I deplore, by the Palestinian leaders of what happened to them in 1948 and thereafter. And yet they could not be in the position they are in without that entirely concrete and minutely, intensely lived experience of loss and dispossession for which 1948 is both origin and enduring symbol. So there is an eerie dynamic by which the reliving of our mistakes and disasters comes forward collectively without the force or the lessons or even the recollection of our past. We are perpetually at the starting-point, looking for a solution now, even as that 'now' itself bears all the marks of our historical diminishment and human suffering.

In both the Israeli and Palestinian cases there is, I think, a constitutive break between the individual and the whole, which is quite striking, especially insofar as the whole is, as Adorno once put it, the false. Zeev Sternhell has shown in his historical analysis of Israel's founding narratives (*The Founding Myths of Israel*) that an idea of the collective overriding every instance of the particular was at the very heart of what he calls Israel's

---

[13] Rosemary Sayigh, *Too Many Enemies: The Palestinian Experience in Lebanon* (London: Zed Books, 1994).

nationalist socialism.[14] The Zionist enterprise he says was one of conquest and redemption of something referred to almost mystically as 'the land'. Humanly the result was a total subordination of the individual to a corporate self, presumed to be the new Jewish body, a sort of super-collective whole in which the constituent parts were insignificant compared to that whole. Many of the institutions of the state, especially the Histadrut and the land agency, over-rode anything that might smack of individualism, or of individual agency since what was always of the utmost importance was the presumed good of the whole. Thus, according to Ben Gurion, nationhood mattered more than anything else: consequently, frugality of lifestyle, self sacrifice, pioneer values were the essence of the Israeli mission. Sternhell traces out with more detail than anyone I know what sorts of complications and contradictions were entailed by this vision—how, for example, Histadrut leaders and military men got higher pay than the labourers who were, in the going phrase, conquering the wasteland, even though an ideology of complete egalitarianism (often referred to abroad as 'socialism') prevailed.

Yet this did not evolve once Israel became an independent state. 'The pioneering ideology, with its central principles—the conquest of land, the reformation of the individual, and self-realization—was not an ideology of social change; it was not an ideology that could establish a secular, liberal state and put an end to the war with the Arabs.'[15] Nor, it must be added, could it develop a notion of citizenship since it was meant to inform a state of the Jewish people, not of its individual citizens. The project of Zionism therefore was not only this entirely new modern state but, as Sternhell puts it, the very negation of the diaspora.

It would be extremely difficult to find within the parallel Arab dominant ideology or practice of the period after 1948—whether we look in the annals of Baathism, Nasserism, or general Arab nationalism—anything like a con-cerned attention paid to the notion of citizenship. Quite the contrary, there was if anything a mirror image of Zionist corporatism except that most of the ethnic and religious exclusivity of Jewish nationalism is not there. In its basic form Arab nationalism is inclusive and pluralistic generally, though like Zionism there is a quasi-messianic, quasi-apocalyptic air about the descrip-tions in its major texts (of Nasserism, Islamism, and Baathism) of revival, the new Arab individual, the emergence and birth of the new polity, and so on.

As I noted earlier, even in the emphasis on Arab unity in Nasserism one feels that a core of human individualism and agency is missing, just as in

---

[14] Zeev Sternhell, *The Founding Myth of Israel: Nationalism, Socialism, and the Making of the Jewish State*, trans. David Maisel (Princeton, NJ: Princeton University Press, 1998).

[15] Ibid., 46.

practice it is simply not part of the national programme in a time of
emergency. Now the Arab security state already well described by many
scholars, political scientists, sociologists, and intellectuals, is a nasty or sorry
thing in its aggregate, repressive, and monopolistic in its notions of state
power, coercive when it comes to issues of collective well-being. But, once
again, thunderingly silent on the whole matter of what being a citizen, and
what citizenship itself entails beyond serving the motherland and being
willing to sacrifice for the greater good. On the issue of national minorities
there are some scraps here and there of thought, but nothing in practice given
the fantastic mosaic of identities, sects, and ethnicities in the Arab world.
Most of the scholarly, scientific literature that I have read on the Arab world—
the best and most recent of which is critical and highly advanced—speaks
about clientelism, bureaucracies, patriarchal hierarchies, notables, and so on,
but spends depressingly little time talking about *muwatana* (citizenship) as a
key to the socio-political and economic morass of recession and de-develop-
ment that is now taking place. Certainly accountability is left out of the
critical picture more or less totally.

I am not the only one to have said, though, that one of the least discour-
aging consequences of 1948 is the emergence of new critical voices, here and
there, in the Israeli and Arab worlds (including diasporas) whose vision is
both critical and integrative. By that I mean such schools as the Israeli new
historians, their Arab counterparts and, among many of the younger area
studies specialists in the West, those whose work is openly revisionist and
politically engaged. Perhaps it is now possible to speak of a new cycle opening
up in which the dialectic of separation and separatism has reached a sort of
point of exhaustion, and a new process might be beginning, glimpsed here
and there within the anguished repertoire of communitarianism which by
now every reflecting Arab and every Jew somehow feels as the home of last
resort. This communitarianism is likely to be exacerbated for a while by the
terrible events of 11 September and their political and military aftermath. It is
of course true and even a truism that the system of states in the region has
done what it can do as a consequence of 1948, that is, provide what purports
to be a sort of homogenized political space for like people, for Syrians,
Jordanians, Israelis, Egyptians and so on. Palestinians have and continue to
aspire to a similar consolidation of self-hood with geography, some unity of
the nation, now dispersed, with its home territory. Yet the problem of the
Other remains, for Zionism, for Palestinian nationalism, for Arab and/or
Islamic nationalism. There is, to put it simply, an irreducible, heterogeneous
presence always to be taken account of which, since and because of 1948, has
become intractable, unwishable away, *there*. 11 September has brought this
out with alarming intensity, as Ariel Sharon justifies his policies of collective

punishment against the Palestinians by associating himself and Israel with the US campaign in Afghanistan.

How then to look to the future? How to see it, and how to work towards it, if all the schemes either of separatism or exterminism, or of going back either to the Old Testament or the Golden Age of Islam or to the pre-1948 period, simply will not do, will not work, so far as any peace, much less a Just Peace, is concerned? What I want to propose is an attempt to flesh out the emergence of a political and intellectual strategy based on Just Peace and just coexistence based on secular equality. This strategy is based on a full consciousness of what 1948 was for Palestinians and for Israelis, the point being that no bowdlerization of the past, no diminishing of its effects can possibly serve any sort of decent future. I want to suggest here the need for a new kind of grouping, one that provides a critique of ideological narratives as well as a form that is compatible with real citizenship and a real democratic politics. In the context of my opening remarks about Just Peace, what I want to discuss now is the dynamic, developing nature of Just Peace at the point where precisely most peacemaking efforts normally stop.

1. We need to think about two histories not simply separated ideologically, but together, contrapuntally. Neither Palestinian nor Israeli history at this point is a thing in itself, without the other. In so doing we will necessarily come up against the basic irreconcilability between the Zionist claim and Palestinian dispossession. The injustice done to the Palestinians is constitutive to these two histories, as is also the crucial effect of Western anti-Semitism and the Holocaust.

2. The construction of what Raymond Williams termed an emergent composite identity based on that shared or common history, irreconcilabilities, antinomies and all. What we will then have is an overlapping and necessarily unresolved consciousness of Palestine–Israel through its history, not despite it. An acknowledgement—as yet unknown in Israeli mainstream discourse—of the injustice committed against the Palestinians. Since no comparable injustice was committed against Israel by the Palestinians, none should be sought.

3. A demand for rights and institutions of common secular citizenship, not of ethnic or religious exclusivity, with its culmination first in two equal states, then in a unitary state, as well as rethinking the Law of Return and Palestinian return together. Citizenship should be based on the just solidarities of coexistence and the gradual dissolving of ethnic lines.

4. The crucial role of education with special emphasis on the Other. This is an extremely long-term project in which the diaspora/exilic and research

communities must play a central role. There are now at least two or perhaps more warring research paradigms, most if not all of them based on the lamentable clash of civilizations model, which is so misleading and constitutively bellicose: to its credit this series of interventions acknowledges the transitional state of research on Israel–Palestine, its precarious, rapidly evolving, and yet fragmentary and uneven character. The need to focus on equality and coexistence.

Ideally of course the goal is to achieve consensus by scholars and activist intellectuals that a new, synthetic paradigm might slowly emerge which would reorient the combative and divisive energies we have all had to contend with into more productive and collaborative channels. This cannot occur, I believe, without some basic agreement, a compact or entente whose outlines would have to include regarding the Other's history as valid but incomplete as usually presented, and second, admitting that despite the antinomy these histories can only continue to flow together, not apart, within a broader framework based on the notion of equality for all. This of course is a secular, and by no means a religious, goal and I believe it needs to start life by virtue of entirely secular, not religious or exclusivist, needs. Secularization requires demystification, it requires courage, it requires an irrevocably critical attitude towards self, society, and others, at the same time, keeping in mind the imperatives or principles of justice *and* peace. But it also requires a narrative of emancipation and enlightenment for all, not just for one's own community.

For those who challenge all this and call it utopian or unrealistic, my answer is a simple one: show me what else is available today as a way of thinking about and moving towards a Just Peace. Show me a scheme for separation that is not based on abridged memory, continued injustice, unmitigated conflict, apartheid. There just is not one, hence the value of what I have tried to outline here.

9

The Concept of a Just Peace, or Achieving Peace Through Recognition, Renouncement, and Rule

Pierre Allan and Alexis Keller

What is a Just Peace? It describes a process whereby peace and justice are reached together by two or more parties recognizing each others' identities, each renouncing some central demands, and each accepting to abide by common rules jointly developed. While this book has examined alternative aspects of this question, we wish to go beyond in this concluding chapter by proposing a general and synthetic concept. In Chapter 3, we underscored the limits of the liberal theory of the 'law of nations' by demonstrating how it had been devised and applied to justify the extinction or assimilation of indigenous peoples. We revealed its homogenizing legal discourse and illustrated that it was trapped in a European vision of international relations.[1] Finally, we pointed out that some thinkers were aware of the cultural diversity to be found within modern states themselves and had therefore called for the 'principle of recognition' to be used in relations between peoples. In doing so, they foreshadowed the arguments used by contemporary culturalists such as Edward Said and Bhikhu Parekh.[2] In Chapter 5, the development of an international ethical scale allowed putting the concept of Just Peace in a comparative perspective. It is neither an absence of war, nor does it stem from an imposed solution as in a Carthaginian peace. Just Peace is morally superior to 'stable peace' where no party considers the possibility of threatening force and the idea of a war stays totally outside of cognition in terms of its practice. On the other hand, Just Peace is superseded by 'positive peace'

---

[1] From this perspective, Max Weber was right to underline the close link between liberalism and European expansion. See H. H. Gerth and C. Wright Mills, *From Max Weber* (London: Routledge, 1948), especially 71–2. We owe this bibliographical reference to Richard Tuck.

[2] See Edward W. Said, *Culture and Imperialism* (New York: Knopf, 1993) and Bhikhu Parekh, 'The Poverty of Indian Political Theory', *History of Political Thought*, 13/2 (1992), 535–56.

where exploitation and 'structural violence' tend to disappear, and distributive justice enters the picture. Morally, Just Peace is also much less requiring
than the concept of Global Care. From a deontological viewpoint, Just Peace is
legitimate. From a consequentialist perspective, it solves the problem of conflict.

The ideas set out below are based on the assumption that a Just Peace
cannot be achieved by pitting the liberal belief in cultural 'neutrality' against
the culturalists' faith in the 'principle of recognition'. Liberals set great store by
state relations and generally agree to 'recognize' other cultures. They do so in
keeping with what Rawls termed 'reasonable pluralism',[3] but solely on their
own terms, according to their own world view. Recognition is only acceptable
within their own conceptual universe since it is, in their view, a universal one.[4]
Culturalists, on the other hand, argue that demands from indigenous peoples
are blotted out by traditional European thinking or mindset. In response, they
strive to have their voices heard by using a distinct language, blocking off
dialogue between the two schools of thought.

We argue that it is possible to go beyond this academic quarrel by rooting
the concept of Just Peace in a process that is a language-oriented one.
Together, negotiators build a new common language, and with that, redefine
some elements of their identity. The aim of our 'bottom-up' approach is to
propose an accommodation process whereby negotiators seek to agree to a
fair and lasting peace by crafting it in a manner deemed just by all relevant
protagonists. Peace achieved in this way is just because it entails gradual
recognition by the negotiating parties of a series of conventions. It is just
because it is expressed in a shared language that respects the sensitivities of all
parties. And it is just because it does not reflect a blinkered vision of law.[5]

---

[3] John Rawls, *The Law of Peoples: with 'The idea of Public Reason Revisited'* (Cambridge, MA:
Harvard University Press, 1999), 4–5.

[4] As James Tully explains, this approach is based on a 'separate, bounded and internally
uniform' conception of culture whereas in fact, 'not only do cultures overlap geographically and
come in a variety of types. Cultures are also densely interdependent in their formation and identity.
They exist in complex historical processes of interaction with other cultures. . . . Cultures are not
internally homogenous. They are continuously contested, imagined and re-imagined, transformed
and negotiated, both by their members and through their interaction with others. . . . The meaning
of any culture is thus aspectival rather than essential.' James Tully, *Strange Multiplicity: Constitutionalism in an Age of Diversity* (Cambridge: Cambridge University Press, 1995), 10–11.

[5] In this case, the definition of justice itself will, to some extent, have to be negotiated
between the parties involved, recognizing that there is some inevitable tension between the
idea of justice and the idea of reconciliation. As shown by Herbert Kelman, such a process
usually experiences different kinds of justice that an agreement might try to achieve, such 'as (1)
substantive justice, achieved through an agreement that meets the fundamental needs of
both sides, (2) future justice, achieved through the establishment of just institutions, arrangements, (3) procedural justice, achieved through a fair and reciprocal process of negotiating
the agreement, (4) emotional justice, achieved through the sense that the negotiations have

Based on our language-oriented approach, we claim that four conventions or principles are required to negotiate a peace perceived as just and legitimate, a Just Peace: thin recognition, thick recognition, renouncement, and a common rule. They are adjusted to prevailing circumstances and are prerequisites for a Just Peace as well as the steps making it possible. As in Just War theory, all conditions are necessary, and if together all are satisfied, then they are sufficient for a Just Peace. Unlike Just War doctrine, our conventions also describe a process and not simply a set of requirements.

1. THIN RECOGNITION

The first such convention is *thin*[6] *recognition*: each party needs to recognize the other as such. Parties recognize each other as agents, as autonomous 'entities' that have a particular identity, a history, a culture, and usually their own common language. In other words, they accept each other as human beings. This thin recognition proceeds simply on the acceptance of the other,[7] of its having the right to exist and continuing to exist as an autonomous agent. At this level of a thin or minimalist recognition, the 'thickness' of the other agent, while being accepted in principle, is not recognized as such, and remains in the background. Simply, the other is accepted as a full-fledged negotiating partner and the negotiation may not succeed. Most crucial is that the parties recognize each other as the key for solving the conflict. It is this acceptance of the other as such, as an essential element in the conflict at hand that is a central feature of a Just Peace.

In this sense, our perspective is analogous to Kant's minimalist 'cosmopolitan right', 'the right of a stranger not to be treated with hostility when he arrives on someone else's territory', a 'right of resort', allowing each

---

seriously sought and to a significant degree shaped a just outcome'. See Herbert C. Kelman, 'Reconciliation as Identity Change: A Social-Psychological Perspective', in Yaacov Bar-Siman-Tov (ed.), *From Conflict Resolution to Reconciliation* (Oxford: Oxford University Press, 2004), 122–3.

[6] We borrow Michael Walzer's conceptual distinction between 'thin' and 'thick' morality but do not follow his theory of morality. Instead, we make use of it to distinguish between two forms of recognition (see later on 'thick' recognition). Walzer himself in *Thick and Thin: Moral Argument at Home and Abroad* (Notre Dame, IN: University of Notre Dame Press, 1994, p. xi) borrows the idea of 'thickness' from Clifford Geertz. See Clifford Geertz, *The Interpretation of Cultures* (New York: Basic Books 1973).

[7] Obviously, not all conflicts are between two parties only. Expository purposes make us speak of only one other party and we do not wish to imply that 3, 4 or *n*-party Just Peace processes do not happen.

human being 'to attempt to enter into relations' with others,[8] such as trade. However, it does not imply the knowledge of the other party's identity, simply the recognition that he has a separate one and that one can enter into potentially fruitful interchange with him. It has a universalist bent, because even Paul Feyerabend, the relativist epistemologist and philosopher of science, agreed at the end of his life that all individuals finally represent a universal human. In his autobiography, Feyerabend wrote: 'I am coming to the conclusion that each culture is potentially all cultures and that special cultural traits are variable manifestations of a unique human nature.'[9] All this shows that a common humanity makes for both some communication as well as some lineaments of morality among different persons, communities, and cultures.

In Chapter 3, the value Montesquieu, Rousseau, and Chief Justice John Marshall attached to 'mutual recognition' between peoples was shown. Marshall referred in 1832 to the Royal Proclamation of 7 October 1763 in which the British Crown set out its views on relations between North America and the Amerindian nations. The Proclamation unmistakably recognized indigenous peoples as autonomous nations, and did not define them using traditional Eurocentric Enlightenment discourse. Instead, it drew on a raft of symbolic benchmarks that Timothy Shannon called 'intercultural diplomacy' in a fascinating article.[10] According to Richard White and Francis Jennings, a number of negotiations between Indians and Europeans took account of cultural differences.[11] British envoys acknowledged the Indians' lack of European-style legal and political institutions, without passing judgement on that fact. They observed the different types of government through confederation and counsel, consensual decision-making, power rooted in authority rather than coercion, and respect for ancestral traditions. European negotiators then adapted their approach to the Amerindian culture and

---

[8] Immanuel Kant, 'Perpetual Peace: A Philosophical Sketch', in Hans Reiss (ed.), *Kant: Political Writings* (Cambridge: Cambridge University Press, 1991), 105–6.

[9] Paul Feyerabend, *Tuer le temps: Une autobiographie* (Paris: Seuil, 1996), 192 (our translation) which was the last book he finished writing just before dying in 1994.

[10] Timothy J. Shannon, 'Dressing for Success on the Mohawk Frontier: Hendrick, William Johnson and The Indian Fashion', *The William and Mary Quarterly*, 53 (1996), 13–42. Shannon shows the crucial role played by fashion in the negotiations of 1740 between Iroquois Confederation and the British colonies of North America. The European negotiators respected the preference of the American Indians for some clothes and some colours and this allowed for a real exchange between the two populations that accepted each other as they were, that recognized each other at a 'thin' recognition level.

[11] Richard White, *The Middle Ground: Indians, Empires and Republics in the Great Lakes Region, 1650–1815* (Cambridge: Cambridge University Press, 1991); Francis Jennings (ed.), *The History and Cuz Of Iroquois Diplomacy: An Interdisciplinary Guide to the Treaties of the Six Nations and Their League* (Syracuse: Syracuse University Press, 1985).

refused to dismiss its peoples as 'inferior' on the evolutionary scale. In 1763, for instance, they agreed that all negotiators would speak their own language, wear traditional dress, and abide by their political and social customs. It is this acceptance of the other as an essential figure in the conflict at hand that constitutes the first convention which is, in some sense, a liberal one.

2. THICK RECOGNITION

Thick recognition is our second convention in which each party needs to understand the other's fundamental features of its identity. Only then can each actor truly understand the situation as it appears from the other's perspective, a necessary condition for finding a formula for a Just Peace. Mutual empathy—which does not necessarily entail sympathy—is crucial here. Thus an intersubjective consensus of what each side profoundly needs to remain 'self', and thus, satisfied, should be developed in a Just Peace process.

Here, we are not asking for an overall consensus. Nor are we requiring the kind of societal consensus necessary in some of the societies studied by anthropologists whereby differences are solved by long palavers and where each individual has in some sense the power of vetoing the collective decision. All we require for a Just Peace is a minimal understanding of the internal support a proposed just solution would have for each significant or relevant group or sensitivity within each actor. According to the identity of an actor, support may stem from the agreement of the legitimate leaders in a representative democracy, or the consent of the major groups supporting an authoritarian system or any other significant domestic political force or sensitivity which may block a Just Peace formula.

The notion of identity is therefore crucial. Despite their undeniable rigidities, identities are potentially changeable (and in fact negotiable) for two reasons. First, unlike territory and resources, they are not inherently zero-sum game; though they are perceived and debated as such in intense conflicts, it is in fact not the case that one's identity can be expressed only if the other's identity is totally denied. If the two—or more—identities are to become compatible, however, they have to be defined anew or redefined. And here is the second reason they are changeable: they can be redefined because they are to a large extent constructed out of real experiences and these experiences can be presented and ordered in different ways. As Herbert Kelman put it: 'In fact the reconstruction of identity is a regular, ongoing process in the life of any national group. Identities are commonly reconstructed, sometimes gradually and sometimes radically, as historical circumstances change, crises emerge, opportunities present themselves, or new elites come to the fore.'[12] Thus, there is clearly room for manoeuvre in a group's self-definition—particularly with respect to the definition of group boundaries and the priorities among elements of a group's identity.

The discovery that accommodation of the other's identity need not destroy the core of the group's own identity makes these changes possible, and this kind of learning is usually taking place during the negotiation process. Therefore, to find a common ground between identities, it is essential to genuinely understand the core identity of the other. Thick recognition implies full acceptance of the humanity of the other—including the contradictory elements of human experience and their societal dimensions.

But it is not sufficient to understand the other: it is just as important to understand oneself. Surprisingly, most social scientific approaches start from the premise that actors are knowledgeable of themselves and concentrate on how the nature of the other is defined. Most often, the rationality of the other is posited in order to be able to rationally enter into social intercourse with him.[13] However, we argue that those representing a party need to fully understand the core identity of their own party in order to be able to devise a solution that will be, sometimes only with time, recognized and accepted by their own people. For example, is Israel to be understood foremost as a nation-state in search of its security, or *the* Jewish State, the Jewish State on *holy lands*, or simply *a* state that welcomes all Jews the world over, or a Jewish *democratic* state? What are the essential features of its ontology? What constitutes the deeper core characterizing it is the crucial question since other definitions of Israel can be envisioned besides the ones mentioned here.

Closely connected with thick recognition is the notion of consent. As shown by James Tully, it is a keystone of modern constitutionalism and comes from a Roman law maxim: *quod omnes tangit ab omnibus comprobetur*—what touches everybody needs to be approved by everybody.[14] As we saw in Chapter 3, Locke, Vattel and other proponents of modern international law did not see fit to apply this maxim to indigenous peoples, thereby dismissing them as individuals or cultural minorities within a sovereign state. They crossed over the principle of consent by claiming, not without bias, that

[12] Herbert C. Kelman, 'Negotiating National Identity and Self-Determination in Ethnic Conflicts: The Choice between Pluralism and Ethnic Cleansing', *Negotiation Journal*, 13 (1997), 338.

[13] Some advanced game-theoretic treatments of this question however also start with the necessary stage of self-definition; on this issue, see Pierre Allan and Cédric Dupont, 'International Relations Theory and Game Theory: Baroque Modeling Choices and Empirical Robustness', *International Political Science Review*, 20/1 (1999), 23–47.

[14] See Tully, op. cit., 116–23.

colonization benefited the Amerindians. They firmly believed that European trading powers were superior to communities of hunters and farmers. As Locke put it, 'Americans are [...] rich in Land and poor in all the Comforts of Life; [...] yet for want of improving it [their land] by labour, [they] have not one hundredth part of the Conveniencies we enjoy; And a King of a large and fruitful territory there feeds, lodges, and is clad worse than a day labourer in England.'[15] Clearly it was in the indigenous peoples' interest to become a part of the trading system.

Commenting critically on John Locke's arguments in *Worcester v. the State of Georgia*, Chief Justice Marshall pointed out in 1832 that the British Crown had incorporated the idea of mutual consent—and therefore thick recognition—into the treaties signed with Amerindians and concluded that the US government was bound to respect that undertaking.[16] Under no circumstances did the British Empire's right of discovery or conquest endow it with authority over indigenous populations. At most, it gave Britain the edge over some European nations to settle and buy up land from native dwellers. Throughout the colonization process, Amerindian nations—here the use of the term 'nation' as 'autonomous entities' is crucial—had negotiated the handover of land and the drawing of borders in exchange for a pledge to respect the boundaries of the territory assigned to them through treaties. Marshall argued that the Indians would never have agreed to give up some of their land if they had not believed that the convention of 'mutual consent' would prevail. In sum, Marshall used the convention of *thick recognition* as the cornerstone of his argument, thus going beyond liberalism, this in a culturalist vein.

3. RENOUNCEMENT

The third necessary convention is *renouncement*: concessions and compromises are necessary to build a Just Peace. Some symbols, positions, and advantages need to be sacrificed. In other words, it is not sufficient to find a win-win formula, but an essential ingredient lies in sacrifices, that is, costs, that each party needs to make with respect to the other. Just Peace cannot be had on the cheap, with mutual benefits only. Rather, it is a human experience that

---

[15] John Locke, *Two Treatises of Governement*, ed. Peter Laslett (Cambridge: Cambridge University Press, 1988), § 41, 296–7.
[16] *Worcester v. the State of Georgia*, 6 Peter 515 (U.S.S.C. 1832), reprinted in John Marshall, *The Writings of John Marshall, Late Chief Justice of the United States, upon the Federal Constitution* (Littleton, CO: FB Rothman Press, 1987), especially 435–45.

requires a visible and obvious rapprochement on the human level and that requires visible sacrifices from both parties. In essence, although a catharsis such as the one following the Second World War between the USA and Japan is not necessary, it is indispensable to have both parties recognize that they each make some significant concessions to the other, such as the USA accepting the continuation of Emperor Hirohito's reign—while at the same time organizing a victor's tribunal and executing top Japanese military. These concessions do not necessarily have to be 'heavy', but they always need to *signify* a real sacrifice.

Thus, a Just Peace demands painful concessions. Apart from the division of territory, sovereignty, and power, negotiations are often marked by one overriding factor, a symbolic, initially non-negotiable issue around which the conflict is structured. That issue may be state unity, religious freedom, constitutional reform, or the role of a language. In Northern Ireland, the defining factor is the union with Great Britain. Canada's conflict is embodied in the issue of language. In Kosovo, religion divides hearts and minds. Each side must give up symbols, elements of prestige, positions or principles, which, for some, justified the continued conflict.

In many ways, the *Edict of Nantes* (1598) was based on the principle of renouncement. It differed in wording and content from other edicts of its time. It contained an explanatory preamble, the avowed purpose of which is to 'address' the two conflicting parties. It sets out the specific reasons why they should give ground, but also reassures all parties that their true identity remains untouched. The text is complex, granting protestants too much (infamous safe places) and yet not enough (limited freedom to worship), but it is also pioneering. It sealed France's rejection of the one religion dogma and granted all citizens freedom of conscience. As such, it was part of a bid to achieve a Just Peace. It sowed the seeds for two basic principles of individual liberty: the separation between religion and politics, and the distinction between public and private spheres. Henry IV and the commissioners who negotiated the *Edict* settled the Huguenot issue and showed caution and tolerance in integrating Protestants as full-fledged French citizens. In doing so, they enabled two religions to coexist peacefully. For this they needed—some might say imposed—the idea of compromise, that is, renouncement as a political keystone of 'religious peace'.[17] The stable peace which resulted was in a sense a development from the peace negotiated at Augsburg in 1555.[18]

---

[17] See Olivier Christin, *La paix de religion. L'autonomisation de la raison politique au XVIe siècle* (Paris: Seuil, 1997); Thierry Wanegffelen, *L'Edit de Nantes: Une histoire européenne de la tolérance (XVIe-XXe siècle)* (Paris: Le livre de poche, 1998).

[18] Cf. Stephen D. Krasner, *Sovereignty: Organized Hypocrisy* (Princeton, NJ: Princeton University Press, 1999), 79ff.

More recently, the *Geneva Accord,* signed on 1st December between the Israelis and Palestinians,[19] complied with the third principle of renouncement. Jerusalem and the right of return were crucial in this respect. All other negotiating factors were organized around those two issues. At the outset, each side was well aware of the need to break major taboos, that is, renouncing. The Palestinian team agreed to sacrifice one of the cornerstones of Palestinian ideology, the 'right of return'. On this point, Article 7 is categorical: 'The Parties recognize that UNGAR [United Nations General Assembly] Resolution 194, UNSC [United Nations Security] Resolution 242, and the Arab Peace Initiative (Article 2.ii.) concerning the rights of the Palestinian refugees represent the basis for resolving the refugee issue, and agree that these rights are fulfilled according to Article 7 of this Agreement.' The Article specifies that the solution lies in 'a choice of permanent place of residence'. This is to be, 'an act of informed choice on the part of the refugee to be exercised in accordance with the options and modalities set forth in this agreement'. The wording leaves no room for ambiguity: there is no 'right of return' to the State of Israel.

The Israelis, in turn, had to cross a line over Jerusalem. As an age-old symbol of Jewish spiritual aspirations and nationhood, the Holy City was at the heart of the Israeli delegation's act of renouncement. The text is equally uncompromising on this point. Following President Clinton's proposal, the state of Palestine would hold sovereignty over the Muslim, Christian, and Armenian neighbourhoods of the Old City of Jerusalem. Talks on the Jaffa Gate and the Citadel were admittedly heated, garanteed arrangements for Israelis regarding access, freedom of movement and security were adopted, but the text shows no ambiguity. To secure compromise-driven peace, both sides had to relinquish a dream. The Geneva Accord is therefore 'relevant' to both sides in this respect. It expresses their hopes, affirms their deep-rooted identities and sets out their dreams. But it also paves the way for each side to relinquish a key demand. As such, it represents progress towards renouncement, the price of a Just Peace.

4. RULE

Rule constitutes our fourth and final convention. Just Peace cannot be only in the minds of peoples, a subjective feeling among negotiators, a sentiment of justice and peace between them. For a Just Peace to be durable, it needs to

---

[19] See in particular Alexis Keller, *L'Accord de Genève: un pari réaliste* (Paris and Geneva: Seuil and Labor et Fides, 2004).

be shown in the open, in the public sphere. It requires explicit rules of settlement, legitimate rules of acceptable behaviour, and objective yardsticks allowing all—both parties and outside observers or guarantors—to approve of the solution found. We posit *rule* in the generic sense of common principles, norms, and accepted behaviours. Typically, the rule between parties to a Just Peace is grounded in law, which is seen as a way of shaping the first three. Law is a means of guaranteeing an 'objective' approach. Usually, law addresses the problem of human nature at two levels. It provides authoritative rules of conduct for all to observe in the pursuit of their own ends, rules which provide order in that they establish legitimate expectations for such conduct. It also establishes conventions for interpreting, creating, and changing the rules.[20] In a pluralistic society, the conventional character of law is an advantage in that it sets out common rules for people of all moral persuasions to follow without vesting authority in one particular moral rationale for the rules. This second meaning of law is very important for our purpose. It means a shift away from law as a set of abstract and absolute rights to an approach much more closely associated with the view of law as social process. For us, law is but one of the tools for creating and implementing norms and rules likely to promote a Just Peace.

The Hague Conferences and Conventions of 1899 and 1907, followed by the setting up of the League of Nations in 1919 and the United Nations in 1945 all testify to the growing role of international law. Modern international law no longer seeks to legitimize just wars, unlike its predecessor, *jus gentium* or the law of nations. Instead, its goal is to render existing legal standards truly objective, thus guaranteeing security and peace for all peoples. To that end, various conflicting laws are to be confronted with each community retaining its rules, principles, assessment criteria, and written or unwritten laws. Yet a solution deemed satisfactory according to one tradition of thought is unacceptable to another. Each tradition has its own innate belief as to what constitutes the most rational take on themes such as peace and justice, and their members' judgements are shaped by that belief. If that is indeed true, two conclusions may be drawn.

First, rational debate on law is not possible between traditions, only within a given tradition, be it Eastern, Western, Asian, etc. Advocates of opposing views within a tradition may still agree on a sufficient number of key beliefs to engage in debate, but followers of one tradition are unable to explain these beliefs to members of a rival tradition or indeed to learn from them how to alter radically their own view of things. Second, since each tradition expresses

---

[20] On this point, see Hart's discussion in H. L. A. Hart, *The Concept of Law* (Oxford: Oxford University Press, 1961), especially chs. 4 and 5.

its beliefs using its own terms and concepts, there appears to be little hope of reaching agreement outside the borders of each legal system. Dialogue between different cultures on specific key issues seems too flawed to reach full understanding. We seem to be doomed to live with competing beliefs and incompatible perceptions of the world, with only patchy communication between them. Is this indeed true, though? Is it really impossible to settle on a legal language shared and accepted by all? Therein lies the challenge posed by relativism (impossibility to choose between traditions) and perspectivism (impossibility to claim that one holds the truth inside a school of thought).

Tzvetan Todorov and Ashis Nandy provide us with useful insights to solve this dilemma and think about a way to create channels between rival traditions.[21] Both are concerned with the process of 'othering' by means of which a self understands the relationship between itself and some other and it is an understanding with practical implications. Both offer richly rewarding insights into cross-cultural understanding, notably Todorov's idea of 'nonviolent communication' and Nandy's notion of a 'dialogue of visions'. Through a conversational process that does not assume Western superiority, they argue it is possible to achieve a dialogue between cultures and the degree of mutual understanding needed to sustain international society. In essence, their concern is that of engaging in dialogue with the other in order to understand those who are different in their owns terms and that means avoiding repeating the same form of past injustices.

A similar route to achieving cross-cultural understanding is Andrew Linklater's application of Habermas' 'discourse ethics' to international relations.[22] Discourse ethics refers to the ground rules for dialogue between culturally different communities. It proceeds on the assumption that cultural difference is not a barrier to dialogue aimed at breaking down practices of exclusion and is concerned particularly with overcoming the exclusion of communities from the debate about issues that affect their vital interests. To qualify as a true dialogue in conformity with the procedural rules of discourse ethics, participants must 'suspend their own supposed truth claimed [and] respect the claims of others'.[23] Linklater acknowledges that the result of dialogue may be no more than an agreement to disagree. Political interests may be too entrenched to allow the possibility of thinking from the standpoint of others. Therefore, 'discourse ethics' may sometime be politically naïve if not curi-

---

[21] Tzvetan Todorov, *The Conquest of America: The Question of the Other* (New York: Harper Torch, 1992) and Ashis Nandy, *Traditions, Tyranny and Utopias: Essays in the Politics of Awareness* (Delhi: Oxford University Press, 1992).

[22] Andrew Linklater, *The Transformation of Political Community: Ethical Foundations of the Post-Westphalian Community* (Cambridge: Polity Press, 1998), especially ch. 3.

[23] Ibid., 92.

ously apolitical. In fact, Linklater's project is grounded in, and intended to be a contribution to, critical theory, which is in many ways a continuation of Enlightenment themes. Enlightenment thinking celebrated reason, the autonomy of the individual and the autonomy of reason. As Kant put it, Enlightenment depended on 'freedom to make public use of one's reason in all matters'.[24] And, as previously shown, those lacking the capacity for reason were seen as ignorant and being ignorant marked out 'others' beyond the boundaries of the moral community to which Europeans belonged. Thus, although very useful, Linklater's approach does not offer a satisfactory solution to finding a common and acceptable language among traditions.

Without falling into the trap of a purely semantic investigation, we believe that there is a way to devise a language that reflects the idiosyncrasies of opposing traditions. It may be that one or both of them will require considerable development before acceptable common ground can be found. But one path leading to that end is the building of the fourth convention, rule. The chances of success are not so much influenced by the concepts available to negotiating parties and their openness to recognition. Instead they may well lie primarily with their talent for *linguistic invention*.[25] This will also determine the range of options available for rejecting, amending, and rewording beliefs, reinterpreting texts, and deriving new power structures.

Rule is the arena where each party's cultural conventions on recognition and renouncement are reinvented, fleshed out, and modified. By crafting and then drafting a common acceptable convention using the terminology of both negotiating traditions, it allows the features of the just solution to be objectified by a 'text'. This term is to be seen in the widest sense, including the essential symbolic features such as shaking hands, having a common meal, a reciprocal invitation to visit the leaders' private home, and so forth. Rule is therefore functioning as a kind of 'system of interactional expectancies', to use Lon Fuller's terminology, including the public acceptance of the proper ways of acting with respect to each other.[26] It requires a common language to be set forth, respecting the particular identities of each, making their concessions

---

[24] Immanuel Kant, 'An Answer to the Question: "What is Enlightenment?"', in Hans Reiss (ed.), *Kant: Political Writings* (Cambridge: Cambridge University Press, 1991), 55.

[25] This expression will sound familiar to those aware of the debate on the *linguistic turn*, identified with the form of historical critique developed by the *Cambridge School*. It consists in the historical adaptation of Wittgenstein's method of dissolving philosophical problems by examining the conventions that governed a language during a period of time in which both problems and solutions arose. For an introduction to this method in a comparative perspective, see Melvin Richter, *The History of Political and Social Concepts* (Oxford: Oxford University Press, 1995), especially ch. 6.

[26] Lon L. Fuller, *The Principles of Social Order: Selected Essays of Lon L. Fuller* (Durham, NC: Duke University Press, 1981), 219–20.

clear to all, and defining the rights and duties of each in securing a Just Peace that is seen by both as a lasting one. Of course, history continues and the world changes, and therefore that does not imply that this Just Peace will necessarily be, as in a Kantian perspective, a perpetual one. Rather, rule allows for the open and public acceptance of peace and justice solving the conflict at hand.

In a way, our fourth convention also has a certain familiarity to the concept of 'regime' in international relations theory. In the classic definition by Stephen Krasner, a regime is a set of 'implicit or explicit principles, norms, rules, and decision-making procedures around which actors' expectations converge in a given area of international relations'. But, whereas a regime usually pertains to a number of actors, 'rule' is more of a bilateral relationship. However, because the regime's principles and norms are 'beliefs of fact, causation, or rectitude' and 'standards of behaviour defined in terms of rights and obligations', normative dimensions are central to the agreement at hand, and it comes about by parties sharing them in their expectations.[27]

So far, however, we have not explained in detail how we arrive at this common language. The answer is given, we believe, by Ludwig Wittgenstein's approach to the concept of understanding.[28] In one of the most famous passages of his *Philosophical Investigations*, Wittgenstein compares language to an ancient city: 'Our language may be seen as an ancient city: a maze of little streets and squares, of old and new houses, and of houses with additions from various periods; and this surrounded by a multitude of new boroughs with straight regular streets and uniform houses.'[29] This analogy is used to make us understand that language, like a city, has grown up in a variety of forms through practices overlapping in many ways the endless diversity of human activities. Like a city it does have a multiplicity of possible paths. 'And this multiplicity is not something fixed, given once for all; but new types of language, new language-games, as we may say, come into existence, and others become obsolete and get forgotten.... Here the term 'language-*game*' is meant to bring into prominence the fact that the *speaking* of a language is part of an activity, or of a life-form.'[30]

---

[27] See Stephen D. Krasner, 'Structural Causes and Regime Consequences: Regimes as Intervening Variables', in Stephen D. Krasner (ed.), *International Regimes* (Ithaca, NY: Cornell University Press, 1983), 2.

[28] Our reading of Wittgenstein has been much influenced by Stanley Cavell's work on Wittgenstein. See Stanley Cavell, *The Claim of Reason: Wittgenstein, Skepticism, Morality and Tragedy* (Oxford: Oxford University Press, 1979).

[29] Ludwig Wittgenstein, *Philosophical Investigations*, trans. G. E. M. Anscombe (Oxford: Blackwell Publishing, 2001), 7.

[30] Ibid., 10.

Consequently, it is impossible to articulate a comprehensive rule that stipulates the essential conditions for the correct application of words in every instance, just as there is no such comprehensive view of a city. Wittgenstein explains that 'a meaning of a word is a kind of employment of it. For it is what we learn when the word is incorporated into our language.'[31] Furthermore, '[l]anguage is a labyrinth of paths. You approach from one side and know your way about; you approach the same place from another side and no longer know your way about.'[32] Wittgenstein thus shows that understanding a general term is not the theoretical activity of interpreting and applying a general theory in distinct cases. It is rather the *practical* activity of being able to use it in various circumstances. It implies the employment of examples which make obvious a connection with other cases, so that a person understands why or why not the term should be used in this case.

How do I explain the meaning of 'regular', 'uniform', 'same' to anyone? I shall explain these words to someone who, say, only speaks French by means of the corresponding French words. But if a person has not yet got the *concepts*, I shall teach him to use the words by means of *examples* and by *practice*. And when I do this I do not communicate less to him than I know myself. In the course of this teaching, I shall show him the same colours, the same lengths, the same shapes, I shall make him find them and produce them, and so on. . . . I do it, he does it after me.[33]

This final sentence introduces an important aspect of Wittgenstein's concept of understanding: the process of understanding a term by assembling examples always take place in *dialogue* with others who see things differently. As James Tully put it: 'Since there is always more than one side to a case, one must always consult those on the other side. As a result of exchanges of views by denizens from various neighbourhoods and the finding of examples which mediate their differences, a grasp of the multiplicity of cases is gradually acquired. Understanding, like the *Philosophical Investigations* itself, is dialogical.'[34] In that sense, Wittgenstein's philosophy furnishes an alternative way of building an intercultural dialogue by enabling the interlocutors to modify their languages and their 'pictures of the world'.[35] It is barely the case that a whole practice and an entire world-picture get changed suddenly and at once in all their components. Some parts stay hardened for some time and can be used as a common frame of reference, as a starting point of understanding one practice from the viewpoint of another. Nevertheless, this dialogical way of apprehend-

---

[31] Ludwig Wittgenstein, *On Certainty*, trans. Denis Paul and G. E. M. Anscombe, ed. by G. E. M. Anscombe and G. H. von Wright (New York: Harper Torchbooks, 1972), 10.

[32] Ludwig Wittgenstein, *Philosophical Investigations*, 69.

[33] Ibid., 70.

[34] Tully, op. cit., 110.

[35] Wittgenstein, op. cit., 15.

ing others provides us with a process that does not entail comprehending what they say within one side's own language. In sum, Wittgenstein's theory gives us a solid base to anchor our concept 'rule'. It not only allows us to 'do things with words', following John Austin's terminology,[36] but it also permits us to go beyond the usual opposition between liberalism and culturalism.

Differently put, after the highly 'subjective' thick recognition and re-nouncement, it is necessary that the agreement be fully communicated to the relevant publics. It needs to be publicized, thus entering the public sphere not only of each party, but also of all outside observers and third parties, helping to cement the agreement. The requirement is of a commonality between the parties, in the sense of the public acceptance of the proper ways of acting with respect to each other. The common language set forth, respecting the particular identities of each, making their concessions clear to all, and defining the rights and duties of each in securing a Just Peace is the key ingredient for making it a lasting one. Because for a Just Peace to be durable, explicit rules of settlement, legitimate rules of acceptable behaviour, and intersubjective yardsticks allowing everyone of significance to approve the solution found, all need to be settled in common.

These four conventions thus define both a Just Peace and point towards the necessary features of a process leading to it. In fact, by neither specifying some general rules of justice nor the content of the peace, but focusing only on some very general forms the process of a Just Peace needs to proceed through, we have developed a formal concept. Akin to Thomas Kuhn's theory of scientific change, it only gives the form of a Just Peace development, and says little about its contents.[37]

5. JUST PEACE COMPARED TO OTHER INTERNATIONAL ETHICAL CONCEPTS

Based on Pierre Allan's international ethical scale,[38] we present a comparative table of the eight international ethical concepts which provide for empirical measurement of different deeds and situations evaluated normatively. They are all positioned with respect to the four conventions required for a Just Peace. This coding obviously does not render full justice to each, since it is

---

[36] John L. Austin, *How to do Things with Words* (Oxford: Clarendon Press, 1962).
[37] Cf. Thomas Kuhn, *The Structure of Scientific Revolutions*, 2nd edn. (Chicago, IL: Chicago University Press, 1970).
[38] See Allan, Chapter 5 of this book.

only through Just Peace that each is envisioned. However, it is a useful exercise because it allows one to focus on some of the essential differences between those varied ethical stages of international life.

By definition, Just Peace satisfies its own four criteria, that is, they are all present, giving us the four 'yes' on the line corresponding to a Just Peace. Quickly moving through the table starting at the first line, with the concept of genocide, we observe that none of our conventions is satisfied there. Since the other is negated, not even a thin recognition is present, and even less so a thick one. Obviously, there is no renouncement when the other is to be exterminated. As for rule, neither common language nor sharing takes place. Consequently, we have four 'none' in that first line.

In war, there is some thin recognition, but no thick recognition, but for strategic and strictly interest-based rational considerations pertaining the enemy to be vanquished. No renouncement exists in war either. But even a surrender, and even when unconditional, is nevertheless governed by a series of practices and rules that pertain to a given epoch.

Non-war or Hobbesian peace is characterized by thin recognition of the (potential) rival or enemy, whereas the state of nature prevents thick recognition in favour of the malign version of the Security Dilemma. There is no renouncement there either, but some rules apply, such as diplomatic ones.

The case of Just War versus Just Peace is particularly interesting. Briefly put, they share thin recognition as well as rule, while there is neither thick recognition nor renouncement in Just War, contrarily to those essential requirements for obtaining a Just Peace. An essential parallelism lies in the fact that both are based on a series of necessary and sufficient conditions in order to deserve the adjective 'just'. This is due to the central deontological requirements of both concepts. Thin recognition is somewhat similar to the legitimate authority central to Just War doctrine. Thick recognition is much more complex and includes considerations such as the essential just cause element(s) of a Just War, as well as the right intention, and the last resort requirements of that theory. It is probably here that our concept is closest to a fundamental ethical value: truth. Finally, rule is a richer concept than the necessary public declaration of the Just War requirements—but of course at the same time containing it.

Continuing our journey along the lines of Table 9.1, with stable peace we have a concept that is clearly close to Just Peace, while both thick recognition and renouncement are only imperfect there. They exist in part, but are not perceived as fully just.

Positive peace goes beyond a just one, with thick recognition pertaining to other actors besides those directly involved in a Just Peace, and with further rule in the sense of not only a self-sufficient rule ensuring peace among parties, but also distributive justice beyond.

Table 9.1. Just Peace compared to the concepts of the International Ethical Scale

	Thin Recognition	Thick Recognition	Renouncement	Rule
Genocide	None	None	None	None
War	Some	No	No	Some
Non-war	Yes	No	No	Some
Just War	Yes	No	No	Yes
Stable peace	Yes	Some	Some	Yes
Just Peace	Yes	Yes	Yes	Yes
Positive peace	Yes	Yes, also for others	Yes	Very much
Global Care	Yes	Yes and sympathy	Very much	Very much

Finally, Global Care extends justice in a more humane way, and substitutes some of its 'coldness' with a warmer humane sympathy. Renouncement is maximal there, of course, and so is rule in our sense of that word and concept.

This classification exercise is somewhat arbitrary because although the meanings of our four conventions are quite rich, their richness does not fully include the multiple meanings and depth of all other categories. But comparison fleshes out some major similarities and exposes major differences. Since such an exercise is rarely done in the field of international morals, we submit it as preliminary with a heuristic value, while intending to leave the development of these comparisons to future work.

Before concluding, we need to show in what ways our approach departs from a classical, liberal, as well as legalistic perspective.[39]

6. SOME LIBERAL OBJECTIONS TO OUR CONCEPT OF A JUST PEACE

A liberal objection[40] to our approach has argued that our sort of peace is hardly distinguishable from the kind of peace envisioned by the liberal

---

[39] Many other objections can be raised. For example, some communitarian theorists share the view that demands for the recognition of cultural diversity—one of the preconditions for building a Just Peace—is a threat to the conceptions of a given community. Therefore, when they ask the crucial questions such as 'Whose Justice?' or 'Which Rationality?', the answers are always the same: European justice, Western rationality, male traditions of interpretation set within a European view of history. Where do they really develop a true dialogue with Non-European traditions set within non-European views of history? They carefully analyse a change in Greek syntax from Homer to Aristotle or the evolution of the Scottish tradition. But the long contests of non-European cultures remain unnoticed. An excellent example of such view is to be found in Alasdair MacIntyre, *Whose Justice? Which Rationality?* (Notre Dame, IN: University of Notre Dame Press, 1988).

[40] Made by an Oxford University Press anonymous reviewer of this book project whom we would like to thank for her or his incisive comments, especially this one with which we firmly disagree.

idealists such as Woodrow Wilson, Lowes Dickinson, Henry Brailsford, and Alfred Zimmern who wrote after the First World War. Although sounding reasonable at a first glance, this liberal notion of peace cannot—or only with great difficulty—apply to a peace between different cultures. Following Kant, liberal peace is defined in legal terms and is envisioned on the model of the Westphalian peace between states or sovereign entities. This 'legalistic' approach is founded on legal norms, which claim a universal scope. However—and this is a central weakness of this approach—it only rarely enquires about the origin of these norms and its authors. It clearly dissociates law from morality. For its liberal partisans, a Just Peace is a peace through law based upon the respect of *existing* international legal norms. What liberal authors forget is that their conception has difficulty in solving conflicts such as civil wars characterized typically by fundamental cultural disagreements between different communities—even though they belong by definition to the same institutional or 'legal' community.

Why is it difficult for liberals—policymakers as well as academics—to understand the question of mutual recognition between different parties having an identity, history, and culture that is quite different? Because cultures make demands that are identity-defining, and some of these usually defy the 'cultural neutrality' that is one of the foundations of liberalism. Liberals see these demands as a threat to the constitutional order. The usual liberal solutions are assimilation, integration, or the elimination of cultural diversity—rather than affirming it and recognizing it.

Indeed, the classical liberal treatment of difference allows for private spaces within which people can get on with their own chosen affairs and a public realm ordered around a set of minimum shared presumptions. But the relegation of difference to a private world of private variation has been experienced as a command to keep distinctive feature a secret, and the shared presumptions that control the public world have proved unfair and unequal in their treatment of different groups. For instance, in the liberal mindset, the separation of church from the state has long been considered the solution to problems of religious differences, but it achieves this by requiring all religions to adopt a similarly self-denying attitude that will limit the relevance of religious precepts to practices in the private sphere. Part of the dissatisfaction with liberalism's approach of difference is that it relies on the idea of toleration as a substitute to recognition. We only tolerate what we do not like or approve of and yet where difference is bound up with identity, this is hard for the tolerated to accept.[41] Furthermore, the defence of toleration by liberals is very often given by reference to a principle of respect for persons as autonomous

---

[41] See Susan Mendus, *Toleration and the Limits of Liberalism* (London: Macmillan, 1989).

agents—also called the autonomy principle. Such defence aims at explaining why toleration is a central value of a liberal society and also at explaining when and why it is to be limited.[42] There are nevertheless difficulties inherent in such an account. Despite its attempt to present toleration as good by itself and not merely a prudential policy, the argument from respect must, ultimately, rely on an analysis of rights and duties and such analysis may differ from one person to another and from one society to another. Justifying toleration by reference to the principle of respect inevitably generates towards the question 'what grounds that principle?'. Consequently, toleration could be perceived as non-egalitarian, resting in some way on a distinction between majority norms and minority deviance, and incorporating some implied preference for a particular way of life. It is perhaps not a coincidence if, nowadays, people do not find tolerance satisfactory for solving cross-cultural understanding.

The limits of the liberal tradition in dealing with diversity are also the result of history. As shown by Dianne Otto, liberalism and law have mutually constituted each other in ways that links the concept of sovereignty to the state.[43] The liberal state places personal liberties and rights above religious, ethnic, and other forms of communal consciousness. Thus, the liberal conception of sovereignty enshrined in law makes it difficult for indigenous cultural identity to be included. Some liberals would respond to that by arguing that the liberal state allows for cultural identities to flourish.[44] Nevertheless, the indigenous way of defining sovereignty clearly contradicts such an argument. For instance, Maori leaders differ from orthodox European politico-legal understandings of sovereignty. Roger Maaka and Augie Fleras explain that at various times, *tino rangitiratanga* [the Maori term for sovereignty] has encompassed the following: Maori sovereignty, Maori nationhood, self-management, *iwi* nationhood (an *iwi* is a confederation of tribes), independent power, full chiefly authority, chiefly *mana*, strong leadership, independence, supreme rule, self-reliance, Maori autonomy, tribal autonomy, absolute chieftainship, trusteeship, self-determination.[45]

---

[42] See Joseph Raz, 'Autonomy, Toleration, and the Harm Principle', in Susan Mendus (ed.), *Justifying Toleration: Conceptual and Historical Perspectives* (Cambridge: Cambridge University Press, 1988), 155–75.

[43] Dianne Otto, 'A Question of Law or Politics? Indigenous Claims to Sovereignty in Australia', *Syracuse Journal of International Law and Commerce*, 21 (1995), 701–39.

[44] Liberals such as Will Kymlicka and Daniel Weinstock have thus argued in different ways that a fair degree of recognition and accommodation of cultural diversity is possible within the constitutional traditions of liberal societies. See, Will Kymlicka, *Liberalism, Community and Culture* (Oxford: Clarendon Press, 1989) and Daniel Weinstock, 'The Political Theory of Strong Evaluation', in James Tully (ed.), *Philosophy in an Age of Pluralism: the Philosophy of Charles Taylor in Question* (Cambridge: Cambridge University Press, 1994), 171–93.

[45] Roger Maaka and Augie Fleras, 'Engaging with Indigeneity: Tino Rangatiratanga in Aotearoa', in Duncan Iveson, Paul Patton, and Will Sanders (eds.), *Political Theory and the*

Numerous authors have consequently underlined the tendency of liberalism to continue to superimpose upon constitutional diversity. Bhikhu Parekh, for example, observes that the modern state is 'a deeply homogenizing institution'.[46] Even a liberal writer such as Isaiah Berlin—who has assembled, one by one, works of modern European political philosophy—documents the importance of calls for uniformity and unity in liberal thought. Berlin showed that diversity was only rarely taken into account and was usually seen as a threat to public order.[47] And feminist authors have underscored how liberal theories (and even communautarian ones) have, in their quest of an imaginary unity, systematically put aside other theories, which gave more place to differences. In particular, they have identified liberalism with an abstract individualism that ignores its own gendered content and have criticized the homogenizing ideals of equality that require us to be or become the same.[48]

The liberal view of peace therefore has a fundamental problem with the convention of *thick recognition*, which is central to our perspective and which it cannot always accommodate. Each party has to be able to understand the other's fundamental identity features, in particular the differences it needs to remain 'self'. The recognition of these differences typically requires reaching out of a universal scheme equally applicable to all parties. Bhikhu Parekh observes that nowadays the presence of rival identities entails problems that cannot adequately be dealt with by the dominant liberal theory of the state. 'In multi-ethnic and multinational societies whose constituent communities entertain different views on its nature, powers and goals, have different histories and needs, and cannot therefore be treated in an identical manner, the modern state can easily become an instrument of injustice and oppression and even precipitate the very instability and secession it seeks to prevent.' Parekh concludes that 'since we can neither write off the modern state nor continue with its current form, we need to reconceptualise its nature and role. This involves loosening the traditionally close ties between territory, sovereignty and culture.'[49]

Rights of Indigenous Peoples (Cambridge: Cambridge University Press, 2000), 99, quoted by Paul Keal, *European Conquest and the Rights of Indigenous Peoples* (Cambridge: Cambridge University Press, 2003), 148.

[46] Bikhu Parekh, *Rethinking Multiculturalism: Cultural Diversity and Political Theory* (London: Macmillan, 2000).

[47] See Isaiah Berlin, *Against the Current* (London: Hogarth Press, 1979) and *The Crooked Timber of Humanity* (New York: Random House, 1992), especially the last chapter.

[48] See Anne Phillips, *Engendering Democracy* (University Park, PA: The Pennsylvania State University Press, 1991). See also Gisela Bock and Susan James (eds.), *Beyond Equality and Difference* (London: Routledge, 1992).

[49] Parekh, *Rethinking Multiculturalism*, 185 and 194.

Fundamentally, we are arguing in favour of a line of reasoning that is geared to the existence of multiple institutions, legal traditions, and the presence of plural identities in the way parties see themselves. This makes it impossible to resolve the problems of a Just Peace by one all encompassing original position (as under universalism) or even by two sets of overarching original positions, one within each 'nation' and another among the representatives of all nations. The existence of many identities is a central feature of the world in which we live and cannot be ignored in exploring the demands for recognition. As Armartya Sen persuasively argues:

although we cannot escape the need for critical scrutiny of respective demands, this is not a reason for expecting to find one canonical super-device that will readily resolve all the diversities of obligations that relate to affiliations, identities, and priorities. The oversimplification that must be particularly avoided is to identify global justice with international justice. The reach and relevance of the former can far exceed those of the latter.[50]

---

[50] Amartya Sen, 'Justice across Borders', in Pablo de Greiff and Ciaran Cronin (eds.), *Global Justice and Transantional Politics* (Cambridge, MA: The MIT Press, 2002), 50.

Suggested Readings

Allott, Philip (1990) *Eunomia: New Order for a New World*. Oxford: Oxford University Press.

Alston, Philip and James Crawford (eds.) (2000) *The Future of UN Human Rights Treaty Monitoring*. Cambridge: Cambridge University Press.

Appleby, Scott (2000) *The Ambivalence of the Sacred: Religion, Violence and Reconciliation*. New York: Rowman & Littlefield.

Archibugi, Daniele (1995) 'Immanuel Kant, Cosmopolitan Law and Peace', *European Journal of International Relations*, 1/4: 429–56.

Aron, Raymond (2003) *Peace and War: A Theory of International Relations*. New Brunswick, NJ: Transaction Publishers.

Barash, David (2000) *Approaches to Peace*. Oxford: Oxford University Press.

Bartholomeusz, Teresa (2002) *In Defense of Dharma: Just-War Ideology in Buddhist Sri Lanka*. London: RoutledgeCourzon.

Bayefsky, Anne F. (ed.) (2000) *The UN Human Rights Treaty System in the 21st Century*. The Hague: Kluwer Law International.

Beitz, Charles R. (1979) *Political Theory and International Relations*. Princeton, NJ: Princeton University Press.

—— (2000) 'Rawls's Law of Peoples', *Ethics*, 110: 669–96.

Bell, Christine (2000) *Peace Agreements and Human Rights*. Oxford: Oxford University Press.

Best, Geoffrey (1994) *War and Law Since 1945*. Oxford: Oxford University Press.

Bonanate, Luigi (1995) *Ethics and International Politics*. Cambridge: Polity Press.

Boulding, Kenneth E. (1978) *Stable Peace*. Austin, TX: University of Texas Press.

Buckley, William Joseph (ed.) (2000) *Kosovo: Contending Voices on Balkan Interventions*. Grand Rapids, MI: William B. Eerdmans.

Bull, Hedley, Benedict Kingsbury, and Adam Roberts (eds.) (1990) *Hugo Grotius and International Relations*. Oxford: Clarendon Press.

Campbell, David (1993) *Politics Without Principle: Sovereignty, Ethics, and the Narratives of the Gulf War*. Boulder, CO: Lynne Rienner Publishers.

Carr, Edward H. (1942) *Conditions of Peace*. London: Macmillan.

Christin, Olivier (1997) *La paix de religion*. Paris: Seuil.

Clausewitz, Carl von (1968) *On War*.[1832]. Harmondsworth, UK: Penguin.

Coates, Anthony J. (1997) *The Ethics of War*. Manchester: Manchester University Press.

Cochran, Molly (1999) *Normative Theory in International Relations: A Pragmatic Approach*. Cambridge: Cambridge University Press.

Cohen, Ben and George Stamkowski (eds.) (1995) *With No Peace to Keep*. London: Greenpress.

Cohen, Raymond (1991) *Negotiating Across Cultures: Communication Obstacles in International Diplomacy*. Washington, DC: United States Institute of Peace Press.

Dower, John (1986) *War Without Mercy: Race and Power in the Pacific War*. New York: Pantheon Books.

Doyle, Michael W. (1997) *Ways of War and Peace: Realism, Liberalism and Socialism*. New York: W.W. Norton.

Drèze, Jean and Amartya Sen (eds.) (1990) *The Political Economy of Hunger*, 3 vols. Oxford: Clarendon Press.

Dufour, Alfred (1984) 'Grotius et le droit naturel du dix-septième siècle', in *The World of Hugo Grotius (1583–1645)*. Amsterdam-Maarssen: APA-Holland University Press.

Engster, Daniel (2001) 'Mary Wollstonecraft's Nurturing Liberalism: Between an Ethic of Justice and Care', *American Political Science Review*, 95/3: 577–88.

Etziono, Amitai (2004) *From Empire to Community: A New Approach to International Relations*. New York: Palgrave.

Eyffinger, Arthur (1996) *The International Court of Justice 1946–1996*. The Hague: Kluwer Law International.

Fahey, Joseph J. and Richard Armstrong (eds.) (1992) *A Peace Reader: Essential Readings on War, Justice, Non-violence and World Order*. New York: Paulis Press.

Fisher, Roger and William Ury (1981) *Getting to YES: Negotiating Agreement Without Giving In*. Boston, MA: Houghton Mifflin.

Flechter, Joseph (1966) *Situation Ethics: The New Morality*. London: SCM Press.

Foot, Rosemary (2000) *Rights beyond Borders: The Global Community and the Struggle over Human Rights in China*. Oxford: Oxford University Press.

—— John Gaddis, and Andrew Hurrell (eds.) (2003) *Order and Justice in International Relations*. Oxford: Oxford University Press.

Forde, Steven (1998) 'Hugo Grotius on Ethics and War', *American Political Science Review*, 92/3: 639–48.

Frost, Mervyn (1996), *Ethics in International Relations: A Constitutive Theory*. Cambridge: Cambridge University Press.

Galtung, Johan (1969) 'Violence, Peace and Peace Research', *Journal of Peace Research*, 6/3: 167–91.

—— (1971) 'A Structural Theory of Imperialism', *Journal of Peace Research*, 8/3: 81–117.

Gauchet, Marcel (1989) *La révolution des droits de l'homme*. Paris: Gallimard.

Giesen, Klaus-Gerd (1992) *L'éthique des relations internationales: les théories anglo-américaines contemporaines*. Bruxelles: Bruylant.

Gilligan, Carol (1993) *In a Different Voice: Psychological Theory and Women's Development*, 2nd edn. Cambridge, MA: Harvard University Press.

Grotius, Hugo (1925) *Law of War and Peace*, trans. Francis W. Kelsey. New York: Bobbs-Merrill.

Gurr, Ted R. (2000) *Peoples versus States: Minorities at Risk in the New Century*. Washington, DC: United States Institute of Peace Press.

Haggenmacher, Peter (2000) 'La paix dans la pensée de Grotius', in Lucien Bely (ed.), *L'Europe des traités de Westphalie*. Paris: Presses Universitaires de France.

Hampson, Fen O. (1996) *Nurturing Peace: Why Peace Settlements Succeed or Fail*. Washington, DC: United States Institute of Peace.

Harbour, Frances V. (1999) *Thinking About International Ethics: Moral Theory and Cases from American Foreign Policy.* Boulder, CO: Westview Press.

Hashmi, Sohail H. (1993) 'Is There an Islamic Ethic of Humanitarian Intervention?', *Ethics and International Affairs,* 7: 55–73.

Hekman, Susan J. (1995) *Moral Voices, Moral Selves.* University Park, PA: The Pennsylvania State University Press.

Held, David (1995) *Democracy and the Global Order: From the Modern State to Cosmopolitan Governance.* Cambridge: Polity Press.

Helmick, Raymond G. and Rodney L. Petersen (eds.) (2001) *Forgiveness and Reconciliation.* Philadelphia, PA: Templeton Foundation Press.

Hendrickson, David C. (1993) 'The Ethics of Collective Security', *Ethics and International Affairs,* 7: 1–15.

Henkin, Louis (ed.) (1991) *Right Versus Might: International Law and the Use of Force,* 2nd edn. New York: Council on Foreign Relations.

Hinsley, Francis H. (1963) *Power and the Pursuit of Peace: Theory and Practice in the History of Relations Between States.* Cambridge: Cambridge University Press.

Hobbes, Thomas (1996) *Léviathan,* ed. Richard Tuck. Cambridge: Cambridge University Press.

Hoffmann, Stanley (1981) *Duties Beyond Borders: On the Limits and Possibilities of Ethical International Politics.* Syracuse, NY: Syracuse University Press.

—— (1987) *Janus and Minerva: Essays in Theory and Practice of International Politics.* Boulder, CO: Westview Press.

—— (1996) *The Ethics and Politics of Humanitarian Intervention.* Notre Dame, IN: University of Notre Dame Press.

—— (2000) *World Disorders: Troubled Peace in the Post-Cold War Era,* updated edn. Lanham, MD: Rowman & Littlefield.

—— (2004) *Gulliver Unbound: The Imperial Temptation and the War in Iraq.* Lanham, MD: Rowman & Littlefield.

Holmes, Robert L. (1989) *On War and Morality.* Princeton, NJ: Princeton University Press.

Howard, Michael (2000) *The Invention of Peace: Reflections on War and International Order.* London: Profile Books.

Hume, Cameron (1994) *Ending Mozambique's War: The Role of Mediation and Good Offices.* Washington, DC: United States Institute of Peace Press.

Jackson, Helen Hunt (2003) *A Century of Dishonor* ([1881]. New York: Dover Publications.

Jackson, Robert H. (1993) 'The Weight of Ideas in Decolonization: Normative Change in International Relations', in Judith Goldstein and Robert O. Keohane (eds.), *Ideas and Foreign Policy: Beliefs, Institutions, and Political Change.* Ithaca, NY: Cornell University Press.

Johnston, Douglas and Cynthia Sampson (eds.) (1994) *Religion: The Missing Dimension of Statecraft.* New York: Oxford University Press.

Kacowicz, Arie M., Yaacov Bar-Siman-Tov, Ole Elgstöm, and Magnus Jerneck (eds.) (2000) *Stable Peace Among Nations.* Lanham, MD: Rowman & Littlefield.

Kant, Immanuel (1991) 'Perpetual Peace: A Philosophical Sketch', in Hans Reiss (ed.), *Kant: Political Writings*. Cambridge: Cambridge University Press.

—— (1996) *The Metaphysics of Morals*, ed. and intro. Mary J. Gregor and Allen Wood. Cambridge: Cambridge University Press.

Keal, Paul (2003) *European Conquest and the Rights of Indigenous Peoples*. Cambridge: Cambridge University Press.

Keeley, Lawrence H. (1996) *War Before Civilization*. Oxford: Oxford University Press.

Kelsay, John (1993) *Islam and War: A Study in Comparative Ethics*. Louisville, KY: John Knox Press.

—— and James T. Johnson (eds.) (1991) *Just War and Jihad: Historical Perspectives on War and Peace in Western and Islamic Traditions*. Westport, CT: Greenwood Press.

Kent, Ann (1999) *China, the United Nations, and Human Rights: The Limits of Compliance*. Philadelphia, PA: University of Pennsylvania Press.

Küng, Hans (1997) *A Global Ethic for Global Politics and Economics*. London: SCM Press.

—— and Dieter Senghaas (eds.) (2003) *Friedenspolitik: Ethische Grundlagen internationaler Beziehungen*. Munich and Zürich: Piper.

Lederach, John Paul (1997) *Building Peace: Sustainable Reconciliation in Divided Societies*. Washington, DC: United States Institute of Peace.

Levi, Zeev (2001) 'On the Peace Concept in Judaism and in Jewish Thought', *Gesher*, 43 (Summer): 66–71.

Linklater, Andrew (1998) *The Transformation of Political Community: Ethical Foundations of the Post-Westphalian Era*. Cambridge: Polity Press.

Little, David (1994) *Sri Lanka: The Invention of Enmity*. Washington, DC: United States Institute of Peace.

—— and Scott W. Hibbard (1997) *Islamic Activism and U.S. Foreign Policy*. Washington, DC: United States Institute of Peace.

—— John Kelsay, and Abdulaziz A. Sachedina (1988) *Human Rights and the Conflict of Cultures: Western and Islamic Perspectives on Religious Liberty*. Columbia, SC: University of South Carolina Press.

Locke, John (1988) *Two Treatises of Governement*, ed. Peter Laslett. Cambridge: Cambridge University Press.

Loriaux, Michel (1992) 'The Realists and Saint Augustine: Skepticism, Psychology, and Moral Action in International Relations Thought', *International Studies Quarterly*, 36: 401–20.

Macintyre, Alasdair (1984) *After Virtue: A Study in Moral Theory*, 2nd edn. Notre Dame, IN: University of Notre Dame Press.

McElroy, Robert W. (1992) *Morality and American Foreign Policy: The Role of Ethics in International Affairs*. Princeton, NJ: Princeton University Press.

Mapel, David R. and Terry Nardin (eds.) (1999) *International Society: Diverse Ethical Perspectives*. Princeton, NJ: Princeton University Press.

Maalouf, Amin (1989) *The Crusades through Arab Eyes*. New York: Schocken Books.

Montesquieu (1989) *The Spirit of the Laws*, ed. Anne M. Cohler, Basia C. Miller, and Harold S. Stone. Cambridge: Cambridge University Press.

Morgenthau, Hans J. (1978) *Politics Among Nations: The Struggle for Power and Peace,* 5th rev. edn. New York: Knopf.

Mortimer, Edward and Robert Fine (eds.) (1999) *People, Nation and State: The Meaning of Ethnicity and Nationalism.* London and New York: I. B. Tauris.

Nardin, Terry (ed.) (1996) *The Ethics of War and Peace: Religious and Secular Perspectives.* Princeton, NJ: Princeton University Press.

—— and David R. Mapel (eds.) (1992) *Traditions of International Ethics.* Cambridge: Cambridge University Press.

Noddings, Nel (2003) *Caring: A Feminine Approach to Ethics & Moral Education,* 2nd edn. Berkeley, CA: University of California Press.

Orend, Brian (2000) *Michael Walzer on War and Justice.* Cardiff, UK: University of Wales Press.

Osgood, Charles (1962) *An Alternative to War or Surrender.* Urbana, IL: The University of Illinois Press.

Padgen, Anthony (1995) *Lords of All the World: Ideologies of Empire in Spain, Britain and France, 1500–1800.* New Haven, CT: Yale University Press.

Pakenham, Frank (1951) *Peace by Ordeal: An Account from Firsthand Sources, of the Negociation and Signature of the Anglo-Irish Treaty, 1921.* Cork: The Mercier Press.

Powers, Roger S. and William B. Vogele (eds.) (1951) *Protest, Power, and Change: An Encyclopaedia of Nonviolent Action from ACT-UP to Women's Suffrage.* New York: Garland.

Rawls, John (1999) *The Law of Peoples: With 'The Idea of Public Reason Revisited'.* Cambridge, MA: Harvard University Press.

Raymond, Gregory A. (1997) 'Problems and Prospects in the Study of International Norms', *Mershon International Studies Review,* 41: 205–45.

Rigby, Andrew (2001) *Justice and Reconciliation: After the Violence.* Boulder, CO and London: Lynne Rienner Publishers.

Roberts, Adam (2002) 'The So-called "Right" of Humanitarian Intervention', in *Yearbook of International Humanitarian Law* 2000, 3. The Hague: T.M.C. Asser Press.

—— and Benedict Kingsbury (eds.) (1993) *United Nations, Divided World: The UN's Roles in International Relations,* 2nd edn. Oxford: Clarendon Press.

—— and Richard Guelff (eds.) (2000) *Documents on the Laws of War,* 3rd rev. edn. Oxford: Oxford University Press.

Rosenne, Shabtai (1995) *The World Court: What it is and How it Works,* 5th edn. Dordrecht, The Netherlands: Martinus Nijhoff.

Rosenthal, Joel H. (1999) *Ethics & International Affairs: A Reader.* Washington, DC: Carnegie Council on Ethics and International Affairs and George Washington University Press.

Rothberg, Robert I. and Dennis Thompson (eds.) (2000) *Truth v. Justice: The Morality of Truth Commissions.* Princeton, NJ: Princeton University Press.

Rousseau (1997) *The Discourses and Other Early Political Writings,* ed. Victor Gourevitch. Cambridge: Cambridge University Press.

—— (1997) *The Social Contract and Other Later Political Writings*, ed. Victor Gourevitch. Cambridge: Cambridge University Press.

Ruddick, Sara (1995) *Maternal Thinking: Toward a Politics of Peace*, 2nd edn. Boston: Beacon Press.

Said, Edward W. (1993) *Culture and Imperialism*. New York: Knopf/Random House.

—— (1996) *Peace and Its Discontents: Essays on Palestine in the Middle East Peace Process*. New York: Vintage Books.

—— (2003) *Orientalism* ([1978], repr. with a new preface. London: Penguin Books.

—— (2004) *From Oslo to Iraq and the Road Map*. New York: Pantheon Books.

—— (2004) *Humanism and Democratic Criticism*. New York: Columbia University Press.

Sayigh, Rosemary (1994) *Too Many Enemies: The Palestinian Experience in Lebanon*. London: Zed Books.

Schneewind, Jérome (1998) *The Invention of Autonomy: A History of Modern Moral Philosophy*. Cambridge: Cambridge University Press.

Sells, Michael (1996) *A Bridge Betrayed: Religion and Genocide in Bosnia*. Berkeley, CA: University of California Press.

Sikkink, Kathryn (1993) 'The Power of Principled Ideas: Human Rights Policies in the United States and Western Europe', in Judith Goldstein and Robert O. Keohane (eds.), *Ideas and Foreign Policy: Beliefs, Institutions, and Political Change*. Ithaca, NY: Cornell University Press, pp. 139–70.

Singer, Peter (2002) *One World: The Ethics of Globalization*. New Haven, CT: Yale University Press.

Skinner, Quentin (1996) *Reason and Rhetoric in the Philosophy of Hobbes*. Cambridge: Cambridge University Press.

Smock, David R. (1992) *Religious Perspectives on War: Christian, Muslim, and Jewish Attitudes toward Force after the Gulf War*. Washington, DC: United States Institute of Peace.

—— (1995) *Perspectives on Pacifism: Christian, Jewish, and Muslim Views on Nonviolence and International Conflict*. Washington, DC: United States Institute of Peace.

Snyder, Jack (2000) *From Voting to Violence*. New York: W.W. Norton.

Stern, Paul and Daniel Druckman (eds.) (2000) *International Conflict Resolution after the Cold War*. Washington, DC: National Academy Press.

Sternhell, Zeev (1998) *The Founding Myth of Israel: Nationalism, Socialism, and the Making of the Jewish State*, trans. David Maisel. Princeton, NJ: Princeton University Press.

Todorov, Tzvetan (1992) *The Conquest of America: The Question of the Other*. New York: Harper Torch.

Tuck, Richard (1999) *The Rights of War and Peace: Political Thought and the International Order from Grotius to Kant*. Oxford: Oxford University Press.

Tully, James (1994) 'Aboriginal Property and Western Theory: Recovering a Middle Ground', *Social Philosophy and Policy*, 11(2): 153–80.

—— (1995) *Strange Multiplicity: Constitutionalism in an Age of Diversity*. Cambridge: Cambridge University Press.

Vattel, Emer de (1758) *Le droit des gens ou principes de la loi naturelle*. London.

Vitoria, Francisco de (1991) *On the American Indians and On the Law of War*, ed. Anthony Pagden and Jeremy Lawrance. Cambridge: Cambridge University Press.

Walter, Barbara (2002) *Committing to Peace*. Princeton, NJ: Princeton University Press.

Walzer, Michael (1994) *Thick and Thin: Moral Argument at Home and Abroad*. Notre Dame, IN: University of Notre Dame Press.

—— (2000) *Just and Unjust Wars*, 3rd edn. [1977]. New York: Basic Books.

—— (2004) *Arguing about War*. New Haven, CT; and London: Yale University Press.

Welch, David A. (1993) *Justice and the Genesis of War*. Cambridge: Cambridge University Press.

—— (1994) 'Can We Think Systematically About Ethics and Statecraft?', *Ethics and International Affairs*, 8: 23–37.

Wollstonecraft, Mary (1993) *A Vindication of the Rights of Woman*. [1792]. Oxford: Oxford University Press.

Wright, Quincy (1964) *A Study of War*, abridged edn. [1942]. Chicago: The University of Chicago Press.

Zartman, William, Daniel Druckman, Lloyd Jensen, Dean G. Pruitt, and H. Peyton Young (1996) 'Negotiation as a Search for Justice', *International Negotiation* 1/1: 79–98.

Index